T0277296

# MAKE YOUR OWN RULES

# MAKE YOUR OWN RULES

## STORIES and HARD-EARNED ADVICE from a CREATOR in the DIGITAL AGE

## ANDREW HUANG

**SIMON ELEMENT**

New York  London  Toronto  Sydney  New Delhi

SIMON
ELEMENT

An Imprint of Simon & Schuster, LLC
1230 Avenue of the Americas
New York, NY 10020

First Simon Element hardcover edition February 2024

SIMON ELEMENT is a trademark of Simon & Schuster, LLC

Simon & Schuster: Celebrating 100 Years of Publishing in 2024

For information about special discounts for bulk purchases,
please contact Simon & Schuster Special Sales at 1-866-506-1949
or business@simonandschuster.com.

The Simon & Schuster Speakers Bureau can bring authors to your
live event. For more information or to book an event,
contact the Simon & Schuster Speakers Bureau at 1-866-248-3049
or visit our website at www.simonspeakers.com.

Interior design by Kyle Kabel

Manufactured in the United States of America

10  9  8  7  6  5  4  3  2  1

Library of Congress Cataloging-in-Publication Data has been applied for.

ISBN 978-1-9821-9041-5
ISBN 978-1-9821-9042-2 (ebook)

*To everyone who creates.*

# Contents

# Introduction

On paper, my life should have gone a very different way. I shouldn't have become any sort of artist. I was a painfully shy child of immigrants who valued doing things by the book. I had no industry connections when I started out. I'm Chinese—an egregiously underrepresented demographic in many creative fields—and I also have severe, medically unexplained hearing issues (not great for a musician). No one would bet on someone like me to attract a following or to make a living from my art. I'm the exact kind of person who should have ended up working in an office.

But I find myself writing from inside a music studio that was built—every brick of it—with the proceeds of my creative output. There's a trail behind me of hundreds of songs in my discography. I built an online audience in the early 2000s before social media existed, and I've now grown a YouTube channel with over 2 million subscribers and 300 million views. I've done commercial work for some of the biggest brands in the world, and I've released numerous products of my own, including music hardware and a chart-topping mobile app. My online classes have been taken by tens of thousands of students. The part that remains the most beguiling to me? I now have several people on staff to help with production, business, and administrative affairs. I *am* the office.

This book's structure—just like my music—plays around with style and form. I tell stories, I assign homework, I share pie charts about finances. This is all included because to me it's all connected. If you're familiar with my videos, you know I'm always sharing what I'm learning, and I have a lot to share with creators about creating.

I won't be just telling my story to fans, and I'm certainly not writing *Social Media Success for Dummies*. Why? Because I learned a crucial lesson through songwriting that I believe applies to all the arts. Generic characters, and generic stories, are no good. A blank slate, like a "dummy"—something able to have anything projected onto it—is the least relatable creature of all. We relate to imperfect, human characters with specific facets, whether we as readers mesh or collide with them. That's how we learn about each other and ourselves. This is a window into my life and mind, and as you look into it I hope you'll also find your own reflection.

What I want to share is how I bypassed the path set before me to create my own fun, weird, and creatively charged life—both the specific decisions and strokes of luck that make up my story, as well as the overall approach that has allowed me to be flexible and successful in art and business alike. It's not a single approach that I hope to prescribe; it's an attitude of profound openness that sees all approaches as valid.

Often, creative ideas, attitudes, and working methods seem to be at odds with each other or mutually exclusive. Do you create for yourself or for others, plan or improvise, chase inspiration or let it come to you? Across different seasons of our lives—or even moments of our days—there's much more room than we usually give ourselves to try something different from what we, or the world, usually expect. Living in this fluidity is a massive advantage when everyone else is trying to categorize and stabilize, valuing solid ground over taking flight.

This mindset has been behind every move I've made and every idea or follower or dollar that's entered my orbit. It's what brought me to where I am now and whatever it was that may have enticed you to read this book. I've developed a perspective that jumps over any wall and entertains any possibility. I've cultivated an energy that turns anything in my path toward my goals, whether it's a millimeter of leverage or a mountain of an obstacle. This openness is an approach not just to music or my career but to life in general; it lets me see past traditional expectations to make up my own rules. It's a perspective anyone can adopt, and I believe that anyone who does can be immeasurably more effective and fulfilled in their work and life.

I want to share this and everything else I've learned about "making it" as an online-first creator. Openness is a huge part of my work—I'm not secretive about any of my process, and I create a lot of videos about how my music is made because I love being able to give others tools and techniques that can elevate their own practice. In this book, I channel that same openness into detailing the development of my creative outlook and my career. While my journey has been my own, and some of the specifics may not be replicable simply because time and technology move so quickly, there are salient and timeless principles in these pages that anyone can draw from to enrich their own creative pursuits.

The book is divided into four parts. Each details my story and the lessons it has taught me, and each contains prompts and assignments to encourage the application of those lessons in your own creative life.

**Part One** is about becoming an artist—or nurturing the artist you already are. I discuss finding your voice and your workflow. What are your interests and values? How can you encourage growth and productivity in your creative life?

**Part Two** deals with making public-facing work: how you can reach people, present yourself, communicate your ideas, and find an audience. In this section, I ruminate on why so many artists feel dirty about self-promotion, and offer guidelines on how you can effectively market your work in a way that feels right for you.

**Part Three** is concerned with money. I go into a lot of detail about what revenue streams in a creative occupation can look like, because this often opaque information is exactly what I wish I knew when I was trying to get my career off the ground. I discuss building a business, determining your value, strategies for success, and the quest for work/life balance.

**Part Four** is about authenticity. As my career has progressed, my work has only become truer to who I am and what I want to do—and there's a world of difference between how that feels and what it's like to chase what the world tells you to. Authenticity can be more complicated than it seems, and it looks different for everyone. We all have to wrestle with finding and holding on to ourselves—and it's well worth it to do so.

Many people have told me that my videos, music, and online classes have been a font of inspiration for them as they pursue their craft; in *Make Your Own Rules*, I hope to provide insights both deeper and broader with regard to art's creation, promotion, monetization, and overall place in our lives. In my experience of creative work, the process is just as important as its outcomes. As a process, art is fun, it's self-expression, it's escape, it's therapy. As a product, it can make a public impact, and maybe even be lucrative. In both cases, it can be an amazing way to connect with other people. It can change lives. It's certainly changed mine.

# PART ONE

# Foundations

# Chapter One

There's a home movie of me as a toddler taken by my dad on a rented camcorder. I'm kneeling in the kitchen with crayons all around me, one gripped in my little fist as I scribble furiously on yellowed tiles. The sheets of paper I started drawing on lay abandoned nearby; I've moved on to cover half of our kitchen floor in squiggles and spirals. This was not a one-time event—it was a regular activity that my parents let me indulge in. They realized there was no stopping me, so they'd just clean it all up afterward, every time.

The look on my face is pure concentration. I'm breathing deeply. I seem to be working deliberately: *scribble-scribble-scribble*, hop over to another area, *scribble-scribble-scribble*. The crayon makes a fierce scraping noise as it drags across the laminate. This is not a polite scribble; I'm whipping my whole arm back and forth.

All of this is heightened by what's happening offscreen. From the adjacent room, my mom, a skilled pianist, tears through Chopin's *Fantaisie-Impromptu in C# minor*. The piece is filled with wild flourishes and tempestuous chords. The notes pouring into the kitchen heighten the feverishness of my art making. With this soundtrack, I'm not just a kid with a crayon—I'm a possessed visionary, delirious and determined, driving my paraffin wax daggers into the ground to birth a masterpiece.

The scene foreshadows how I would end up spending much of my adult life: lost in creative flow, a camera on me, music playing. But most significantly: I wasn't just coloring outside the lines—I was entirely off the canvas.

What I most appreciate now about that home video is what it tells you about the people who don't appear in it: my parents. From early on they gave me the gift of free creative exploration and, as much as they could, the tools and outside encouragement to do that exploring. Maybe it's not an uncommon scene for young children to draw all over their kitchens, I don't know. But for a child of *Asian immigrants*? No way. And with my dad delightedly filming, and my mom not even concerned enough about it to be in the same room? We're in untrodden territory.

My younger brother, Lucas, and I were brought up within a lot of the cultural dynamics that would be considered typical of a Chinese family: regimented schedules, committed work ethic, high standards for academic performance, an importance placed on social status. You needed to excel at everything you did (there was the implication that otherwise it wouldn't be worth doing at all). For many first-generation Chinese kids like me, the only acceptable career aspiration is to be a doctor, and if you can't manage that, then you'd better *at least* become a lawyer.

Despite all these classic cultural norms, there was this one misfit notion that made its way into my parents' outlook—I'm still not sure how—that had them telling us, often: "The most important thing is that you do what makes you happy. The point of life is to enjoy it."

And so, as long as our grades were As, we finished our chores, and we were respectful of our elders and authority figures, they helped my brother and me pursue our interests. If their expectations for excellence were being met, then it was no problem if I played guitar for four hours a day, spray-painted a mural on my bedroom walls, or brought a toad back from my cousin's cottage to be rehomed in our garden. (That toad lived in our backyard for *years*.) Lucas started playing the drums at school and showed a talent for it, so that Christmas he got a drum kit. Let me reiterate: *The Asian parents bought their eleven-year-old a drum kit.*

There was no chance we were going to become doctors.

Making art is the easiest and hardest thing in the world. It's completely free-form. The only rules are the ones you give yourself. You can explore whatever interests you and shape your creations any way you see fit. At the same time, it takes a colossal amount of work to *get good*—to be able to execute ideas the way you envision them and create work that connects with others. It takes immeasurable dedication and exertion to reach a place where the creative act feels effortless and confident—and then it's easy again. (Well, at least, the skills you've worked on the most feel easy . . . most of the time.)

My musical education began when my mom introduced me to the piano. Before I could speak, I sat in her lap as she maneuvered my hands gently across the keys, piecing together the melodies of nursery rhymes. At age four I started lessons ("Why can't *you* teach me, Mom?" "Because I'll get mad at you!"), which began my relationship with scales, chords, keys, rhythm, structure, dynamics, and, thorniest of all, *practice*.

You don't really understand practice as a kid. You don't get that you're strengthening neural pathways and developing remarkable control in the muscles of your hands. You're just bored. You're forced to play the same thing over and over by your teacher on Tuesday nights, and then every other day of the week by your Asian parents. But you *do* notice that every once in a while, after doing something a hundred times, you can now do it faster. A couple hundred more times and you can do it without needing to think about it. Past a certain point, the notes of a tricky passage flow out of you almost as effortlessly as a breath of air. It's a tremendously satisfying feeling that, usually, makes up for all that boredom.

It took me a long time to realize that the concept of practice carries over into areas other than playing and performing. You can practice writing music (and even listening to it). Most surprising of all, I discovered as an adult that you can even practice having good ideas. But I'll get into that later.

Every Tuesday night, for over ten years, Lucas and I would go to piano lessons. During these lessons, one of us would be with Mrs. Eisner in her living room, playing Bach and Beethoven and learning to identify intervals and rhythms by ear. While that was happening, the other sat at a table in her basement with a theory book and manuscript paper, etching out answers to exercises in classical notation. After an hour we'd switch places.

The process was rarely enjoyable, but the results were gratifying. Slogging through all that boredom gave me what felt like superpowers. I had fun playing pieces twice as fast as they were meant to be played. I could identify the chords in a song as I was hearing them. I could hear a melody and immediately know how to play it back.

Eventually, I realized I had the tools to create songs of my own, and that realization remains my sharpest memory from those childhood piano lessons. I was in Mrs. Eisner's basement; I'd finished my theory exercises early. I wandered over to her electric keyboard, its fake wood finish blending in with the wood-paneled walls around it, and clicked it on. I reached for the slider marked VOLUME and turned it down so as to not disturb the lesson upstairs. In front of me were the black and white keys representing the twelve notes in Western music. These keys had been in my life every day for years—either upstairs where I got my lessons or at home when I practiced. But for whatever reason it was at *this* moment, noodling around on a cheap keyboard with built-in speakers on low volume, that I had the epiphany every musician eventually has. *Every song I've ever heard is made out of these notes*: all the classical pieces I'd been practicing, the Elton John and Loreena McKennitt songs that my parents loved, even music by Madonna and Nirvana and whatever else my school friends deemed cool at the time. I knew there were different instruments involved, and I had an inkling that special equipment could record and enhance these sounds, but at the core of it all I understood: everyone's just rearranging these same notes.

And right then, this epiphany not even a minute old in my mind, I started working on my first original composition. I tried different sequences of notes. I tried to guide them into something expressive and beautiful. I experimented with chord formations I hadn't used before. These musical pitches suddenly seemed new to me, less rigid than the shapes prescribed by the notation I'd learned to follow. They were open, elastic, and mysterious, hinting at infinite possibilities. And as I listened to what I was creating, I had my second musical realization of the day. *This sounds really, really bad.*

Two things tend to happen when we encounter the idea that all popular forms of music use an incredibly limited number of notes. The first is that it makes music seem simple. A major key contains only seven notes, yet it's responsible for some of the most rapturous moments of human experience. Even if we count those notes' recurrence across different registers, a song with a five-octave range in a standard key signature would use thirty-five notes at most.

The supposed simplicity turns out to be a deception. There's a world of nuance behind those notes—timing, phrasing, dynamics, timbre, articulation . . . not to mention the fact that you can combine any number of notes you want at a time. You could compare it to a piece of writing, like this one. I plan to use only twenty-six letters. But whether or not somebody knows the alphabet gives no indication of whether they're able to communicate anything meaningful, beautiful, or interesting.

Ultimately, though, the illusion of simplicity is a good thing, because it leads to the second thing that happens. It makes you believe that you can make music. The notes people have been playing for ages, the same ones used by Tchaikovsky, Duke Ellington, Dolly Parton, Jimi Hendrix, and Beyoncé, are available to *you*. If that spark of interest is strong enough to sustain you through learning the parts of music that are complex or challenging or boring, there isn't much more you need.

Besides the small number of notes, many other aspects of music can similarly be accessed and executed by anyone. The first time a school friend saw me playing the electric bass he remarked, "So you just press the string down with one hand and pluck it with the other?" Yes—it's an action that even toddlers can perform. The work is in doing it so much that you're able to press and pluck in the right places and at the right times with speed, precision, and expression. The mechanics of playing piano are even simpler: you press the keys down. One practice technique even involves holding your hands above the keys and letting your fingers fall as naturally and gently as possible onto the keys, letting gravity work more than your muscles. It seems paradoxical—*you're trying not to try*. But at the heart of it that's what practice is: putting in effort to make something effortless. Anyone can press a piano key and anyone can allow gravity to act on their body. Anyone willing to spend time exploring what's possible through these acts can discover just how accessible music is.

Unfortunately, the instruments are not always accessible. The arts are the first thing targeted in schools when budgets get cut, and far too many schools have had their music programs entirely removed. This is shameful and short-sighted. Not only do many students find music more enjoyable and engaging than other subjects, numerous studies have shown the enormous benefits that music education brings to the rest of kids' studies and their lives. It fosters discipline, memorization skills, multitasking, coordination, cooperation, and listening. It's a source of personal expression and stress relief. It opens doors to many cultures that would otherwise remain unexposed to these young minds. It's disheartening to know that so much of this will be missing from many children's early development.

On the flip side, technology's relentless advancement has put us in an unprecedented position where many tools and educational resources are more widely available than ever before. Fantastic software and tutorials can be found for free online. In some cases, release-ready work can be created on a smartphone. Many tools can be manufactured more affordably—there are perfectly playable $200 guitars and $30 ukuleles. In fact, so many pianos have been built at this point that if you live in a decent-sized city, you can probably find one for free in your online classifieds. You'll probably have to pay a couple hundred dollars to have it moved, but maybe you'll get lucky like I did and find one down the street. The distinctive piano you can see in some of my older videos (white and, inexplicably, stuccoed) was stored for years in a neighbor's garage after his mother died, and I enlisted three friends to wheel it a few blocks with me and hoist it up my front steps and into my living room. Years later I passed it on for free to the next tenant, who was very happy to have it. Whatever you need to start exploring your creativity, some version of it probably exists that is more accessible to you than it would have been even a generation ago.

I've known too many people who have put off creating art because they don't feel they have what they need yet, whether it's skills or equipment or the right environment. But I don't believe you have to get all set up first—with your practice and your knowledge and your state-of-the-art gadgets in your optimized dedicated workspace—to *then* start creating. You should be creating at every point along your journey. It will even help the processes of learning your craft and familiarizing yourself with your tools. Perhaps you're sitting on your ideas, waiting until some day when you feel better prepared to execute them. I've been guilty of this many times, but I've learned that waiting just causes those ideas to shrivel and your progress to falter. Execute *now*, to the best of your abilities and with the tools available to you. The worst-case scenario is that you learn a bunch about yourself and your process, improve your skills a bit, and create something you can use in the future as a reference or building block if you find your ambitions for your project still outpace your current faculties. The best-case scenario? You create something beautiful that touches other people's lives and is a stepping-stone in your career, as well as a piece you can enjoy for the rest of your life. It's win-win. Create *now*.

## SELF-REFLECTION

Is there any part of your creative journey you're postponing? Perhaps you're waiting for the right time, place, or equipment to get started, or maybe you're leaving ideas unfinished because you're afraid they won't live up to your hopes.

Whatever the case may be, ask yourself: What is one thing you can do *today* to make real progress, however small, on your creative goals?

I grew up with an enchanted artifact: my family's small black boom box. Every part of its interface was delightful and satisfying to use. The needle glided smoothly as I turned the dial between radio stations. There was a long antenna I'd extend and retract over and over, feeling each segment catch and slide into the next, and there were chunky mechanical buttons for the dual tape deck that gave me control over sound and time: PLAY, STOP, FF, REW, REC.

REC was a life-changing button. I was familiar with the other buttons from listening to my parents' collection of tapes, but one day when I was four or five, probably only because she needed to find an activity for her overactive child, my mom showed me how to record. We chose a tape we wouldn't mind recording over and she pointed out a pinprick hole on the top of the boom box, which was, inexplicably, its built-in microphone. She pressed PLAY and REC at the same time. The machine sounded its familiar soft whir, the spindles spun, and the slender tendrils of tape skimmed forward.

"And now you can record yourself," she said.

STOP.

REW.

*Louder, more urgent whirring.*

PLAY.

"And now you can record yourself," said the boom box in my mother's voice.

My world changed forever. The magic of being able to make a sound and play it back unleashed my imagination. Suddenly, sound seemed malleable, something I could manipulate physically like playdough. It was one thing to talk, sing, or play the piano. But something about being able to *capture* sound, to collect it from the air and drop it like a trinket into a glass jar, spoke to me on a deeper level than any of my other five-year-old play. This was power, and it was palpable.

I immediately recorded myself singing the Spider-Man theme song.

SELF-REFLECTION

When was the moment you first felt powerful when making art? What was it that opened your eyes to the possibilities before you?

# Chapter Two

Growing up in an Asian family against a white Canadian backdrop in Ottawa, I was often ostracized for looking different. Even with the kids who took the chance to get to know me, I still felt I was at a great distance because I wasn't culturally on their level either. My otherness was always apparent.

My parents were well assimilated for their generation: advanced degrees, respectable jobs, perfectly spoken English, and a love for the Western music and films of their teenage years. But they didn't exactly keep me and my brother abreast of what was new, and ABBA and *The Sound of Music* weren't going to cut it in schoolyard socializing. I was an eight-year-old who didn't know who Michael Jackson was or how to play baseball. At lunch I would attract ridicule for bringing out shrimp-flavored crackers, or dried noodles that I would eat uncooked, just snapping off knotted chunks after sprinkling them with the powdered flavor packet. During recess, as any racialized kid knows, there were special insults and aggressions reserved just for us.

My parents tried to instill us with knowledge and understanding of our Chinese heritage. For years my brother and I even went to an extra half day of school every Saturday to learn to speak and write the language. But the otherness that all things Asian had bestowed on me made me disdain it all. And anyway, even if I'd leaned into these Chinese roots, would I have fit in better anywhere, with only a couple of other Chinese kids in school to befriend? And with no shared upbringing or connections with people in any Chinese-speaking region, could I even hope to fit in if I ever found myself there?

With this as my experience, I rejected the Chinese culture I came from, and I rejected the Canadian culture that was around me and not letting me in.

I'd make friends, slowly, with the other misfits. In the social hierarchy of school, the cool kids and the losers were the first to be established each year, and the handful of us that were left behind sorted ourselves out weeks or months later. We'd gradually reveal our quirks—doing gymnastics, reading books about outer space, having a pet salamander—and I'd gravitate toward the kids who liked writing short stories or drawing maps of made-up places. Or sometimes I'd simply befriend the other people of color. But it was rare for the immigrant kids to find the same depth of community among each other, because our backgrounds and experiences were all mixed up. What we shared was our otherness, not a common ground but an absence of it. We were planets without suns, drifting alone.

When I was very young, I didn't understand the full extent of the othering or the reasons behind it. I just felt different. And as layer upon layer of differentness built up over time, it coalesced into that resolute rejection of almost everything. I could usually ignore these feelings, but their embers were always glowing inside somewhere. Resentment that I was different. Resentment that I had to work harder than everyone else to find acceptance. Resentment that it was never total acceptance—never the acceptance the white kids had for each other, the way they could loll about in a world they inherited from their parents and thus owned outright.

For those of us who weren't white, there was different treatment, if not outright bullying. The name-calling or physical aggression, though, could at least be easily recognized. There were subtler infractions you would feel as a person of color that were trickier—soft enough that sometimes you weren't sure they were real, so automatic that you thought even those who perpetrated them were often unaware. Peers including you less in conversations. Teachers holding you to a higher standard of behavior. When meeting someone new, a hint of surprise in their face when they realize you're a native English speaker. And incessantly, at every turn, "Where are you from? No, where are you really from? Well, where's your family from?"

The racism was just invisible enough that you could believe it wasn't a big issue. *I'll just work a bit harder—at following the rules, at speaking up, at showing people that the stereotypes don't apply. I'll answer the stupid questions. I'll let the name-calling bounce off me. I'll just do all of that. For the rest of my life. No problem.* I almost started to count myself lucky. My parents had it worse. Black and brown folks have it worse. *The things I have to put up with are nothing in comparison*, I would tell myself. *They don't matter. They don't have damaging effects. They've actually made me stronger.*

I also appreciate, though, that being ostracized from such a young age gave me a perceptive advantage over most of the kids I grew up with. By fitting in so easily, they fit in without thinking about what that meant. I saw through the norms and the arbitrary customs, the things that were done because that's how everyone else did them or that's how they'd always been done. I rejected gender expectations and did anything considered "feminine" if it suited me, whether that was simply painting my nails or leaning into all manner of gentler or more ebullient personality traits that have had people mislabeling me as gay to this day. I saw through the shape of the education system—preparing us not to live well or to improve the world, but to do as we're told without asking questions or challenging authority. Adherence to nationality struck me as absurd—every border between every country was made up by people, and they have all changed over time. Countless things seemed to me like just made-up rules for how life should be done, even if they were trivial things. Why are waffles not a dinner food? Why are we hauling this tree into our living room and decorating it with a bunch of balls each winter? Eventually I'd stop celebrating my birthday. I didn't reject anything for the sake of it—I was just hyperaware of how many ideas or judgments about life were simply made up by others, and so it was easy for me to leave behind any that I didn't care for. I was already ostracized; letting myself be a little weirder wouldn't feel much different.

But when you do that much rejecting, you aren't left with a lot. You're out there on your own. The only thing I embraced was music, and I was trying to embrace as much of it as I could—probably because I couldn't find true connection elsewhere. And even with all this music, I couldn't connect with the associated histories or cultures. But the sounds! They made me feel so many things I could not name—sometimes things that I seemed to feel more deeply than any of my other emotions. Eventually I'd realize that it was *sound* as much as music that I connected to—music was simply the highest form of sound expression. I had always appreciated the timbres of people's voices, the sound design in television programs, or even the noises household objects made when they were struck. From a young age I would rhythmically clack my teeth together at different intensities to replicate drum beats of songs I had in my head. Teachers would reprimand me for constantly tapping my pencils or my desk. I filled up tape after tape in the family boom box with my songs and sound effects. I started devouring sound as a child and never stopped, and for a long time it was my only identity.

While I always enjoyed music, during most of my childhood I was much more interested in visual arts. My dad enjoyed working with pastels—and his mother painted brilliant watercolors—so I had opportunities to experiment with those mediums. But for the most part I just loved to sketch. It was a constant creative itch. My parents could leave me with a pencil and a stack of paper destined for the recycling bin and I'd have the time of my life. But the scales tipped in favor of music when I found the right outlet. Like so many kids from so many generations, rock music was the great galvanizing force of my adolescent years. Its high energy and irreverent attitude gave it a special place in my teenage heart, propelling the way I acted and dressed, the events I went to, and the people I wanted to hang around with.

The shift from an art obsession to a music obsession happened in sixth-grade music class. Here, the instrument selection process was seriously flawed. If you already played one of the available instruments, you would keep at it. That part was fine. For everybody else? We got to *look* at the instruments—flute, clarinet, saxophone, trumpet, French horn, tuba, electric bass, drums—and then just . . . choose. There was also a quota for each instrument and a collective goal to, apparently, be able to perform arrangements of such classics as John Williams's *Jurassic Park* theme—so we had to choose instruments one by one as the teacher called on us. Inevitably the last straggling few would be stuck with the unwanted instruments, which for some reason were flutes and tubas.

Naturally the drums were the first to go. We all eyed Lee with envy as he ambled over to take a seat behind the kit, picked up a drumstick, and *THWACKED* the snare appallingly loudly.

"Who's next?" Mr. Merritt had a thick brown mustache and always spoke like a sportscaster giving a play-by-play.

I knew there was only one other cool instrument. I shot my hand up as high as I could, along with most of the rest of the class. Miraculously, the mustache angled over in my direction: "Aaaand how 'bout Andrew! What'll it be?"

And that's how I became a bass player.

It's a wonder that instruments were learned at all in this environment. Mr. Merritt went around the room showing different sections the rudiments of the instrument each student had chosen—where to place your fingers, how to wet a reed, the goofy shapes you had to make with your mouth to get any sound out of a horn. Spit valves caught everyone's attention regardless of whether or not they were playing an instrument that had one. Over time, as you blow into a wind instrument, saliva builds up inside it, and there's a small key you can press to let it out. Pros might bring a small towel to collect their spit. In sixth-grade music class, though, kids were told to just eject it right onto the floor. Dribbling onto the faded blue music room carpet, it mixed with the drool of a thousand students who had come before: a multigenerational tapestry.

The basics of sheet music were somehow conveyed to students who'd never seen it before. And after weeks of squeaking and honking, we were able to play a squeaky, honky rendition of a John Philip Sousa march. Slowly, painstakingly, we learned other pieces and the students' technique improved, though even by the end of the year the squeaks hadn't all been eradicated. Meanwhile, I was having a blast with the electric bass. It felt like a weapon in my hands. Its low notes vibrated through me as I played it. Sometimes I would press my chin against its body as I plucked notes, feeling the deep resonances shake my skull.

But guitar soon became my true love—*the* instrument of rock and roll. My dad had an old acoustic twelve-string that had lived in the back of a closet for years, and suddenly it had all my attention. I found that my proficiency on bass translated into a head start on wringing listenable sounds out of the guitar, and unlike the piano I was actually excited to practice it. My fingers developed hard calluses, and my free time was spent scouring the primitive internet for "tabs"—a simplified form of music notation made up of lines and numbers representing the guitar's strings and fret positions—so I could learn my favorite songs.

The obsession exploded in high school as all kinds of new music met my ears. I had an amazing music teacher, Lionel Tanod, who managed to conduct the boisterous lot of us to play increasingly challenging music while also giving us an education in the history and characteristics of a multitude of genres. Baroque, classical, romantic, blues, bebop, cool jazz, bossa nova, even musique concrète reached our ears through his tutelage. At the same time, I was learning about current music through the divergent friend groups I drifted between. Sylvia and I shared a love of pop. Catherine opened my ears to punk, ska, and reggae. A lot of kids were listening to hip-hop, and there was a contingent of metalheads I would sometimes jam with. Lee, the drummer, showed me everything about alternative rock after hearing my skill develop on bass and inviting me to join his band. (It was a microcosm for so many musical projects I would later be involved in: me, the least cool person in the group, always overeager to schedule practices, always trying to refine our song structures instead of just jamming, and always the one in charge of trying to get a half-decent recording.) On my own, I was exploring online rabbit holes of electronic music: techno, drum and bass, acid, and a particular favorite, the unfortunately pretentiously named IDM—Intelligent Dance Music.

With each new genre I heard, I fell in love all over again. They were all glorious to me, and I was fascinated by how varied and expressive each form was. This all led to a tipping point, a little shift in my outlook that would echo for the rest of my life. Sitting in music class as a fourteen-year-old with Mr. Tanod introducing me to yet another genre I hadn't been aware of, I made a decision I've never gone back on: I wouldn't try to be a single type of musician. I would never be defined by one instrument or by a particular genre. Why was there any need to confine myself? I would consume it all and create it all.

SELF-REFLECTION

What are the educational foundations of your creative life? Take a moment to consider where and from whom you learned about your craft. How and what did you learn? What information might you have missed? Did your education bring with it any baggage, such as standards, assumptions, bad habits, closed mindsets, or restricting beliefs?

From before I was creating my own music I had developed a bit of a recording habit. I enjoyed making "radio shows" with my brother or my friends, where we'd enact skits that we came up with or introduce songs we'd then splice in from other tapes. We might partially listen back to our work, but mostly the joy was in the creating.

After having that epiphany about being able to compose my own music, another boom box feature became more important than any other: *overdubbing*. On one of the tape decks there was the REC button, which I'd used constantly since my mom had shown me how. In its place on the otherwise identical second deck was a different button: DUB. This allowed you to record a new sound while *also* recording whatever was playing from the tape in the first deck.

Once I started writing my own music, the DUB button allowed my ideas to become real. I would record an instrument, and then record an overdub of another instrument. I'd rewind the two tapes, pop them out, and switch their places. The tape with two layers would play back and be recorded on the tape with one layer, replacing its contents, and I'd be adding a third layer on top. So there was only one chance at mixing each additional layer—if its overdub ended up being too loud or quiet I'd rewind both tapes and play or sing the whole part again. The sound quality degraded a bit with each pass, but it was tolerable to my inexperienced ears up to about five layers, after which it would sound a bit too harsh.

Working with such a limited setup, I unknowingly gave myself a great education in making records. I had five layers to work with— ideally fewer, for better sound quality—and each one had to be a single, complete take. This meant I had to have my entire song worked out in my head before I even hit REC (*writing*). I would have to be able to perform each part well, because redoing an entire take was the only way to fix a mistake (*practice*). The parts themselves would have to be well thought out because I had to capture all the energy and emotion of my piece in just these few layers (*arrangement*). I even learned some basics about mic technique (experimenting with my distance from the boom box) and mixing (feeling out adjustments I made with each recorded layer in order to have it sit properly with the others—loud enough to be heard but not enough to overpower everything that came before).

The process was laborious, but even this had a benefit: it showed me which ideas I truly valued. If a song wasn't good, I wouldn't be compelled to record take after take, balancing each layer, honing each performance. It was too time-consuming a process to undertake for a half-baked idea I wasn't that excited about.

Most of all, it taught me that I could always enjoy creating with whatever tools were available to me. I wasn't holding off until some day in the future when I could get my hands on proper equipment or studio time. All I thought was, *This boom box has a microphone? Let's go.* I was compelled to create every day and everywhere. Even at school I'd siphon as much of my attention as I could toward my songs, jotting down lyric and melody ideas in the margins beside my notes about Shakespeare and mitochondria.

By my late teenage years, consumer technology had advanced enough that I could finally work with audio on a computer, and this was when the guitar took a back seat to *making beats*. Being able to arrange and manipulate sounds digitally provided so much more freedom of expression. I could produce pieces that came much closer to what I heard in my head, and I no longer had to contend with the lo-fi quality of my boom box and cassette tapes. I became obsessed with computer music production. My high school was less than a ten-minute walk away, so I started going home every lunch break and spare period I had to work on music. While walking I'd listen to whatever I was currently enamored with—Miles Davis, Wu-Tang Clan, Autechre . . . When I got home I'd try to create my own version of what I heard on those albums.

One particular lunch break, I was getting ready to leave when I crossed paths with my good friend Jen.

"Wait, don't go home!" she said, her eyes just slightly desperate.

I brushed her off. "Why not?" I was eager to get to my music making.

"Well . . . a bunch of us were going to hang out for lunch. You should join us."

"Don't you do that every day? I'm going home to make beats!"

Off I went, with Squarepusher ringing in my headphones. His impossibly tight drum rhythms fizzled in my brain, and I strategized about how I could replicate them on the family computer with my pirated copy of Fruity Loops 3. I ended up producing something that sounded more like a lot of elastic bands being vigorously flicked. *That's fine*, I told myself, rationalizing my failure. *It's original.*

I made it back to school five minutes before the bell for the next class rang. I peeled off my headphones and threw them in my locker. Walking through the common area with my books, I saw Jen stand up and frantically wave me over. She was at a table with a group of our friends. They were seated around a cake—white with blue icing—completely untouched. I was simultaneously filled with love and shame as they all turned to me with the smiles they'd been saving for too long.

"Happy birthday!"

Obsession is kind of the only way I know how to do things—people in my life will tell you how much of an all-or-nothing person I can be—and music became the greatest of all my obsessions. As I experimented with composition in my teenage years, the rest of the world got tuned out. I neglected relationships and responsibilities as I holed up by myself and explored sounds. And most years I did not have a friend group who would surprise me with cake on my birthday to neglect—that was close to the end of high school, and I remember those friends warmly because it was so rare for me to feel that kind of bond and acceptance. Most of the time, I struggled to find people I fit in with, so my relationships were often superficial, and I preferred to be alone. I drifted from my family as well. There was a mutual recognition that I was the black sheep, and whether they left me to my own devices or tried to corral me with tenderness or with force I was headed in only one direction—away. Chicken or egg: I couldn't fit in because I was different and had to find interests to pursue on my own, or I wanted more than anything to have time to myself for creative exploration and so I kept everyone at a distance.

This obsessive, isolationist habit ramped up when I turned eighteen and left home to study at York University in Toronto. Every spare moment was spent either making music or trying to find a genre or artist I hadn't yet heard. This was long before streaming platforms existed. Vinyl and CDs were expensive on a student budget, but I would buy as many as I could each month. And while it was possible to pirate downloads of popular releases, it wasn't nearly enough for my appetite—I was always looking for what was next, new, and different.

I became a library junkie. This was where you could find the *really* rare stuff. Folk songs poorly recorded by an academic on an expedition. Documentation of whale songs and bird calls. Early pioneers of electronic music: Daphne Oram, Karlheinz Stockhausen, Morton Subotnick, Wendy Carlos. I would check out discs where the last stamp on the card was from thirty years earlier. There were some that had never even left the library before. Nobody else I knew was into these things; I was discovering all of this on my own, driven by some urge to experience as much music as possible.

In my own music, experimentation and "originality" became my only goals. I tuned guitars so low that the strings would rest limp on the pickups. My piano pieces would change keys every bar. I'd painstakingly match arrhythmic bursts from half a drum kit with atonal bass lines—I'd memorize five seconds' worth of erratic tom and cymbal hits at a time, then find something to play on the bass in the exact same uncountable rhythm, eventually creating the effect of a band that was telepathically tight despite the lack of any actual structure. I'd make other percussion tracks out of literal garbage— crushed light bulbs, food packaging, an empty oil drum I found on the side of the road. I'd accompany folky acoustic guitar songs with the sounds of crunching paper and water bottles being hit together. I'd construct pieces out of digital malformations, cutting and pasting grainy, spectral sounds that resulted from opening nonaudio files like photos in audio editing software.

More and more rejection started to creep into my musical expression. Why was I still using ideas I knew from rock or rap or classical music? Could I come up with something of my own, beyond all that—or even entirely separate from it? I began removing the elements I'd been brought up to believe turned sound into music: song structure, key signatures and time signatures, traditional instrumentation and traditional recording processes. Actually, why not jettison notes and rhythms entirely?

I was listening to ever more obscure experimental music. Musique concrète. Power electronics. Noise. Harsh washes of static, shrill metallic reverberations and low drones, spliced tape, mutated voices, the clicks and glitches of modified or dying electronic devices. In my own work I experimented with more abrasive tones and abnormal structures. Squelchy soundscapes made with obscure freeware. My untrained playing on a borrowed saxophone, shredded beyond recognition with editing and distortion. Half an hour of echoing pulse waves from a modified video game console, slowed down 800 percent and layered with radio static humming through guitar pedals. My creations became rough, sprawling masses of sound.

I went down this path of rejection and abandonment, trying to find what was outside the music I knew, and I discovered a lot. The promise of a new musical language was tantalizing, but it never quite materialized. It started to feel like I was pushing against a wall. I realized that, as much as I enjoyed the thrill of discovery each time I found a new way to manipulate sound, my creations left me unsatisfied.

It all reached a tipping point during yet another of my experiments. Maybe I was taping contact mics to all my furniture, or drawing with thick black marker on a CD to make it play back in tiny stuttering skips, or scraping detuned guitar strings through boutique electronics mail-ordered from a guy in Portland . . . I had spent so long running as far as I could from traditional music, and then I found myself having another epiphany. There's a spectrum between pure silence and pure noise, and all the genres of music I love occupy sweet spots somewhere in the middle—domains where it's still possible to be original, even with all the customs and traditions and precedents. If you make it all the way to pure noise, you're at the end of the road; there's nowhere further to go. You have to turn around. And also: just like your identity, music that's built on rejection doesn't have much of anything in it.

## SELF-REFLECTION

How do your circumstances affect what and how you want to create? Think about both the large and the small:

Your place in time and the technology currently in use.

How much free time you have in a given day or week, and the tools you have access to.

What's culturally popular? How closely are you aware of trends? Do you respond to them? Do you react against them?

We all have limitations. Are you happy working within yours right now, or are you trying to transcend them?

had disappeared into noise for a year. All my spare time had been spent trying to find new ways to misuse my limited equipment or checking out another obscure experimental record from the library. The whole time I wrote off every bit of "normal" music I encountered—standard harmony, traditional song structure, regular old instruments—how boring! I was prioritizing innovation and experimentation, and it had led me to a misguided conclusion that *all* aspects of a piece of music should be innovative or experimental. But that kind of music is just not what most people enjoy—including me. A sound made in a new way that has never been heard before does not have merit simply for its newness. True innovation serves a purpose, and builds upon and improves what has come before. Uniqueness for its own sake is usually empty of substance, like serving a plate of twigs for dinner. *Nobody else is doing this!* Yes, we know. There are several good reasons for that.

So I had filled tapes and hard drives with all of this "unique" music—crackling electronic textures, washes of slowed down and distorted samples, instruments processed to oblivion—and I had immensely enjoyed making it all. But I never wanted to listen to most of it a second time.

This noise journey taught me a lot, though. I didn't have enough self-assurance to know what I wanted or what I liked, and in my explorations I had wandered off and gotten lost. I had started with that teenage decision to be open to anything and everything in music, devoured mountains of others' work from disparate cultures and time periods, and then tried to push past all of it in the name of finding something new. But throwing away your map and compass doesn't mean north and south stop existing. I wanted to be a self-contained, contextless creator of sound, but I had to accept that I—like every artist—existed in a particular time and place. My circumstances and position in history and culture would inform what I would create more than I could ever really know, and this was fine. With this as my new lens, these noise

33

experiments became like a blast of light—filling the negative spaces in my creative leanings, illuminating the contours of what was actually there. As someone who spent his adolescence open-minded but timid and confused, an outsider everywhere he went, it's something I've had to do in many areas of my life—figuring out what was right for me by doing a lot of what was wrong for me.

As I gradually came back to what more people would consider music, I discovered (and rediscovered) the things about it that were special to me, that I loved more deeply. My tastes were still broad, and in some cases incompatible—a song can't simultaneously be made up of simple pop chords and advanced jazz progressions—but I began to pursue only what truly excited me. I could appreciate different genres without having to learn everything about them or incorporate them into my own art.

I was learning about music as a whole, and discovering the reasons for people's shared enjoyment of many of its timeless traits. For instance, most traditional harmony was not actually arbitrarily decided by dead white guys. The pitch relationships that most people agree are pleasing to the ear are based on immutable properties of physics and math—they form the simplest possible ratios between two different rates of vibration. Flick a rubber band and it will oscillate at a certain frequency, but in addition to that fundamental frequency, it will also vibrate to a lesser extent in integer ratios: over half its length (2:1), a third of its length (3:1), a quarter of its length (4:1), and so on. This is called the harmonic series, and it occurs in anything that has a steady vibration. It's simply how sound works—as dependable as gravity. Our common set of musical intervals is derived from the relationships between the smallest numbers in the series. A 1:1 ratio means two notes are playing in unison—they are the same pitch. 2:1 is an octave—one note vibrating twice as fast as the other. 3:2 is a perfect fifth, 4:3 a perfect fourth, 5:4 a major third. While many traditions incorporate different styles of tuning, these simple-ratio intervals have shown up across cultures and centuries. Humans are wired for patterns, and our ears can more easily make sense of these more concordant tones.

Pattern, of course, shows up in rhythm as well. The regularity of a beat is as natural to the world as waves crashing on a beach, or the blood your heart is pumping right now. Music uses uniform pulses such as these but adds ornamentation—accents that land in between them to create energy and dynamics. There's a push and pull between what's expected and unexpected. A completely steady, predictable beat becomes boring quickly, while irregular, unpredictable rhythms provide little for a listener to latch on to—we need that sweet spot. It comes from the same place as our enjoyment of story. We want continuity, but a bit of surprise—not a list of a predictable sequence of events, nor a string of non sequiturs.

Most of this, or all of it, is probably painfully obvious to you if you've spent any time studying music. But even though I took this circuitous—and perhaps naive—route to arrive back at using the same music theory fundamentals I started with, I learned a tremendous amount through the journey. I confronted and removed every building block of the art form, not just theoretically but with my hands and ears. I spent months approaching the creation of sound from every uncharted place I could imagine, peeling it all back to beyond its first principles. This period of exploration still informs everything I do—some part of me is always tapped in to that primal place where music is not melody, harmony, rhythm, instruments, expression, or anything else I might have learned about it, but just constellations of sound waves, and sometimes no waves at all. It was a deepening of the openness that had been sparked in me as a teenager and continues today, allowing me to make quick sharp turns in the creative process, stepping in and out of tradition, technique, and genre.

I realized that just about any sound could be manipulated to become just about any other sound, by layering it or modulating its speed or volume in certain ways. Every sound you hear has traveled through your eardrum as a vibration, and your eardrum can only be in one position at a time. Hearing multiple sound sources together, you're really hearing a combined, single sound—a certain compression or rarefaction of a pressure wave at any given point in time. (Or call it two sounds, one for each ear.) But your brain is able to make sense of this single complex wave and identify its distinct parts. *That was my cat meowing at the same time as the garbage truck driving by, plus the part of "Bohemian Rhapsody" that goes "Magnificooooo!"*

I realized that even when music was forward-thinking, it worked best when it had a connection to the familiar. It might have a couple of elements that diverged from the norm—perhaps drastically—but all its other component parts remained readily identifiable. I noticed this pattern across all genres. A classical composer might experiment wildly with harmony and form, but the pieces would be written for a standard orchestra. An electronic artist would take sound design to new heights, but rely on long-standing, basic dance rhythms. An indie band with a unique blend of instruments from different cultures would write poppy, singable songs with three choruses. Expected and unexpected, predictable and unpredictable.

I also realized that I was being a pretentious nerd. As much as I was learning and as much fun as I was having, being purely "experimental" was a way to hide that I was directionless and uncommitted. What I created had little meaning for me or anyone else. While there was a lot of "extreme" and fringe music that I loved, I had to admit that what I loved even more was . . . *pop*. Glossy, superproduced pop. And rock. And hip-hop. And folk, jazz fusion, electronica, soul, the impressionist classical movement, doo-wop . . . What were all *these* musicians doing with those same twelve notes, and mostly long-established instruments, and often the human voice, and usually 4/4 time?

And what could I do?

## EXPERIMENT AND DISCOVER

Within your field, what's something you've shied away from or never tried? It may be out of fear or simply lack of interest, but is there a version of it that you can attempt to work with as a learning experience? Perhaps it's a style, a medium, a tool, or a type of collaboration.

We grow through challenge. How can you stretch beyond your comfort zone when creating? While your efforts won't always turn into something immediately productive, experimentation almost guarantees fresh discoveries about yourself and your process. It plants seeds for ideas or techniques that expand the library of possibilities you can call upon in your future work.

Set aside time for one such exploration this week. When venturing into the unknown, take notes about the experience. What was successful? What did you learn? What new realizations occurred? Would you try this again, and if so what would you do differently?

I first started sharing my music online when I was a teenager. This was years before any of the social media platforms used today existed, and my internet use at the time would have been considered extremely nerdy. I began to connect with people in online chat rooms and forums. There was the occasional longer-lasting, long-distance pen pal relationship, but I spent a lot of time just chatting with other random lonely people. Sometimes I'd find someone to talk about music with, or even do a remote music project with, but it would usually fizzle out after a few weeks or months. Regardless, the simple act of sharing media, which many now take for granted, was not so easy or ubiquitous back then. When I began to share my music online, I paid for web hosting, learned some basic HTML, and put together my own website where I could post my recordings (which would be listened to by between zero and five of my online friends).

While I had dreams of my music reaching more people, I deliberately didn't connect my creative output to any information about myself whatsoever. I hid my real name, where I was from, and my artistic aims, and no photographs or backstory accompanied anything I released. I subscribed to the idea of the work standing on its own. What did my age or appearance or background matter? In the self-constructed space of the internet, why couldn't I exist as a purely sonic being, untethered from time and place?

It's no surprise that this was my outlook. My experience was that most of the specifics about myself marked me as different from, and usually less than, everyone around me. I hoped I could be judged on my art—the one place I could believe in myself and where I'd dependably found external validation—without turning people away because of my last name or skin color. Thus, my internal platonic ideal was a void, an empty vacuum where nothing would exist except my songs and their listeners. Slightly more realistically, I daydreamed about an art installation consisting of a long row of white headphones mounted on white walls, each headset playing a different one of my pieces on a loop. I felt an affinity with an underground record label I discovered that issued completely unlabeled vinyl, no artists or song titles ever to be associated with the music etched into the mysterious discs it released. (Ironically, and inevitably, I've now forgotten this label's name.) My own early website was only slightly less opaque. Though my projects had names, they sat simply as a numbered list of links inside a pale blue rectangle on an even paler blue background.

I believed that the work standing on its own shouldn't mean only that it stand apart from me—it should also stand apart from everything else. Each piece should be its own world, to be experienced at face value without the context of its origins, its creator's body of work, or even the rest of music history.

It was a mindset that captivated me, but I know now that it came from a place of privilege. Music for me never *had* to have meaning. I didn't have deep pain for it to speak to. I didn't have a connection to anything like war or slavery, and so I didn't have a connection to protest songs and spirituals. My parents' careers took off when I was still fairly young, so I also didn't have a connection to the everyday struggles many people face. Music for me was entirely aural entertainment, and while it could rouse strong emotions, they were just part of its enchanting diversion, like enjoying the plot turns of a Hollywood movie.

It took me years to see the roots of my inclination toward this isolationist approach. These ideas of artistic insulation and so-called purity were in fact direct expressions of who I was at the time—a person without any meaningful connection to any culture, unwilling to share anything of himself, not even knowing much about himself, and certainly confused about what he did know. Someone who, because he could never really fit in, chose to push everything away—the only control I felt I could exert.

## SELF-REFLECTION

You're shaped by your upbringing, but hopefully not trapped by it. Can you identify what interests and personality traits arose naturally within your environment? Which traits or ideals were instead reactions *against* the world you found yourself in? What parts of yourself did you have to fight to keep alive? Which were developed for protection?

Once you've identified these traits, ask yourself: Which are worth holding on to and which are worth letting go? What would be a fruitful process for you to steer the pattern of your entrenched emotions and thoughts? Consider setting aside time for deeper reflection, a conversation with a trusted friend or family member, or establishing a small new habit to nudge you in a healthier, happier direction.

We often seek some kind of fulfillment when we create, and who we are affects what and how we create. The smoother path to fulfillment starts with clearing away the aspects of ourselves that are no longer—or never were—truly part of us.

# Chapter Three

When I was twenty, I lost an enormous amount of my hearing overnight. Nothing had happened the previous day—I hadn't been injured, I wasn't at a loud concert. I put my headphones on in the morning to work on some music and it sounded off. It was much quieter in my right ear than in my left, and it seemed to lack a little treble and a lot of bass. I checked that I hadn't accidentally changed some settings somewhere in my music setup. It looked fine. Maybe my headphones were broken. I put them on backward, each cup to the opposite ear it had been on. Nothing changed about the sound—the right side was still distinctly quieter. I flipped the headphones around many, many times, not wanting to believe it. There was something wrong with my hearing.

In the ensuing two decades I've been to a lot of ENTs and audiologists, and the experience is always the same. I describe my predicament in detail. They don't seem to believe me, because hearing is usually lost gradually, with the high-end frequencies affected much more. It doesn't just vanish all of a sudden without some kind of physically traumatic event.

We do a hearing test. I enter a padded booth and put on a set of beige headphones. (Headphones are always black for music production and beige for medical purposes.) I listen to beeping tones at different frequencies and volume levels while holding a little joystick-like device.

Every time I hear a beep, I press the button on the joystick. The beeps happen at regular intervals, so I know when I'm missing them. We're mapping out the edges of the range of my hearing, the spots where I can just barely detect a sound if I'm in a completely quiet, isolated environment.

After a few minutes, they ask me to step out of the booth. They're surprised to find that the test results they've plotted on their little graph are exactly what I described. A gradual tapering above 5 kilohertz (kHz). A decline below 700 hertz (Hz), with an increasingly sharp slope as the frequencies go lower. Much greater loss in the right ear than the left. Their tests don't even go below 250 Hz. I can give myself a better version of these tests on my computer at home with a sine wave generator and a spectrum analyzer. They're only concerned about the general range of human speech—250 Hz to 6 kHz—because the only help they can try to offer anyone is some kind of hearing aid, aimed at mildly improving day-to-day communication by increasing the volume of sound being fed to the ear. There's no explanation for what happened to me. And there's no remedy for hearing loss. It's almost always permanent.

For the first few months after this issue arose, I used to hope that maybe some benign thing just went wrong—there was a blockage somewhere, or a cramp that prevented something that needed to vibrate from vibrating. Now I just hope I can find an explanation. But there never is one.

I learned to compensate—somewhat—for the deficits in my hearing. I knew the shape of the frequencies I was missing, and I paid extra attention to what I might need to work on in those areas as I arranged and mixed my music. I tried every type of device that could help. There were headphones that paired with apps that performed hearing tests and then did equalization according to the profile of your ears. There were large pads I could strap to my torso that vibrated in response to bass frequencies (designed for EDM producers to be able to feel the thump of a club system without cranking the volume in their apartments). I would mix with my hand on one of my speaker cones, comparing the feel of its vibrations with those of other songs. I asked other music producers for feedback on my mixes, and eventually, when I could afford it, I began hiring my friend Marty to do a mix pass on most of the work I put out. Since getting a subwoofer in my studio, I've left it on maximum. Between the pressure it pushes out (you can actually feel it move the air sometimes) and the eye I continually keep on my spectrum analyzers, it's the only way I can get an inkling of what's happening in the sub-bass ranges of my work.

The maddening thing is that once in a while, every few years, a bunch of my hearing will come back. It isn't what it used to be, and it isn't consistent—the bass might be back just a little bit, or it will be exaggerated, like it sometimes is when you have a bad cold and some sounds feel as if they're puncturing your skull. But the bass will be there, maybe for a day or for a week, and then it will be gone again.

I also have seasons where things get worse—I'll have bouts of tinnitus (a high-pitched ringing; thankfully it never stays for very long) or the volume of my hearing will fluctuate, becoming some degree louder or quieter for minutes or hours at a time. One of these times coincided with a week of dizzy spells, which just as suddenly stopped and never reappeared. Often with intense cardiovascular exertion I'll experience severely dampened hearing for ten to twenty minutes, which is sometimes accompanied by a thin fizzing sound, as if a little creature living in the back of my brain is enjoying a carbonated beverage.

I noticed a few years after I first lost my hearing that I was experiencing mild diplacusis, a condition common to people with asymmetrical hearing loss, where the pitch of a note can be experienced inaccurately, and differently between the two ears. Thankfully this goes unnoticed most of the time, and affects only the highest frequencies I can still hear by a few Hz. These are not pitches that are typically sung or played on an instrument, but are nevertheless contained as overtones in many sounds. If I play ascending sine wave octaves, I can hear things ever so slightly getting progressively flatter above 2 kHz, with a more pronounced effect the higher I go. At a certain point I no longer perceive them as pure tones; they take on a blurry, shimmering quality.

Sometimes all of this drives me crazy. Sometimes it absolutely devastates me. None of the tools I have will really let me enjoy music as fully as I could before. Getting my music sounding as good as it can takes a lot more time, effort, workarounds, and help from others. It can be aggravating.

At age twenty, it was enough to make me question whether I should continue pursuing music at all—but far from enough to make me come anywhere near stopping. I was already an unlikely case for musical success. This was just another aspect about me that I would attempt to transcend.

My parents warned me for years that if I wanted to do music professionally, the odds were I'd become a guitar teacher for the rest of my life, but there was no choice but music in my mind. I'd been attracted to the classical composition program at York because I'd heard it was more open to the avant-garde than other schools. At the beginning of my university years, in 2002, the choices for postsecondary education involving any music making were limited almost entirely to studying classical and jazz, with a few scarce programs focused on the recording arts. I had more classical background than anything else, but I wasn't accomplished enough to be a performer, so classical composition seemed like the best fit. I was excited—I'd been crafting original pieces in all kinds of genres with my little setup at home, so how much more could I hone these skills with formal training?

Not much, it turned out. I had discovered for myself most of the writing and arranging techniques that were brought up in class. Dynamics, structure, space, variation, layering, tension, resolution, surprise . . . Already knowing about these things, of course, didn't automatically make me a good composer. But I was still a bit let down.

Our first assignment was to write a piano sonata. I turned in something competent but not terribly inspired. The chords were choppy and the melody wasn't very emotive. I'm not sure if I felt restricted by some assignment guideline or if it was just the word "sonata" and its association with three-hundred-year-old European music that led me to create something completely banal. In any case, two weeks later the sheet music was handed back to me with a fitting grade—75 percent. The number was written with a circle around it in red ink beside my staff lines, along with half a sentence of feedback remarking on the banality.

Students were offered the opportunity to play their pieces for the class. They'd sit at the piano while the rest of us watched from our semicircle formation of desks around it. Notes would ring out, we'd

45

applaud politely, and our professor—a wiry old man with thick glasses and long, scraggly hair—would make some comment or ask others what they thought, which elicited two or three surface-level, single-sentence snippets of feedback. I didn't volunteer my piece.

I augmented my education as I had done for years: on my own, on the internet. I hunted for ways to improve my creations, which outside of class had little to do with classical music. They were various fusions of the modern influences I'd leaned into most since returning from my noise explorations: rap, indie rock, and anything electronic. Every new music production tip was like a drug hit; I chased my highs by trawling message boards. *Parallel compression! Move the claps slightly ahead of the beat! If you only have one microphone, point it at the drummer's crotch!*

The internet also fostered a new habit in me: gear acquisition. I'd been working with a spartan setup for years, but the growing internet offered views of fascinating-looking toys: instruments and equipment that promised to make your music better—or at least more fun to create with than whatever you already owned. I spent the most time on eBay, looking for deals on guitar pedals or occasionally a budget synthesizer. I found I could sometimes flip a purchase that I didn't end up using, maybe inching out a 10 percent profit. It wasn't much, but I told myself it was like getting paid to try out music gear.

On the next composition assignment, I tried much harder. We were to write a string quartet. Perhaps the parameters were freer, or I just had more ideas, but I was proud of my composition this time around. I thought I had made something poignant, with interesting phrasing and subtle, elegant departures from standard tonality. I could imagine the violin singing its melody with a mournful vibrato, buoyed by the other strings swelling beneath it. I hoped my teacher would find it moving. I handed it in with confidence.

Two weeks of student life went by.

*Writing a paper.*

*Falafel wrap.*

*Music history class.*

*Smoking weed and writing mediocre poetry.*
*Falafel wrap.*
*Counterpoint class.*
*Trawling message boards.*
*Falafel wrap with friends, and somehow deciding once again that our drink for the night would be vodka mixed with Kool-Aid.*

Then the day arrived when our composition assignments were to be returned. All my hope and pride deflated as I received my manuscript with another red circle with a red 75 inside it. No attached commentary.

This time around—no string quartet at our disposal—we didn't listen to anyone's pieces in class. It was just on to the next lecture topic about how to create a twelve-tone row, or Beethoven's clarinet parts in the *Eroica*. Was this really how I was going to learn to compose? Trading in sheet music for a number, listening to an old man talk about music written in other centuries? This was ostensibly a class about creating music, *and we never created music during class.* In school I often daydreamed about the music I wanted to be working on instead; now those daydreams started to include ways I would rather learn—or teach—music.

As the end of the school year approached, I needed to start looking for a summer job. My experience consisted of absolutely random employment I'd had throughout high school: data entry (my accuracy had not been great), construction (which makes me sound tough and capable, but in reality my job was hanging doors in a school), and on Thursday nights I'd help with a mix of things at my mom's pediatric practice: reception, filing, weighing babies, and testing the acidity of their pee. One summer I also worked for the city of Ottawa's parks department to . . . guard a pond? I would linger under a sign reading NO SWIMMING 1PM–7AM and tell people not to swim between one p.m. and seven a.m. Supposedly this was for "conservation" reasons, but most of the employees thought it was because rich people in the giant houses nearby wanted it to be quiet. I also trimmed hedges and cleared dirt paths from time to time, but the day-to-day of this job was: *Keep people out of the pond.*

All that is to say: I was looking for my first job in a new city, and my experience did not make me a very employable person. Pond guarding. Door hanging. Pee testing. So, with all this in mind, I tried to make my job applications stand out in another way.

This comic strip cover letter got me an assistant manager job offer at one of Canada's largest record store chains.

In composition class, we were given our final assignment for the year—a completely open project. We were encouraged to experiment and embrace the avant-garde. We were given a rough length guideline but that was it.

I should have been excited to have a chance to break out of all the classical conventions we'd been focusing on—after all, that's what I'd been doing in my creative output outside of class: experimenting with form, harmony, rhythm, instrumentation, sampling, and electronics. Maybe there was a way I could weave all of that into something that would show my professor I *was* creative, that I *did* have something unique to offer, but by this point I was too jaded by my experience in the program. It hadn't helped me make any meaningful strides toward my creative goals. I put off thinking about how I'd approach this project for a while. I was occupied with other music composition business anyway.

I never did take that record store job, because the same week it was offered to me, I had an idea that changed my life. I was still spending far too much of my free time on eBay. There was a rhythm to it—getting excited about a new auction, seeing what I could sell off to be able to make the purchase, coming in at the last second with a "snipe" bid, and enjoying my new gear until the next exciting auction came along. The peripherals of my little music setup were always shifting, and I recycled the same $500 for years trying out new things: a long-neck banjo, a mixer with motorized faders, a theremin built into a baby doll's head. (A theremin is played without being touched; antennas or light sensors detect the proximity of your hands to the instrument, one controlling volume and one controlling pitch. You could conjure eerie, gliding tones out of thin air by waving your arms around this decapitated baby head. Whoever built it also made its eyes light up red. Great for any live show.)

Maybe it was the dread of spending another summer at a job I wouldn't like, or maybe I had just let eBay permeate and percolate in every corner of my brain. For whatever reason, a thought reared its head: *I will auction my music skills.*

I'd been creating all this music in various genres, and between the music theory I'd been taught and the music production skills I'd taught myself, I knew I could create at least a half-decent facsimile of most kinds of music. Maybe people would hire me to make something custom for them. Would anybody want that?

I put together a listing describing my idea. *If you win this auction, I will create a piece of music for you in any style.* I went on to describe my experience and listed my equipment, as well as specifying a delivery window (one to two weeks) and maximum length (three minutes). I provided no audio examples. The starting bid: $1.

*Click.* The listing was published. I had no reason to believe this would lead to anything, but I believed it anyway.

*Six hours of sleep.*

*Toast.*

*Bus ride, transfer, bus ride.*

*Music history class.*

*Coffee.*

*Composition class.*

*Falafel wrap.*

*Bus ride, transfer, bus ride.*

In this pre-smartphone era, I might not use the internet for the first eight or ten hours of my day. It seems inconceivable now.

I lived in a house with Jen, my high school friend who'd gotten me that birthday cake I'd almost missed, and another roommate we'd found online. (Side note. His name was Michael Bolton—like the singer—which he hated. It was the exact same situation as the Michael Bolton character in *Office Space*. Our Michael Bolton was adamant that everyone address him instead as Max Power.)

I arrived back in my room, throwing my bag on the floor as I raced to my desk. I turned on my computer and checked my eBay listing. Someone had bid $30. It had worked! How had they come across my listing? I never did end up finding out.

Then I noticed there had been seven bids. I clicked to unfold the chronological list of them all. *Four* people had bid on my auction so far, and two of them were now engaged in a bit of a back and forth. I checked the page counter. The listing had been viewed more than fifty times.

There were still a few days to go on the auction. I had seen how these things tended to unfold. A new listing would go up and there would be a few excited but low bids. It would then die down for the bulk of the auction's duration, gathering awareness from other prospective buyers but fewer bids. Then in the final hours, or even the final minutes, the price would shoot up as the most serious parties angled for their deal.

My auction followed this pattern exactly. Over the next few days, the price slowly climbed to $50. On the final day, I watched as these same two usernames who had been in a bidding war since the beginning duked it out for the win. The auction ended with a bid of $105 from bunnygirl45. I was ecstatic.

This was my first client, bunnygirl45—known offline as Vanessa. Over email we sorted out what she wanted: an instrumental track in the industrial style of Nine Inch Nails. But she had an extra request she hoped I could accommodate. Could she record herself singing with the microphone on her webcam, then send me the vocal to mix in? I told her yes, of course, no problem.

I got to work on a first draft of the track, which took only two hours. A pulsing synth bass line, heavy programmed drums, some atmospheric sound effects, and distorted guitars coming in for the choruses. I was a longtime NIN fan and knew it didn't measure up to Trent Reznor's exacting production style, but I felt I'd captured the tone nonetheless. I figured I'd send Vanessa a working draft and get her feedback before sinking a lot more time in. I exported the track and attached it to an email.

Within a couple hours I heard back:

OMG!!! IT'S PERFECT!!! THIS IS SO GOOD!!!!

It seemed I had already surpassed Vanessa's expectations. She was ready to lay down her vocals. I didn't think the track was ready, but who was I to argue with a happy customer? $105 for two hours was by far the best wage I'd ever made.

Vanessa took a few days to write her part and then sent me what she had recorded. It was the worst-quality audio I had ever heard. It was worse than anything I'd done with my boom box and tapes at five years old. Was she recording inside a broken TV? Was her webcam made of potatoes? Her voice, timid and breathy, struggled to surface through a froth of static. Half of her lyrics were muffled beyond comprehension, but I could make out enough to ascertain the subject matter of her opus: bunnies. We were making a Nine Inch Nails–inspired industrial rock song about bunnies.

I did the quickest mix job of my life, slapping this file on top of the instrumental I'd made, not touching any of the song's already *PERFECT, SO GOOD* components. A layer of static now rested over everything like snow, and Vanessa's words fought even harder to be heard. Was she really going to be happy with this? Was this worth $105? Maybe I could recommend a microphone to her—even a dirt cheap one would dramatically improve her recording quality. I exported the song and sent it to her.

She loved it. No revisions necessary.

I went on eBay and posted another auction listing.

Time was running out for my final composition project, and I found myself caring less and less about it. I was already writing lots of music, and now I was making money doing it.

For two months at this point, I'd been running a couple of auctions each week, with some of the winning bids approaching $200 (and this was 2004 dollars). I learned that Vanessa's song had been a unique case—nobody else wanted to be involved in the creation of the music. One thing everyone had in common, however, is that they were thrilled with the first thing I sent them and never asked for any revisions, which surprised me, as I'd never been fond of my voice, and I knew my production quality was far from professional.

Most of the songs I created were for special occasions. A personalized song as a birthday gift for a zany friend or a hard-to-buy-for parent. An emotional ballad for someone to play before proposing to their partner, or a celebration song to burst out of the speakers after a marriage pronouncement. I found it hilarious that my basement bedroom recordings were making their way into some of the most special moments in people's lives. Also, many customers requested songs for their pets. I discovered there was a completely untapped market for pet theme songs, and wrote about many dogs and cats, the occasional lizard or ferret, and once a snake.

I learned a lot about these random people (and animals). To be able to personalize the songs, I asked for detailed descriptions of my subjects and lists of their favorite activities, places, foods, and of course music so I could create something in a style they'd appreciate. I'd learn about their aspirations and sometimes got a synopsis of their childhood. The more material the better.

When I started writing a song, the first thing I did was scan all this information for preexisting rhymes and see how I could fit them into couplets. This was just a shortcut to make my job easier, but it made the songs appear cleverer when such a connection could be made within the substance of someone's life. *He's an environmental scientist, and his friends make fun of him for owning too many appliances? This song is writing itself!*

I took a genuine tone for the romantic songs, but I had much more fun with the personalized theme songs. They were meant to be humorous and played for their target at a party in front of their friends. The lyrics would celebrate them while also getting in a few lighthearted digs. It was especially satisfying for everyone involved when I could exploit personal quirks or career predicaments for a punch line. *She spends so long ironing out her shirt creases / No wonder she hasn't finished her PhD thesis!* My job was, essentially, to roast people.

Jen, who had some basic web design skills, helped me set up a website. It wasn't to make my operation more professional—I would've been happy to stay on eBay. It was because I'd had my next idea: *Songs To Wear Pants To.*

In the still-nascent internet of the early aughts, before social media or video streaming existed, only nerds like me had *fun* online. Using a web browser was normally for boring grown-up tasks like sending emails and looking up directions. (In those days, you'd find the route you needed to drive and then *print out the directions on paper.*) But there were people who created fantastic online destinations: *Bitter Films, Homestar Runner,* sites and forums dedicated to music production or favorite bands. I decided I was going to be one of those people.

I was especially inspired by *Exploding Dog,* whose creator would make somber or ironic illustrations based on titles people sent him, and *Eric Conveys an Emotion,* a guy who'd built an audience posting funny photos of himself depicting ever more specific emotions that people suggested. I thought a musical version of those ideas could exist, and so *Songs To Wear Pants To* was born. It was a silly title that came out of nowhere, but I liked the absurdity it promised. (My only other contender was *Magic Song Land,* so . . .)

Anyone visiting this site could suggest an idea, and I would bring to life slapdash executions of the ideas that inspired me most, usually under a minute long. I needed a suggestion to start the site off, so I asked Jen, who told me to make a beat using only the sound of a toilet flushing. It turned out awesome.

Jen shared the website on her LiveJournal, an early blogging platform where she'd developed several online friendships. These people, my friends, and our roommate Michael Bolton/Max Power were the next to suggest song ideas: a song about Jell-O, a song about spoons with spoons as the only instrumentation, a Gregorian chant about people photocopying their bums.

The songs' bizarre subject matter and humor made them quite "shareable"—a word we weren't even using back then to describe viral content. I don't think we were even using the words "viral" and "content" yet in the context of internet media. This was before Facebook and Twitter, so I think people were just emailing my link to their family and friends? In any case, I was having a blast responding to prompts and experimenting with genres I hadn't tried producing before. Within a few days of launching the website, I was getting requests from total strangers, along with hundreds of site visits a day. Within a week, I had an email from the record producer Steve Albini suggesting a song about a wrestling rivalry.

In the sidebar on my website, I made a note to visitors that they could contact me for longer, personalized commissions. I enjoyed creating this content for my new Fun Internet Destination, but I wasn't trying to work for free. To deter people from taking advantage of the free songs I was making, I developed a recurring trope in my content to self-referentially poke fun at the person who had requested the song. A guy who asked me to write a song about his crush, describing only her physical attributes, got a song with the chorus "I don't even care about your personality!"

School concerns faded into the background. I had something else I was working on now. I started skipping classes to be able to create more content, which I justified because it was bringing in commissions. I increased my rates. My audience slowly grew.

With all of this occupying my attention, it was a week before the deadline for my final composition project when I decided what I was going to do. Supposedly this program was open to the avant-garde; I would see how my professor judged nontraditional pieces, music without precedent or parameters.

I got out five sheets of manuscript paper and a pencil and I filled the staff lines with completely random notes. Long, short, high, low, fast, slow. I indicated that it was a duet between a piano and a cello. There were no repeated melodies or rhythms. There was no key signature. The tempo was chosen at random. It took me less than half an hour. I never listened to any of it.

It was sure to sound awful, full of clashing notes, with nothing substantial for the ear to follow and no discernible intent. I did not care. I called it *Untitled*, made no mention of how I'd "composed" it, and handed it in.

Two weeks later the sheets were handed back to me. I looked for the little red circle. How would my professor assess my experimental opus? What grade would he assign five pages of randomly scribbled notes?

Seventy-five percent.

I transferred out of the classical composition program.

# Chapter Four

How to learn music:

1. Never play anything that isn't written down.
2. Never play anything that was composed less than two hundred years ago.
3. Never create anything original.

These are three of the main pillars of music education that many teachers of Western classical instruments swear by. They don't think or speak of them this way, but these precepts are easily inferred from the methods used in their lessons. They believe in developing only skills and techniques that will allow students to reproduce the works of long-dead European composers. In too many music lessons happening around the world, there's no exploring, no jamming, no deviation from centuries-old manuscripts, and the notion of creating original work of your own is never mentioned, as if creating and experimenting can't go hand in hand with learning fundamentals. There's a lot less *listening* than one would expect, and there's even less fun. How did they manage to remove *fun* from music?

In fairness, these methods have produced countless skilled musicians, and these European composers are beloved and respected for a reason. But the products of this type of training are musicians who have developed little to no proficiency with improvisation, composition, or imagination. I'm tremendously grateful that there was some force that compelled me to start writing pieces on my own and exploring music outside of piano lessons. I've met so many classical musicians who can play with marvelous expression and technique yet freeze up if they're asked to do anything without sheet music. They've learned to follow, but not to forge anything new. They seem to live in a world of rules they're afraid to break.

I'm not against this system. In part, I'm a product of it. The world is also a better place for having instrumental virtuosos in it who can bring to life some of the most beautiful music that has ever been written. But I don't think anyone can argue that the Western classical method is a comprehensive approach to understanding, appreciating, and creating music. It's a single shining strand on a loom. I think anyone would benefit from seeing much more of the tapestry.

APPROACH FROM EVERY ANGLE

There's no book or class that's ever going to contain or convey the vast richness of every artistic practice, never mind the fact that new ones are constantly being created. I don't claim to have all the answers, but I can share the way I've come to see music holistically, and the way I still go about learning new things—and I believe this is applicable to any creative field.

It's about approaching things from every possible angle: learning both formally *and* informally, on your own *and* from experts, through studying books *and* getting out into the world. You have your own learning style and will have your own balance of approaches that may best suit you. But I'd still recommend this: wherever you see a dividing line between learning methods, try it from both sides.

I'll share some examples from the domain of music.

### Formal/Informal

The Western classical system—the Royal Conservatory, specifically—was a great education for me. I know I was *just* harping on it, but it's a potent form of musical training. It's just far from the only one.

I benefited tremendously from learning the layout of the piano, all the key signatures and their associated scales, and how to read notation and see how some of history's greatest musical minds constructed their masterpieces. I practiced daily—rarely more than an hour, which is much less than those who excel in the classical world, but still a good amount of time that led to steady improvement and deeper internalization of the material. I played along to a metronome. I isolated elements to practice: just the left-hand or right-hand part; just changing between three specific chord shapes; just the tricky passage from bars 38 to 42. Ear training helped me identify rhythms, intervals, and chord progressions as easily as looking at a picture and saying what colors were in it. I filled several books' worth of handwritten notation, completing music theory exercises, which forced me to create the music mentally—to sonify and hold in my mind several notes at once, or to be able to understand a rhythm in less time than it takes to play.

It's rigorous, and it works. But it's not the only thing that works. Moving along the spectrum from formal to informal, there are so many ways to learn different aspects of music. There are less rigid systems in the classical world, such as the Suzuki and Yamaha methods. There are more casual lessons available for any instrument—many that you could probably find a teacher for in your neighborhood. There are group classes, workshops, open mics, jam nights, worship bands, and drum circles. There are coffee dates with fellow artists. There are ten-year-olds using mobile apps or taking radios apart. Music is everywhere.

I had a lot of formal music education, but I had (and continue to have) significantly more *informal* education: things learned by being in the same room as other musicians, by experimenting on my own, or by exploring the internet (which becomes a better educational resource with every passing day). When it comes to writing, recording, collaborating, producing, mixing, even utilitarian things like restringing a guitar or soldering—none of my knowledge of any of this came from a class-room. Much of it could have—there's a course for just about anything now—and that would also have been helpful. There are lots of tips and techniques you can pick up from an expert that you wouldn't even have known to search for. But there's a certain kind of learning that only happens without goals and guardrails. The classroom is not where the producer learns to direct the energy of a session, where the DJ learns to read a room, or where the songwriter finds their own sound. In a formal setting, you learn about all the things in music that other people have already figured out. In the freedom of informal play and exploration, in the open space where you can create without judgment and follow any idea to the end of a path of your own choosing—that's where you find how *you* fit into music.

## Broad/Deep

It pays to specialize. People who do things the best, who can take things the furthest, often reap the most success. They go deeper than most are willing or able to go and resurface with treasures we would never have imagined. Virtuosic performance, stunning instrument design, true compositional innovation—these things are rarely achieved without years of singular focus.

The opposite, or at least the counterpart, is breadth—absorbing a multitude of sounds and ideas from different cultures, times, and paradigms. There is *so much* to music, it's funny we even use the phrase "learning music" at all. What are we learning? The notes in a major scale? How to build a viola? Granular synthesis? Why sound travels faster underwater? Taking in a broad range of musical experiences and knowledge has a compounding effect—what you learn in one area often brings more understanding to another area you already know.

If there's one thing I'm not humble about, that I might say I'm among the best at, it's having breadth. I've gone deep on going broad. I don't know anyone else who appreciates and approaches the range of music I do to the same degree. Almost every genre requires a shift in perspective, and many listeners enjoy music from a specific, narrower frame of reference. But I've come to appreciate the huge number of worlds within music, some of which overlap, and some of which have nothing in common besides the idea of sound ringing through time. There's music for your body and music for your mind. There's music that entertains and music that changes how you understand the world. There's music that tells a story, music that conjures emotion, and music that is more of a conceptual exercise. It's quite common for the compositional focus of a piece of music to be the melody, harmony, and vocals, but many forms exist that instead emphasize rhythm instruments, electronic textures, or any other number of elements. There is also, of course, music that blends any of the above into its own wonderful concoction.

One of my calling cards is my "found sound" music, wherein I compose and perform pieces using what most would consider to be nonmusical items—things like balloons, pizza, dental equipment, and pants. It's an idea that people love—a mix of fun, surprise, inventiveness, and whatever emotion I've imbued in the composition of any given iteration of this concept. It also makes for an entertaining visual. You've seen thousands of people sing before, but how many have you watched carve a carrot into a whistle? You can plink around on a piano, sure, but what about using the sound of an old upright hitting the ground after being dropped from a crane?

Making music with unorthodox sound sources is strangely captivating, and many an ad agency has approached me for this particular ability. I paid off most of my mortgage by making music with cars, soap, phones, food, sports equipment, and shaving supplies. (Never mind what I said about being humble. I'm great at this too.)

I bring this up as an example of both breadth and depth. The depth is probably easier to see. The amount of music made exclusively using sounds from everyday objects is relatively small, and I believe I'm one of the handful of musicians working this way who've taken it the furthest. When someone has a project that requires this approach, there's a good chance I'll be among the people they'll call.

But it's an approach that's possible only *through* breadth. Creating a compelling piece of music using nothing but frozen fries or water bottles, despite maybe sounding like a simple novelty, requires open-mindedness and a massive synthesis of skills. There's no formal technique for how to mic a tray of fries—that kind of decision is made through the experience of recording many other instruments. Proficiency with sampling and audio manipulation is of course paramount in these found-sound pieces. Not to mention that, when composing them, I'm drawing on a wealth of influences—in part because of the aesthetic demands of a given project, but also because sounds are so much more limited than purpose-built instruments. With everyday items, it's far harder to produce a pitched sound than a percussive sound (hit any two objects together and you have a drum) so I rely on my knowledge of a disparate set of genres that place a heavy emphasis on rhythm and contain expansive repertoires of percussion tones. In my years at York, I studied West African drumming, joined a Brazilian samba squad, and took lessons on the tabla, the beautiful Indian percussive instrument. I've also loved hip-hop since I was a kid (my mom will tell you I was rapping before I was in piano lessons) and have drummed for several bands. Experience with all these musical traditions has served me immeasurably as I've been tasked with creating catchy grooves using an SUV or a bunch of dog food.

I don't have *the* answer regarding where and how much to focus your creative experience and curiosity. I think following instincts and interests is key. What I *can* say about what I've learned is that depth gets results—but depth is tremendously enhanced by breadth.

### Theoretical/Practical

Music theory is resolutely avoided by many who think it's complicated or boring, and I won't lie, many aspects of it are. It's work. But I always encourage people to learn at least the fundamentals, as those principles can open doors for understanding and creating music in many genres. While mastery and fluidity don't come easily, understanding the concepts is much less daunting than many make it out to be; most people I've taught get the hang of it with a few solid days of effort!

There's a misconception that music theory is made up of rules that must be strictly adhered to, but really it's more like a big pile of things that many people tend to agree sound good. There may be elements you disagree with or simply don't want to use, and there are definitely things that *aren't* in the agreed-upon pile that also sound good, but the basics of music theory are a fantastic starting point for understanding how music works and what you can do with it.

Many musicians have approached making music on intuition alone and gotten by fine, but I believe they all could have benefited from understanding some rudiments. Internalizing those concepts allows you to get ideas out faster, communicate better with collaborators, and learn more about the music you love. "The Beatles didn't know music theory!" people argue—the quintessential example I've been hearing throughout my life; it came up when I met my first guitar-playing friend at age thirteen and it's come up innumerable times since then. First of all, if your answer to the idea of learning music theory is to hope that you're a Lennon- or McCartney-level genius, you may find yourself disappointed. But more significantly, while it's true the Fab Four didn't study formally or learn classical notation, their music displays a deep understanding of how to use those twelve notes we all have. If you watch *Get Back* or *McCartney 3, 2, 1*, you can see the band members know a great deal—the names of the notes, the names of many chords, they speak about reharmonizing a chord with a different bass note, they use terms like "octave," "syncopation," "staccato," "3/4 time," "arpeggio." If you dig into their history, you discover that they studied songs they loved by replaying a bar or two at a time from their records, working things out until they could reproduce them flawlessly. They once took a multibus trip to the opposite side of Liverpool because they heard of someone who knew a chord they didn't know. *They went across town to knock on a stranger's door to learn a single chord!* If that's not dedication to learning music theory, I don't know what is.

I should clarify that it's not music notation I encourage people to learn. Classical notation is just a system, a relatively new one in the grand scheme of things, that represents elements of music that existed long before it. (It's useful if you'll be working a lot with classical musicians.) When I encourage others to learn theory, I'm not referring to notation. I'm referring to the understanding of how notes can relate to each other.

Of course, you can't learn to make music by just taking in information about chords and keys. You need practice manifesting it, letting it flow out of you, whether that's through your voice, with an instrument in your hands, or by bringing your ideas to life through composition. You can learn what a major-7-flat-5 chord *is* and still be able to spend your whole life exploring different ways to *use* it. The practical side of the equation is about getting hands-on experience putting the theoretical side to use, as well as exploring and discovering in less structured ways. It's about strengthening your capabilities through time, physical work, and real-life projects. Where the rudiments of music are concerned, this means practicing your instrument, jamming and collaborating with others, performing, and also just experimenting to see what happens.

This is just one example of the axis of theory and practice, but it can apply to writing, mixing, sound design, or just about any other area. It's about gaining technical knowledge to guide you (which might also mean showing you what you *don't* want to do) as well as real-world experience to get you to understand these aspects of music in your body and soul. I've found equal benefit from being able to take in the instruction of teachers and from figuring things out on my own through trial and error. Both are helpful, and neither can replace the other.

Formal/informal, broad/deep, theoretical/practical—these are some of the main divides along which you might try taking a multipronged learning approach, but if any others occur to you they're likely to be worth exploring.

What has been your typical way of expanding your creative skill set, and how could you shake that up?

Here are additional examples for inspiration.

**Passive/Active:** I glean a lot from music just by letting it wash over me. However, I also notice details and structures I never did before when I actively listen while taking notes.

**Private lessons/Group classes:** It's probably worth trying each at least once. Private lessons provide more personal instruction and attention, but it can also be beneficial to be in a room with other students who will have different questions and perspectives than you do. (It can also be a great way to make friends.)

**High pressure/Low pressure:** There are benefits to casual, exploratory learning, and there are benefits to turning up the heat. If you're someone who thrives under pressure and tends to jump right into the deep end, maybe you'd get something different out of a slower, more meditative or open-ended approach. If you often play it safe, what's something that could get you out of your comfort zone?

We were recording the bubbling bong water as Adil took a hit.

I was engineering the session from my laptop. The intro of the song we were working on had a head-nodding beat, a synth pad, and shades of color from Iain's tenor saxophone. But we felt it could use some extra texture, and the bong was right there, having been in regular use that evening. Iain had taken the clip-on mic from his sax and affixed it to the bowl.

I had met these two—both sax players—during my third year at York University. We shared a couple of classes and eventually found ourselves jamming together. I'm not sure who started it—they had been good friends before I met them—but they were the first people I ever saw playing saxophones through guitar pedals. It made for an intoxicating, electrified take on jazz. The classic *wah* effect gave them new expressive possibilities. Reverb and delay turned the notes they blared into swirling atmospheres.

This evening we were set up in the living room of Adil's small student apartment, in the company of his roommate and some friends.

"This is too funny," I said, holding up the bong with the mic attached to it. "We gotta get a picture of this!"

Mobile phones in those days could snap about four pixels at a time, so there was a scramble to find a proper camera, but neither Adil nor his roommate could locate theirs. It probably didn't help that the apartment was currently smokier than a bar. We were starting to fear we'd lose this moment.

"Guys, guys," Iain said, squinting through a cloud. He'd just taken another hit and was smirking at us, holding up the bong in one hand.

He unclipped the mic from it. He clipped it back on.

"We can do this whenever we want."

We named ourselves after a label on the back of one of Iain's pedals: Analog Input. Adil, Iain, and I formed the core of the band: the two of them played sax and synths, while I handled production and vocals. A rotating cast of other students joined us for gigs and recording sessions as different strains of music developed and called for more instruments. I felt totally out of my depth with these virtuosic players from York's jazz program, who were the kind of people who had total dedication to their instrument and would practice six to ten hours a day. Meanwhile, I had enrolled in classical composition, and had let my guitar and piano chops slide in favor of making beats on my computer. As a vocalist, my voice was nasally and untrained. But they liked my beats, and they liked that I could rap fast.

Our sound arose naturally out of the blend of our three personalities and musical interests. We were exploring a hazy fusion of jazz, hip-hop, and electronica, with live sets that left large swaths of time open for improvisation in between tightly structured songs where I'd sing hooks we came up with together and spit my double-time verses. When I wasn't doing that, I'd be triggering beats from my laptop and tweaking improvised vocals through a growing collection of guitar pedals to create strange layers of effects. One technique I came up with during this time was running my voice through a DJ mixer and flicking the crossfader so I could shred a sustained note into rhythmic slivers.

These jazz cats had a real community, and it seemed I had stumbled into friendship with people who knew how to throw a party, so there were many nights spent with us playing a set and then DJing at someone's dorm, a bar, or, once, a decrepit former crack house that an acquaintance was trying to turn into a venue. When Adil's student visa was up and he had to return to Malaysia, we threw a farewell show at Toronto's iconic El Mocambo and the place was completely packed.

During this time, I was also involved in other musical projects. I was part of a duo with my friend Stephen: he would play guitar through my pedals, and I would turn them on and off and twist their knobs, creating an ethereal sound bath. It was a feedback loop—each of us responding to the other to build these shimmering soundscapes. I supported any of my friends who needed a guitar or bass player for a gig, whether we were playing country, pop, folk, or rock. There were a number of people I'd get together with to make beats. (This was in the early aughts, when good samples were not easy to come by online, and sharing drum sounds with each other was an *event*.) I was the only person most of my friends knew who had gotten into recording, so even with my primitive computer setup I made sporadic money as a DIY engineer/producer/mixer.

Working with these people taught me a lot that I would never have learned at school: how to run a session, how to share and build upon ideas, how to hold an audience's attention, the ins and outs of gigging, and so much more. I picked up some knowledge at York, but I quickly realized the traditional classroom setting wasn't an effective way to teach many practical aspects of music creation. There's a lot more to be learned by sitting in with players twice as good as you, or trying to record a band in your bedroom, or getting onstage in a bar full of strangers. One way that school did help here: networking and community building. In just a couple of years, I went from working in complete isolation to thriving within the company of kindred spirits.

One of the biggest takeaways from this chapter in my life was about the power of collaboration and the potency of each individual voice. When musicians work well together, the whole is fantastically greater than the sum of its parts. We make fun of the idea now that a generation of kids was raised to believe they were all special, but I believe it still, because it's clear with every musical exchange I'm a part of. I can bring the same seed of an idea to ten different people and we'll come out with ten totally unique songs. I've worked with beginners and amateurs who may have lacked some of the prowess or experience needed to execute what's in their minds, but all had interesting ideas that no one else would've come up with. Every person in the room—if they're passionate about music and they feel open and encouraged—contributes something one-of-a-kind, something absolutely *them*. Collaborating with anyone will bring out different parts of each of you, creating a blend that would never happen with anyone else. And collaborating with someone who's an *amazing fit* for you? Treasure those relationships, because they're a door to beautiful, life-giving, never-ending magic.

People are complex, and that makes working with people complex, but there are ways to make things go a little smoother. Here are some things to keep in mind to help encourage and maintain healthy, productive collaboration.

**Maintain the creative flow.** Creative sessions generally follow an unspoken rule: *There are no nos*—if you don't like an idea or a direction, it's your job to steer it a bit, improve and build upon it, or suggest something new. While it's occasionally useful to discuss why something isn't working, often it's better to just get on with trying to make it work.

**Be attuned to people's needs.** These always include feeling valued, respected, and heard, and sometimes we also require food, water, and breaks. Keep the energy up by letting it be known whenever you like or love something, whether it's a stroke of genius or an accidental quirk. At the same time, try to be someone whose energy doesn't need to be managed. If someone shoots down your idea, it doesn't mean you're bad. It might be the wrong idea for the moment, or for the project. It might be a brilliant idea that your partner is unable to recognize, or it might have triggered something uncomfortable for them. It also could just be a bad idea—but you'll have lots of good ones too.

**Communicate early and clearly about roles and ownership.** There are basically two ways for a collaborative project to work. Either it belongs to everyone involved, and they all get a fair share of the rewards, or it belongs to one party, and that party compensates everyone else for their contributions.

**Know when the good outweighs the bad.** Sometimes you might have to extricate yourself from a project or, better yet, recognize that you shouldn't get involved in the first place. How can you know? Here's a helpful triangle.

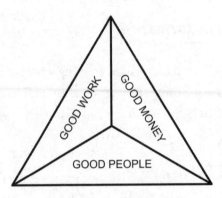

*At least two out of three.*

Any project that hits two-thirds of the triangle is likely to be worth your time, and any that doesn't has a good chance of leaving you frustrated and filled with regret. (I'd also give the base of the triangle a bit more weight.) If you ever get all three, you win! Shout *bingo!* and clear the chips off your scorecard to start again.

As with learning your craft, putting it into practice usually benefits from—and often even necessitates—contradictory approaches. The creative process is rife with conflicts, and a large part of who you are as an artist lies in where you strike the balance between them. One of the most important ideas I wish I'd understood earlier in my artistic journey, or even just in life, is that the world is constantly telling us that things are mutually exclusive, when in fact many can coexist.

No matter what you're hoping to create, I think you'll find it helps to embrace these and many other dualities.

**You need to create *and* destroy; there is growth *and* decay.** For every beautiful, finished work of art, there's a mountain of material that has been thrown away, lost, or left in a drawer. There are countless ideas that didn't work or didn't fit, bad takes, mediocre sketches, loose ends, dead ends, and things that were just forgotten about. It's okay. All of this is fertilizer and soil. You won't have a lush garden without it.

**Making art is both sacred *and* casual.** I take my creative time seriously. I approach it with reverence. It's essential not only to my job but to my mental and spiritual health. At the same time, I'm not precious about what I create. I'm having fun, I'm going with the flow, and I'm throwing ideas around with the nonchalance of a casual conversation.

**Make a mess *and* craft and refine.** There's a time for exploring new things and trying out ideas where you have no clue what will happen. There's also a time to be deliberate and exacting and work toward specific outcomes. If you're meticulous and methodical about your art, perhaps you could benefit from occasionally taking a looser approach. If you always think it should be a good fun time and lose interest when it comes to finishing a project, you might be surprised by what happens when you (sometimes) get serious about it.

**We're after some degree of grittiness *and* polish.** Even as you're putting the final touches on a piece, you often don't want to smooth every edge and scrub away every speck of dirt. For music producers, "filthy" and "clean" are both compliments—but generally we don't want to be told our work is "messy" or "sterile." Everyone has some level of quality they'd like to reach in a project, but usually not at the cost of squeezing out all the elements that make it feel human and real. If precision and purity are on one end of the spectrum, and shoddiness and chaos are on the other, where does your style fall?

**Collaboration *and* isolation are beneficial to the creative process.** Alone or with others, the creative act is a different experience. You may find you work better one way or the other, but perhaps you'll want a blend: isolation in some stages or seasons, collaboration in others. You can be a social butterfly *and* a lone wolf. You can be *both* the artist who's always inviting the crew to the studio for late-night drinks and jams *and* the one who holes up alone in a winter cabin and rises at dawn to meditate before hewing away at a magnum opus. (Just probably not in the same day.)

In my scattered and eclectic fashion, I tend to take things even further than the above; I'm more than willing to straddle lines that people often advise me against. I will publish both dark, deeply serious pieces and lighthearted, comedic ones. I will just as readily release a song I made in an afternoon and one I labored over for years. I will create an album where I'm determined to write and play every part myself, and then another that relies on generative composition processes, machine learning tools, and mountains of other people's samples. Nothing is off-limits, and the only rules are the ones I've made up for the current moment. **DO EVERYTHING POSSIBLE**—that's the Andrew Huang way. And it leads to only *occasional* burnout! (More on that later.)

# Chapter Five

I left York's composition program after being graded 75 percent on five pages of randomly filled sheet music, but I didn't leave the school. Since childhood it had been drilled into me that a university education was basically the most important thing a person could have. Rather than pursue a music degree, I learned I could take a broader smattering of courses and graduate as a bachelor of fine arts, and this is where I can truly credit York's musical openness. It was here that I studied Indian and West African percussion. I took a course on synthesizers and another on microtonal music. Samba was my favorite—I got to strap a massive bass drum called a surdo to my waist and march with a fifty-member squad in Toronto street festivals as we let out the most thunderous, danceable music I'd ever heard. All of this continued to feed my musical appetite.

At the same time, I was sharpening my production skills. At the height of my song commissions I was writing, recording, producing, mixing, and mastering fifteen songs a month for people from all over the world. The website was getting thousands of hits a day. By the time I graduated there was no question about what I was going to do. This was my job now. I made songs for people on the internet. Really interesting people sometimes.

An early commission I had was for romantic purposes. And I don't mean a wedding or a proposal. It was a song "for the bedside," as this client had put it. A mood setter in the vein of sultry lounge jazz, which is about the furthest thing from what I'm able to pull off vocally, but she'd heard the weird pieces I'd been posting on my website and still hired me, so I went for it.

It gets weirder. A part of me wants to believe this was a joke, but the person I was corresponding with took the whole process very seriously. She didn't want to share much about her partner. All she said was that this was part of a Valentine's gift for him, and he was very into planes, so could I please fill the lyrics with as many sensual euphemisms as possible, with the more colorful language replaced with aviation terminology?

For the rest of my life, I'll never be able to hear the word "fuselage" without thinking of this song, and this couple.

The most money I ever made for a personalized song commission was for a birthday gift. Two siblings got in touch about a song for their mother, who was apparently a very wealthy woman. People with tons of money don't just come out and say "I have tons of money," but as they shared details about her it sounded like she lived an ostentatious life.

I didn't charge them a lot just because they sounded rich, but I did charge them more than usual because they had the most demanding song idea I'd yet encountered. Their mother liked swing jazz, so this brother and sister hoped I could re-create the sound of *an entire 1930s-era big band,* and then croon on top of it.

I thought about it. I'd just led a small band at a friend's wedding, and I did all right affecting a deeper tone to my voice for some Sinatra numbers. I could play the upright bass and drums, and then . . . hire my friend Rebecca, who played the trumpet, to do forty layers of parts and pitch shift them around to imitate the different registers and timbres of a full horn section. It would be a lot of work, not only composing all those parts but also notating the sheet music for Rebecca. I decided it was possible, and I launched my fee into low orbit.

Rich son's reply: *It's a bit high, but I spoke with my sister and we definitely think it's worth it. It will be so much more meaningful for Mom than just getting her a custom Gucci handbag or something.*

had a client named Rachel who only ever communicated with me through her assistant. At first I thought nothing of it—another rich person, I supposed—but as I gathered intel to write the lyrics my curiosity was piqued.

She was looking for a triumphant song to congratulate an actor friend of hers. Michael was in the early stages of his career but it was going well: he'd just landed a lead part in a theater production and she wanted to present this song to him on opening night. In came the usual details about his life, his quirks, and a little bit about the show. I was interested to learn that the two of them had met at the same university I went to, but in the theater program. Fellow Torontonians!

But that wasn't what made me curious. At one point this assistant told me she needed more time to gather the last few bits of info because Rachel was extra busy this week, and she let it slip that she was working on a film. I had several friends who worked in film or on commercial shoots—directors of photography, grips, gaffers. The DPs might have an "assistant camera"— someone whose job it was to pull focus or manage the equipment—but none of these people had a personal assistant who would deal with their email correspondence on the job, and they certainly couldn't afford to have one just for general life.

I googled the assistant's name. Several results came up, but one seemed particularly promising: an IMDb page for a major movie that had been released the previous year. I clicked on it and scrolled through. She was listed near the bottom of the crew credits. Beside her name it read: Assistant to Rachel McAdams.

spent several years working this way, creating music in any style for anyone who reached out, never turning down an opportunity. Without realizing it at the time, my mindset shifted. I'd spent so much of my musical life questioning: *How can I improve? How can I be original? Where's my place in all of this?* (And, of course, *What gear should I try next?*) It was always reaching, searching, wondering. That all faded as I got on with actually making music, *finishing* projects and putting them out into the world.

Of all things, I have *Songs To Wear Pants To* to thank for that. I had a small but growing online audience. I had paying clients who expected me to create something from nothing and deliver it in a couple of weeks. I had to learn how to do things quickly and effectively, and most important to just *get things done* no matter what. It's easy enough to put a little time into a project here and there, poking and prodding, trying things out, making progress in millimeters. But in that period in my life, I learned that if you want to finish something it doesn't happen by accident. It happens through determination and deadlines.

I also learned to be resourceful. For the first few years I wasn't making enough money to hire session players or buy any tool that could make my job easier. I needed to quickly study up on genres I'd never worked in before and be able to reproduce them. My gear churn slowed nearly to a halt; I did all my work with an acoustic guitar, an electric guitar, an electric bass, a rudimentary synthesizer, a dilapidated drum set a friend gave me for free, one of those old boxy beige PCs, and a single microphone.

For any instrument I needed that I didn't own, I'd write parts that worked specifically to the strengths of General MIDI, a sort of default set of stock sounds that were ubiquitous on computers and synthesizers of a particular generation—and trust me, it didn't have many strengths. A long, flowing trumpet line would never fly, but a quick brass stab could be fairly convincing. The MIDI banjo sound was always going to be terrible, but tucked lower in the mix beneath some real guitars it did what it needed to do.

I came up with tricks to accomplish commissions where I'd bit off more than I could chew. At one point someone wanted some jazzy piano, which to this day I can't play. So I recorded a pass of digital piano where I mashed the keys around in "jazzy" rhythms—anyone can play dexterously and dynamically if they don't have to worry about what notes they're hitting—and then I spent hours in my software's editing tab, painstakingly clicking and dragging the note data into the jazz harmonies my fingers had never learned.

I was once again giving myself an education, and it turned out to be a holistic one. I found that different areas of knowledge expanded upon one another. My music theory and ear training helped me pick out the chords, scales, and rhythms I came across, allowing me to build an understanding of different genres and techniques. Actively listening to a broad range of music showed me what kinds of writing and production approaches worked well universally, or what things weren't typically done in certain traditions, and therefore where there might be an opening to attempt something novel. Learning about the physics of sound and the technology of digital audio made me a better producer and mixer—it's all about how we manipulate these waves, after all.

The thing that really made me better was just that I worked. A lot. There was no substitute for time spent on my craft. I should've known this from my experience with piano lessons, and from seeing the regimens of the virtuosos at York, but I had never felt that level of drive for mastering a particular instrument. I had the mistaken understanding that practice was mainly about physical training—getting your fingers or your voice to respond with nimbleness and accuracy. The truth is that it's just as much about your mind. I eventually realized that writing and production were my deepest musical passions, but also that they could be practiced. Of course they can: after writing your hundredth song you'll be a better writer than you were when you wrote your tenth.

But these realizations came later. At the time, I was just focused on getting my commissions finished however I could, and in my innocence I thought the main way to get better at writing and production was to accrue more knowledge: deconstruct the writing of others, hunt for production tips in online forums, find out what plug-ins the big-name mixing engineers put on vocals. These kinds of things help as well, but without practical experience—writing and recording and producing and mixing those one hundred songs yourself—they don't amount to much. It's great to know the tools and techniques, but experience is what tells you which to reach for and how to employ them at any particular point in any particular project.

The great news is: *you can give yourself experience.* This isn't like job searching when you're young and underqualified. If you're into making music and you've got a spare hour or two every day when you can give it deliberate focus, powerful things can happen. I've seen it in my online course: when students are committed and have a goal to work toward, a couple of hours a day leads to astonishing improvements. If you have a parcel of time you can dedicate every day, there are so many ways you can use it. Different approaches might speak more to you or be a more realistic commitment, so with this in mind here are some ideas to help structure your time, set goals, and boost your creativity.

If you haven't already, can you find a regular time and place where you can focus on your craft? Can you commit to one or two hours a day? Here are some ideas and goals for how you could approach things in different seasons of your creative life. I've done all of these at different times, and some I return to regularly.

1. **Create every day, judgment free.** Make it a point to set time each day (it could be fifteen minutes, it could be all evening, whatever is feasible to you) to buckle down and create. Do *just the creating*—no editing, no polishing. That means no revisiting yesterday's work to try to make it better—or at least not during this judgment-free window. Let brand-new ideas happen without worrying about them being complete, perfect, or even good. This gets you generating a lot of material and, just as important, it gives you practice at suspending your inner critic. There will be other times for making tweaks and deciding what ideas are worth keeping. This exercise is about letting your expression flow freely, with no fear and no excuses. At worst, you'll have a few projects that don't amount to much, and you'll get a little better at what you do.

2. **Post finished work online every week.** Though you'd be creating fewer overall pieces with this approach than with the previous method—one a week instead of one or more a day—there are greater challenges. You have to complete your project, and you'll open yourself up to judgment from others. However, those two things help each other. Knowing that other people will experience your work, even if it's just a couple of friends or your parents, will push you to higher standards. And bringing your projects to the finish line—making your ideas the best version of themselves that

they can possibly be within a week—will greatly improve their reception (and your satisfaction). The most important thing is that this method helps you practice *finishing*, which is one of the hardest things for any artist!

3. **Timed challenges.** Setting yourself a timed challenge means you'll create a lot quickly *and* practice finishing, but without (necessarily) the pressure of publishing. Also, it's usually pretty fun. Is there something that feels doable, if a little uncomfortable, within a window of free time you'd have most days?

In music, trying to write a full song in an hour is a great way to go—it's a manageable amount of time to come up with something half decent, but also short enough that you have to keep things moving (which is a good habit to have). In the world of professional songwriting, a lot of collaborative songs are written in a single day; everyone's schedule has to align between tour dates, recording dates, and songwriting dates with other people. If you can get good at finishing a song in an hour, writing a song in a day will be a breeze.

One of my most well-known projects is First of October, where fellow YouTube creator and multi-instrumentalist Rob Scallon and I form a band for only one day out of each year (guess which one). The aim is to write *and* record *ten songs in a day*. It's a great creative experience on every level. While many of the pieces turn out goofy, rough around the edges, or a bit short, *every time* we've tried this challenge, we've come up with at least two songs that are absolute gold—favorites of ours and our fans that would never have been written otherwise, and that came together in about an hour each.

My friend Dylan, who produces electronic music under the name ill.Gates, has a different version of a timed musical challenge idea, which he calls "Timer Beats." He does many different versions of it, and you'll have to adjust the stages to suit what you're creating, but an example of a twenty-five-minute Timer Beat would be something like:

    0:00–5:00 – Chop samples.
    5:00–10:00 – Arrange the chops with drums to make a beat.
    10:00–15:00 – Add bass and chords.
    15:00–20:00 – Create a variation or second song section.
    20:00–25:00 – Add impacts, effects, and automation.

As you can see, this example divides the tasks into fairly ambitious five-minute chunks. You can set aside a short block of time and structure what you hope to accomplish in a similar way.

4. **Plan your project and break it down.** If you have a project or even just an idea that's special to you, how will you make it happen? This might feel a bit like school, but it's incredibly effective. Make an outline. Write down what you're aiming for, break it down into its component parts, and break *those* down into smaller and smaller pieces until you have the individual steps you can take.

I'll use the example of creating a song. You'll probably be starting with some idea, even if it's vague, of what you intend it to sound like. There are parts of the process that we know will be necessary—writing, arranging, recording, producing, mixing, mastering. Each of these can be broken down further. For instance, writing might entail coming up with melody, harmony, and in some cases lyrics. There would be some overlap with arranging in that you'd also need to write parts for specific instruments, and you could identify what you anticipate each of those instruments will be. When some people write, they come up with melody, harmony, and lyrics all at once, so perhaps they'd instead choose to break up the writing process into the parts of the song they'll need: intro, verse 1, verse 2, chorus, bridge, etc.

There's no one size fits all for this; it's a matter of finding what the smallest, measurable step is that you can execute without being overwhelmed. With most of my songs, I'm usually fine treating "writing" as a larger, single step. However, when it comes to production and mixing, I'll listen to iterations of my work in progress and make reams of highly specific notes. They might look something like:

- *hi-hat too loud*
- *add plucky synth echoing bass line in verse 2*
- *needs a swell before the bridge*
- *edit mouth click before the word "sky"*

. . . and another ten or twenty items like that. In that part of my process, I need to be very detail-oriented, and it works much better than the single step "open the project and try to make it better" that I used to do.

'm lucky to have stumbled into my song commission business model. If you track down and listen to the work I was doing then, you'll probably cringe. I know I do. For me, their only surviving merit is an occasional bit of inventiveness in the writing or production. I'm not someone who was so naturally gifted that I would have wowed you right out of the gate. I'm floored by what some young producers are able to do after only a year or two of experience. That was not me. I wasn't nearly skilled or competent enough to be working professionally—maybe I could have been somebody's assistant. But was I worth $300 so that your labradoodle could have a theme song? Apparently, a lot of people thought so. This gave me a rare opportunity—I was able to improve much faster than I otherwise would have, because I was working on every aspect of producing finished original recordings, from scratch, for up to sixteen hours a day.

I also inadvertently learned all kinds of things about business and content creation. For instance, a prospective client was much more likely to follow through if I kept my offerings simple, such as giving a choice between a one-minute song and a three-minute song, rather than a multitier breakdown of different costs at each thirty-second mark with dependencies for how many instruments were involved.

I realized that what I was doing, the shareable songs I made for fun on my website, was something like a "freemium" model—getting people participating without needing to spend any money. With the proliferation of social media content nowadays, this has basically become *everyone's* model: coming up with posts that are compelling in their own right and that also serve a business goal—whether promoting a specific product or simply a reminder that a brand exists—for people to engage with as they scroll free-to-use platforms.

A similar idea is that of a *loss leader*, which I also started using to great effect—by far my biggest days for sales of albums or sample packs are the days when I offer one for free. It's often something like a fifty-fold increase in sales. The free thing just gets so many more people in the door. (I'm sure this isn't news to anyone with the slightest experience in business, but I know a *lot* of musicians who need to hear it.)

Through being prolific in my creation and my posting, I learned that action can be more important than planning. Action is what gets results. Giving some thought to strategy and goals is also important, of course, but so much changes once you're actually in the game. You'll find answers you need by taking action, by making too many mistakes rather than too few decisions. As others have said, if you're not going forward, you're going backward. The journey is upstream—you need to keep moving just to stay in the same spot.

I learned that the most valuable skills are the ones that compound. Understanding how you learn best allows you to improve faster. Organization creates room for the important work to flow efficiently. Getting good at switching gears makes you more effective and flexible—identifying in the midst of your unfolding process exactly when you need to be creative or critical, exploratory or focused.

Maybe most important, I learned to follow what was joyful and fun. This is my natural inclination anyway, but I discovered that it was great for business too. A lot of us fall into the trap of making business-y content for business-y goals—a promotional flyer, a post that says nothing except to ask people to click on a link. Believe me, any time you're inclined to do that, just throwing the link up with no explanation and a video of you dancing will get more of the results you want. And I'm sure you can come up with something that fits your niche even better. People engage with fun.

## WHY NOT BOTH?

I find that "quality over quantity" is a useless saying, because while it applies in certain situations, in just as many situations I would say:

    **a.** "Quantity over quality," or
    **b.** "Both."

When you're starting out in creative work, whether it's just making things to try to get better, taking on freelance gigs, or publishing content for all to see, it's my belief that quantity is better. You will reach quality *through* quantity.

There's a balance to this, of course. If you take on so much work that the quality of it begins to suffer, you should definitely scale back. If you're practicing an instrument for hours with bad technique, you might build less-than-ideal habits and muscle memory that will affect your playing—or even your health—down the line. But if you're mindful of these things and stay open to learning and exploring, you can always course correct.

The reason it's more beneficial to aim for quantity is because most of us are smart but lazy creatures who will find and take any available shortcut. If you commit to "getting better at songwriting," you might noodle around on your guitar for twenty minutes here and there. If you commit to "writing a song every day from 8 p.m. to 9 p.m.," you'll write a lot more songs *and* they'll be better.

Also, what does it even look like to aim for quality? Sitting at your desk and declaring "Time to make something really good!" as you crack your knuckles? While there will always need to be space in your process for refining your work, the tendency for most is to get caught in a perfectionism spiral where things are never good enough and we're spending forever on something we're treating too preciously. By aiming for quantity, you force yourself to make bold decisions and move on.

Quantity can be measured. You know when you're hitting your goals. And usually, the more quantity there is, the more quality there will be.

Additionally, there are a few things not traditionally considered "skills" that can also be improved by repetition and consistency.

**1. Idea Generation.** I used to feel my creative ideas were few and far between, and so I'd give each one too much weight and become attached to projects I'd never have spent time on if I were more discerning, or less afraid of admitting the ideas were bad. But quantity is the path to quality. I learned that I could practice *having ideas*. I would set aside a bit of time every day to think of ten ideas. They didn't even need to be exclusive to music: they could be anything from a video concept to a drum pattern to a new way to store shoes. As I kept up this practice, I noticed that I could reach my daily quota of ten ideas faster, and over time I even felt my ideas were getting better. Plenty of them were still bad, and most of them never amounted to anything more than one line written down in my journal. But without these hundreds of ideas, without the daily practice of making connections and searching for something new and interesting, I wouldn't have had a lot of my best ideas. Many of them became videos that now have millions of views.

**2. Creative Flow.** The more I work, the better I work. We each have to get to know our own creative selves, and like any relationship it takes time and attention. Take a moment to do some self-investigation. Do you need cozy darkness when you work, or does your space need to be well lit? How often do you need breaks? Are you fine with skipping lunch when you're on a roll, or do you make poorer creative decisions when you're hungry?

Some people work in flurries of inspiration and can't feel good about reaching for their tools otherwise. Some people show up to their workspace every day at the same time and see where things go. Others stop at a certain time of day no matter what, even mid-thought, to ensure they have room in their day to live the other parts of their lives. Some love to work in the morning, some throughout the night.

I think it's worth giving everything a try. You never know—maybe you often don't feel like being creative, but you realize that the best stuff comes when you sit down and do it anyway. Maybe learning about new techniques and tools fuels your creativity, or maybe it distracts you from actually getting anything done. You can only find out by trying.

You can learn to differentiate between the feeling of being on the cusp of something good versus working an idea to death. You can recognize when you're fatigued and should come back to the project another day, or when you're in an inward-facing season and need to be learning and growing more than executing and publishing.

I was shocked to discover that I'm a morning person. I thought I was a night owl for ages, but it was only because I was so excited about exploring music that I'd keep putting off going to bed. One day I happened to go to bed early, got an amazing night of sleep, and was gently awoken by the rising sun at an hour I'd rarely seen before, and I was an instant convert to the glories of the brand-new day. For a period of time, I was one of *those* morning people: 5 a.m., eyes opening with a twinkle, leaping out of bed and heading right to the studio to take advantage of the hours when the world is its quietest and my mind its freshest. As age has caught up with me, I've pushed those hours a bit later—because these things do change, and when you can measure how you feel against five or ten years of doing the same thing, you notice.

I still cherish mornings more than any other time of day. I know I'll have a bit of an energy slump from 2 p.m. to 4 p.m.; I know that it's better if I don't make any creative decisions after 9 p.m. But if my evening is open and I'm still feeling productive, I can use those hours before bed to prepare for the next day, tidy my space, update software, back up files, or any other number of housekeeping tasks. (This is also a chance for me to listen to others' music, since so much of my day is spent working on my own.) If lightning strikes in my work, I'll allow myself a rare late night, but it comes with the understanding that I'm sacrificing the best of the next day.

Even beyond these broader rhythms of the day, I've become highly attuned to the moment-to-moment flow of my energy. I feel the cues that let me know the quality of my work will start to deteriorate if I continue—the slight drift in attention, the weight behind my eyes. For me, those aren't moments to force myself onward or get more caffeinated, they're immediate signals to change tasks or take a break. One lapse in attention will only beget more; coming back to the work later is the only move. I also recognize the spark that lets me know I'm moving in a great direction—in fact, much of the creative process could be seen as exploring until a spark is found, and then the next one, and the next one.

So pay attention to your body and what happens as you work. When do you tend to lose focus? When work is going well, do you get jittery, or calmer? Maybe your breathing gets shallower, or you get out of your chair and pace the room without consciously deciding to.

In terms of your space and your schedule, try a lot of things out, see what works best for you, and be deliberate about optimizing your work conditions. But every once in a while, maybe shake it up a little. Just to see.

**3. Finishing Projects.** *Finishing* is a problem area for so many creatives I know, myself included. We get stuck and don't know where to take a half-formed piece. We aren't sure if the choices we've made are right. If we've pushed past those difficulties, we're besieged by the high standards we hold ourselves to, always finding some little detail to improve. How do we get to the finish line, and how do we know where that even is?

Finishing can be practiced. I didn't realize this until I was a few years deep into doing song commissions. I was at a party at my brother Lucas's house. At the time, he was deeply embedded in Kingston's music scene, playing in a boisterous indie folk band called the Gertrudes as well as various other outfits that gigged nonstop. It was a houseful of creative musicians, and late into the night a guitar started being passed around. Everyone would play a song or two they'd written themselves. It should have been a perfect moment for me to be a part of, but I realized I had nothing to play.

Could that really be true? I felt like I spent all my time on music. I posted songs on my website constantly. People paid me to create music for them—I was doing ten to fifteen commissioned pieces a month! I had so many ideas, I was working on at least a dozen different-sounding albums . . . But none of them were close to being finished.

With the pressure of an audience for my content and deadlines for my clients, I was finishing projects all week long. I was focused, I was problem solving, I had to-do lists and systems in place for taking each project to its next step until I knew it was complete. And somehow it hadn't dawned on me that those things could be helpful for my "real" music. Somehow I'd felt that my *art* wouldn't require planning or scheduling. Surely I'd just tinker with it when I was feeling inspired and then one day it would be done, ready to send out into the world.

Not so. Not for an "official release" anyhow. I could jam and throw ideas around all day, but there would need to be a more methodical approach if I expected to polish and package my work for an audience, to create something I felt I had done my best on and was worth sharing. Fortunately, I happened to have developed those skills through my song-making business. I had finished hundreds of songs based on the prompts sent through my website, and hundreds more for clients. All I had to do was apply the same work ethic to the albums I wanted to make.

At the party, though, in between everyone's sincere, fragile folk songs, I pulled out a one-minute *Songs To Wear Pants To* bop about how to kill zombies.

## PERFECTIONISM

It's hard work to finish a project. It's easier to endlessly tinker and fool yourself into thinking you're making progress with your minuscule changes. At some point you're making adjustments that won't tangibly improve anyone's experience of your work—or even be noticed at all. This tendency doesn't come from a bad place. As artists we've all put time and work into our craft, and seen improvements as a result. It's worth striving to make something special and aligned with your vision. But it's wise to recognize the point of diminishing returns while it's still in your rearview mirror, or you risk ending up in that perfectionist wasteland where you can't tell what's good or not—a difficult place to escape.

Sometimes, the tweaks start happening too early in the process—before you've finished with all the broad strokes. I've been guilty of this many times. If I felt the sound of a part I'd just recorded could be improved a bit, I'd jump right to polishing, fine-tuning the settings on equalizers, compressors, and reverbs. But this kind of work needs the context of all the other parts in a song playing alongside it. There may be times where it's worth chasing and honing a very specific detail that will be key to your piece, but often it's more effective to get all the big pieces in place first, and then move on to finer and finer levels of detail.

Perfectionism might even be self-sabotage. If you call a piece done, then it's open to judgment. If it's never finished then it can never be released, and if it's never released then there's no chance for it to fail. But then, of course, there's no chance for it to succeed. There's far less room for you to grow. If you're spending all this time fiddling with the same aging ideas, how much capacity do you have to let in fresh inspiration and build on your skills? It goes back to reaching quality through quantity. You could spend a year trying to perfect one song, but if you wrote one a week for the same period of time, you'd almost certainly come up with something better.

Lastly: perfection does not exist. You can always search for something to improve. Your taste and context can also change. What you think is fantastic right now might feel lackluster in the future. What you think is the best creative choice today might feel off tomorrow. For those of us who hold ourselves to very high standards, or find ourselves in that place of endless fine-tuning, it's worth internalizing this. Perfection does not exist.

I have a cue now that tells me I'm finished with something. It's when I start making volume adjustments of less than half a decibel. If I'm so zoned in on a project that I think there's an improvement to be made at this level, I know it's the kind of thing that's going to go completely unnoticed by listeners, including me the minute I step away from the computer. And a lot of the time, even at the computer, I'm probably fooling myself that I can perceive the change. Half a decibel is a barely noticeable difference in volume that a skilled listener, with certain sounds, if they're paying attention, can *maybe* distinguish. In your work, perhaps there's something like this that sits at a difference threshold that can nudge you into considering that you may have crossed over from productivity to perfectionism.

When I recognized that my perfectionist tendencies were holding me back, I resolved to push past them. I scrawled a reminder in thick black marker at the top of a sheet of paper, tore the strip of writing off, and taped it to the top of my computer screen. It read:

## *IT WILL NEVER BE GOOD ENOUGH*

I felt confident this would remind me to focus on results rather than achieving some impossibly high standard. I also immediately liked it as a feature of my workspace. Despite the instruments around my room and the colors on my screen, this stark ribbon of black and white stood out almost threateningly with its forceful message. As I looked at it, though, I found it distracting that the letters were a bit slanted compared to the edge of the paper. I ripped it down, scrunched it up, and uncapped my marker again.

### *IT WILL NEVER BE GOOD ENOUGH*

I didn't even bother tearing this one off the page—I'd written it a bit too messily. I gave it another go.

### *IT WILL NEVER BE GOOD ENOUGH*

This one turned out better, but I still felt some of the inconsistent lettering could be improved.

### *IT WILL N*

I had to stop and laugh at myself in the middle of writing it out for the fourth time. The lesson was literally spelled out in front of me. I taped up the previous one I'd written, and soon I couldn't even remember what had bothered me about the lettering.

This sign lived above my workstation for a couple of years and never failed to draw a comment from anyone visiting. They fell into two camps. Most people were taken aback: "How can you have that in front of you every day? Isn't that so discouraging?" They interpreted the message not as a nudge to focus on moving toward results but as a predetermined judgment on the results, or as a decree that one's goals were unattainable. There was an occasional person, though, whom I knew I shared a deeper connection with when they would read the message and say something like "I need a sign like this" or simply "Yes!" They were, like me, people who had recognized that they were sometimes "productive" to the point of unproductivity; that their pursuit of *creative excellence* often got in the way of *creating*.

In any case, the sign totally worked. To this day, I'm still not perfect.

One weekend during college, I went back to Ottawa to visit my parents. My mom slid a page of a newspaper across the kitchen counter to me. "You might find this interesting," she said. It was an article about a new website that was growing in popularity, where anyone in the world could upload videos that anyone else in the world could watch. It was called YouTube.

# PART TWO

# Making Art in the Digital Age

# Chapter Six

I've always been lucky. My mom says I was "born under a lucky star." I'm in the right place at the right time, and perfect solutions seem to materialize whenever I find myself in a scrape. While I have tremendous privilege—growing up somewhere safe, with a loving family, education access, and financial stability—I benefit from something even beyond that: complete dumb luck. I win raffles. I find twenty-dollar bills on the sidewalk. Multiple times I've forgotten expensive music equipment in a public place and returned to find it still sitting there the next day. The first time I ever heard about four-leaf clovers as a child, I looked over at the patch of grass beside me and immediately found one. My luck is absurd.

My favorite story about the universe giving me special treatment for no reason occurred one afternoon in a Toronto streetcar. It was full, and I was standing near the back. At one stop, a disheveled man boarded, shouting and moving erratically. He walked down the aisle, pausing at every single person to aim vitriol directly at them—all the four-letter words, any insult he could find based on race, gender, or appearance. As is often the case with public transit, everyone did their best to ignore him, though some were visibly taken aback. I braced myself for my turn and wondered if there was some way I could show him compassion. The streetcar was slowing to a stop as he reached me, and when our eyes met he softened. He put his hand on my shoulder, and said: "You're a beautiful man. Find your Rihanna." Then the doors opened and he staggered out into the light.

All of this is to say, I feel it's important to acknowledge the privilege and the luck I've had. I work extremely hard, but lots of people work extremely hard. Lots of people are smart and talented and produce quality work. But a great deal of our careers and our lives are predicated on pure chance, and while I wholeheartedly believe you can benefit from all the lessons and advice in this book, I can't share the rest of my story without telling you: I know, a lot has worked out for me in absolutely improbable ways. I don't know why.

The best eyebrows you will see today," read the front page of Reddit. I'm well aware that I have strange, sharply angular eyebrows (they just grow that way) but this little sentence taught me a great deal.

It was a post that linked to "Pink Fluffy Unicorns Dancing on Rainbows," an inane earworm I wrote whose music video features me playing instruments with a massive smile, staring unblinking straight into the camera lens. Some people interpret it as absurdist humor, others think it's a wonderful children's song. I composed it for a laugh during my *Songs To Wear Pants To* days—someone's entire song suggestion had simply been that title, and it inspired a playful tune I sang in a put-on deep voice accompanied by ukulele and glockenspiel.

"Pink Fluffy Unicorns" has reached far and wide, with 13 million views of the music video, a similar number of plays on streaming platforms, another million views of a behind-the-scenes video about how it was written, 60 million of an animated music video version, and countless fan-made renditions. Many parents and teachers have told me that children sing it without even knowing about the videos—it's just one of those schoolyard things.

People who know the song are mostly familiar with the repetitive, two-bar melody. But if you make it far enough into the original version, you'll hear the self-referential joke I inserted. After the lyrics "pink fluffy unicorns dancing on rainbows" (and no other words) have been repeated ad nauseam, there's a quiz that anyone by that point should be able to ace: "Let's test your knowledge and see what you've learned so far! What color are the unicorns? Where are they dancing? Please use one word to describe the texture of their magical fur . . ." Not all the answers are what you might expect.

The video's weirdness and the song's catchiness were enough to engage many passersby on the internet, but the quiz would send people into fits of laughter, which made it all the more shareable. People sent it to friends and family, and it made the rounds on sites where viral things were shared, eventually reaching a few thousand people a day within the first weeks of its existence. Then fifty thousand in one day when it reached the front page of Reddit, thanks to a gracious eyebrow appreciator.

*The best eyebrows you will see today.* I had to recognize the casual brilliance in that choice of words. It's a master class in salesmanship. It contains lessons I still think about to this day.

1. The "you" in the title brings the reader in—it's not just an author's observation (such as "the best eyebrows I saw today") but a promise, a *guarantee* to anyone who might come across it.

2. It doesn't overpromise. These are only the best eyebrows for today. Tomorrow there will be others. Perhaps you've come across better eyebrows earlier in your life; clicking on this link will fulfill the promise without leaving you disappointed.

3. It makes you curious. What could possibly make these *the best* eyebrows? You'd better investigate.

4. The payoff is immediate. You click the link, the video loads, and this guy has two goofy isosceles caterpillars above his eyes.

5. It overdelivers. Oh, you thought you were just going to see a picture of some eyebrows? Here's a video that will inject happiness directly into your veins (whether you're laughing with me or at me). Here's a song you might sing for the rest of your life. Here's a musician with an eclectic body of work you might love.

6. The headline fits the vibe of what it links to. It's a humorous and bizarre proposition; it hints (in tone if nothing else) at the content you'll get through clicking it.

7. It's relatable. Most of us have eyebrows. We may have no particular interest in them, we may rarely think about them, but if someone says there's a super-wild pair of eyebrows to check out, what are we going to do? *Not* look?

I'm spending so long on this eyebrows headline because these are the insights that everyone publishing online content eventually has to learn (and that even established creators continually struggle with). *What's the most effective way to share my work? What's the angle that will interest more people? How do I make this compelling while still giving people a satisfying payoff?* It's not about "clickbait"—though of course there are those people who will shamelessly use a flimsy, sensationalized premise to get as many clicks as possible. Most creators I know are thinking longer term. They want to deliver on what they promise—they care about their work and they value their relationship with their audience.

I'd learned almost none of this at the time that "Pink Fluffy Unicorns" went viral. The work I'd been creating had been reaching a somewhat consistent but smaller audience, and the success I'd found was mainly through leaning on zaniness—creating stuff so weird that weirdos would share it with other weirdos. I wasn't thinking about titles, thumbnails, audience retention, or even business growth. I was having fun making music and the occasional video, and for years I had the inexplicable good fortune that word of mouth brought in enough clients each month to pay the bills.

It had also been a different world when I started out—2004, a world before social media was part of our lives. I'd created a destination, and my audience was made up of people who'd stumbled across it and were compelled to visit again from time to time. By 2010, when "Pink Fluffy Unicorns" came out, things were rapidly shifting to a situation where most people most of the time would visit the same handful of sites to find content made by anyone else who might be using the same platform. All content was now surrounded by other content, all competing for attention. Bold images and sensational copy became—and have remained—the most dependable and commonly used strategies for disseminating work widely online. I was beginning to see how I would have to adapt.

After learning about YouTube from my mom and that newspaper article, I created an account, but I used it only to occasionally post animations of my songs by *Songs To Wear Pants To* fans. I continued with my commissions, which were going well, and I imagined that's what I would be doing for a job for many years to come. I worked on my own music, and I harbored hopes of "making it" via the traditional artist route, though due to my broad tastes I was far too unfocused for a music industry that loves clean categorizations. I also played shows and managed online presences for a chaotic range of projects: I led an eight-piece folk-rock ensemble, I had aliases for my solo hip-hop and electronic explorations, I still collaborated with my friends from York, and I even performed *Songs To Wear Pants To* live—with a slideshow projecting song requests, which I'd read out, and then deliver punch lines in the form of thirty-second songs. I realized later it was much more of a comedy routine than a music show, and terrifically out of place in the small rock clubs I would get gigs at. But the songs and my stage presence were so over the top and asinine that I'd always win over even the most jaded audience. Once, an engineer spent my soundcheck being surly and giving me attitude, but then after my set he was all smiles and wanted to chat. Another time, I was on a bill with a pop-punk act whose manager approached me after the show to say he thought he was going to witness a train wreck, but in fact he'd love to represent me, and was I available to go on tour in the fall? (I did not vibe with him and said no thanks.)

Eventually, the hodgepodge of projects felt like too much to keep track of. I kept *Songs To Wear Pants To* going because it was my main source of income, but I didn't particularly care about what I was making for clients or as website content. For the music I was creating that was meaningful to me, I decided I should unify it all—however disparate— under a single name. The process took me months, but eventually I came up with . . . Andrew Huang.

**Rejected Artist Names**

The Universe

The Void

The Ocean

Everything Everywhere

Wraith Bomber

Supercomputer

Infinity Unicorns

Magenta

Swampy

Evil Sword

The decision to use my birth name as my artist name didn't come lightly. I didn't like the sound of it to begin with, and I was wary of the racial baggage that would come with it. Since I was young, I'd felt that being a person of color distanced me from my peers; I suspected this would be more pronounced in the world of music, where I was even more out of place. When I played shows, I was almost always the only Asian person onstage—sometimes in the entire venue. Despite being a voracious music listener with wide-ranging tastes, I had discovered barely any Asian artists whose work had penetrated the mainstream, or even the underground. "Huang" was also simply impractical—a name no one pronounced right if they read it or spelled right if they heard it. I spent a long time searching for something else that would encapsulate me and fit with the broad range of genres and moods I was exploring. Ultimately, something happened that at first turned me off of the name even further, and then, in the end, was a deciding factor in using it.

It was the end of 2008 and I had recently gotten married to the whitest of women. I guess that's how I'm introducing my wife in this book. Essa's family roots are in England, with suspicions of German ancestry as well. She's so white that I was the first person in her life to ask her where she was "really from"—and she had to think about it for a while. (When you're white in Canada, you belong automatically. When, like Essa, your family's been in Canada for seven generations, you barely even consider earlier roots.)

Essa was looking for a job at the time, and not worried about it at all. She's the smartest, most confident person I know; she's been offered a position at any workplace she's ever interviewed for. At the job she eventually landed, she worked her way up from an entry-level position to becoming the director of marketing in three years. She's a stellar employee.

During this particular job hunt, though, she decided to try an experiment. Freshly married, we still hadn't settled on what to do with our last names. (I wanted to take hers because the patriarchy sits among the most rejected of all my rejected things, but after an emotional argument with my mom—the only argument we've had in my adult life—I realized it would cause too much family grief to depart that far from the template of socially acceptable choices.) Essa sent out forty résumés for jobs she was perfectly qualified for. Twenty of them used her last name and twenty used mine. Other than that, they were identical. And within a few weeks, the invisible had become visible in a way I never before believed would happen.

A lifetime of microaggressions as well as occasional overt racism directed toward me had shown me plainly that we hadn't reached racial equality, so I expected that the white version of Essa would have a minor advantage. But we were in progressive, egalitarian Canada. So diverse! A cultural mosaic! Look how many refugees we accept! And we were in Toronto—often recognized as the most multicultural city in the world. On top of that, our American neighbors had just elected their first Black president; we were riding on a wave of race relations optimism. So when Essa told me what she'd done, I just laughed, mildly interested to see what would happen. She wasn't expecting particularly dramatic results either. This was just a whim she'd acted on.

She got at least a phone call, if not an in-person interview, from all twenty companies where she'd applied using her last name. And the companies where she had introduced herself as a Huang?

She didn't hear back from a single one of them.

It was maddening, and heartbreaking. The same person with the same skills and experience was applying for all those jobs, but nobody wanted her when she was called Esther Huang.

If job searching is made this much more difficult just because of your last name—one you perhaps married into!—how much more do you face, and how much worse is it, in every other part of your life? When every interaction you ever have is marked by the color of your skin and the shape of your nose?

This episode made it clear to me that I would be at an even greater disadvantage than I'd previously thought if I shared my work under my own name. Now, I had starker and broader confirmation of what I'd felt in my adolescence about being a person of color. Even at the slightest hint of otherness, and even if they don't know they're doing it, people judge you and treat you very differently.

I couldn't change my appearance, but I didn't *have* to be immediately and unmistakably Asian to anyone who just saw my name on an album cover or in a press release. With a pseudonym, perhaps I could fly under the white radar a little longer in some situations. Shouldn't I take any small advantage I could get in an industry that was already in short supply of people who looked like me?

But the longer I thought about it, the more the middle fingers in my mind extended. I was going to be *me*. And I would be so good, and so relentless, that a name could never stop me.

Around this time, I began posting on YouTube more. It started because I felt I'd enjoy making music videos, and that it would be another step toward "professionalism" on the artist side of my career. Essa thought buying a camera was a waste of money and tried to dissuade me—and while that's hilarious given how things have worked out and I'll never let her live it down, she probably felt justified for the first couple of years after that purchase. Here's an example of one of my early "music videos."

*Andrew sits on the couch in his living room. He starts playing an acoustic guitar and singing an original song. He's looking right into the lens. He sings a verse and a chorus. He sings a second verse. He sings a second chorus. He sings a bridge. About two minutes have elapsed at this point. But then the final chorus comes in, and the big moment arrives. Two people who have been hiding behind the couch lift up some sticks with cardboard cutouts of animals attached. They wave the cardboard animals around behind Andrew's head, vaguely in time with the music. They wave them around for the rest of the song. The end.*

Spike Jonze I was not, but I was enjoying working in a new medium, and I did what I usually do: explored it from every angle I could. I tried out every camera setting, I watched tutorials and read articles, and I chatted with the filmmakers who hired me to score their projects, as well as friends of mine who'd gone into commercial videography. Most important, I made a lot of videos: vlogs, skits, time lapses, stop motion animation, countless shallow depth-of-field shots of my houseplants, and more "music videos." Some of these ended up on my YouTube channel. Many of them have been deleted.

Another thing I tried was a video version of my songs-by-request concept, creating music and accompanying videos based on suggestions that arrived in my YouTube comments. This is how "Pink Fluffy Unicorns" came about. Before that video, my YouTube uploads were usually viewed between a few hundred and a few thousand times by a small portion of the small *Songs To Wear Pants To* audience that followed me to YouTube; I thought of YouTube as a video hosting service where I would direct my existing fan base for additional content.

But I began to notice that many comments I received indicated that new people had found me just by browsing. I also noticed that there would always be a bit of immediate activity on a newly published video—a handful of views and comments popping up right after an upload finished—and eventually realized that these early YouTube users had already adopted a new culture. YouTube, for them, wasn't just a repository of one's past work, archived and organized for easy access. This is how I'd been thinking of YouTube, and all of the internet, really: as a library. But YouTube, in more than just the sense of being a video platform, was akin to live television. Viewers wanted to watch what was new, what was *now*. If they were subscribed to a channel, they were excited to be notified of a new upload. There was almost the assumption that the videos on the platform were being published immediately after they had been made. There was, and still is, competition to leave the first comment on a video. YouTube wasn't just a video hosting service—it was a movement, a community, and an entirely new paradigm for creation. People all over the world were building followings for their music, their comedy, their tutorials, or even for simply sharing their thoughts on camera.

YouTube was also growing fast. It didn't exist five years before, and now hundreds of millions of people were using it. It was (and still is) the world's second-largest search engine, behind Google. There was a potential audience far greater than any you could hope to find by driving to different cities and playing in bars. This audience could discover you from the comfort of their homes with just a few keystrokes. On top of that, this new world had no gatekeepers! Unlike more traditional routes, the distance between creator and audience had shrunk to nothing but the speed of your internet connection and your access to a camera.

I had slowly made these realizations over the few short years of YouTube's existence, but they were driven home by having a viral video.

By that point, though, I felt I was late to the game. So many people had already spent years growing audiences for their channels, and I was convinced I'd missed the best window of opportunity. As it turns out, I was one of the earliest—especially in the world of music—to see the possibilities. I can't pretend it was like flipping a switch and seeing the future; it would be a few more years before I went all-in on YouTube. At this point, it simply became an additional avenue where I felt it would be worthwhile to concentrate my creative efforts. And it was a lot of fun.

**Aim for the eyes.** Our experiences on mobile devices are primarily about what we see. Many people keep devices silent while browsing, so regardless of whether you work in a visual medium, you should be asking yourself how you can use visuals to their greatest effect. This might be by using bright colors or high contrast, creating a distinct visual identity for your brand, or appearing in eye-catching clothes or interesting locations in photos and videos.

**Take up real estate.** Though we can scroll endlessly, there's a finite amount of space on our screens. If you can make your posts bigger—by using a taller aspect ratio for media, or even by adding spaces between lines of text—you can attract more attention simply by virtue of having a little less other content visible around yours.

**Be part of the action.** Engage with other people's posts, both those in your community and those getting lots of platform-wide traction at any given time. Adding value to a conversation is a great way to intrigue new people to visit your profile. To step it up a notch, create content around what's currently trending. Share your perspective on the hot topics of the week, or do some remixing. Whatever everyone is excited about at the moment, can you incorporate it into a quick creation?

**Make your bio count.** A cute saying underneath your profile picture is fun, but it doesn't help anyone. Sum up what you do, link to your work, and if finding gigs is part of why you're on a platform, let people know how to go about hiring you.

**Connect with potential collaborators.** Leave meaningful comments and send kind, genuine messages. Share other people's work if it resonates with you, and tag them. This won't lead to something every time, or even most of the time, but it's how you'll find creative kinfolk.

**Don't spam.** Throwing your link into a hundred conversations will usually go completely ignored. Posting more than a few times a day, especially if it's self-promotion, will probably turn people off. Your posts should provide value. Even if ultimately the aim is to get the word out about your work, you have to give a little something to your audience: a laugh, a good story, a bit of inspiration.

**Don't post right away.** Unless you're trying to jump right onto a rocketing trend, let the idea for a post sit for a few hours or even a couple of days so the cogs in your brain can turn a little more—you may find some small but effective tweaks you can make. You might find a better way to say something, or realize that you would have regretted saying it. It's also important to post at times of day that are optimal for your audience—when people who follow you are actually online. Most platforms will let you dig into these analytics. You might finish your work or have a brilliant thought at 3 a.m.—wait until your world is awake to share it.

- Ask a question you're interested in discussing—either put it out into the ether or directly ask an expert you respect.
- Share about a tool or strategy you use.
- Review a product you use.
- Create a poll to see how opinions are divided about something in your field.
- Post about what's currently trending in your field.
- Post a funny thought about something in your field.
- Post a strong opinion about something in your field.
- Take a photo or video of a visually captivating part of your process.
- Share a tip about how you create your work.
- Write about what influences your work.
- Post an early or alternate draft of a piece that people can compare to the final version.
- When you do share your work, keep it conversational. Talk about how excited you are that it's finished. Ask people what their favorite part is or what they think about a certain detail. Share a story about how or why you created it.

There was a magic to early YouTube. Everyone who participated in it as a creator knew they were into something well outside the mainstream. While now there are millions of creators, established best practices, and niches as large as any TV channel used to be, in YouTube's early years creators bonded around the simple fact that we were all exploring uncharted new territory. I became friends with vloggers, comedians, dancers, entrepreneurs, makeup artists, and people who ran channels about anything from cooking to crafting to landing trick shots with basketballs. While the platform had exploded in popularity, it was still a time of mostly short and candid videos. The things that were heavily viewed tended to be kids or animals doing cute things, or mild injuries that had been caught on camera—very *America's Funniest Home Videos*. Things that are now commonplace—like planning out your content or talking to your camera—weren't the norm, and the few of us who did those things seemed like excited nerds. (Which is exactly what we were.)

In the early YouTube community, it seemed like everyone was enthusiastic about helping each other and in it for the fun more than anything else. Pockets of these sentiments still exist but, unsurprisingly, with growth, commercialization, and widespread adoption of social media and influencer culture, it's a very different world now. That's not to say that community no longer exists, it's just much more splintered now, with many prioritizing growth over fun. That's fine—social media has become a viable career path now, and I'm among the multitudes who are glad that they can work for themselves and build businesses out of their interests thanks, in large part, to these online platforms.

And community is still one of the best ways to grow. Many of us dream that someone in the upper echelons of our industry will recognize our brilliance and reach out to catapult us up to a more prestigious sphere—which does happen occasionally, and of course makes for a great story. But most of the major stepping-stones in our journey arise out of building a strong network of relationships—people around our own level and in our own circles we can collaborate with, share knowledge with, and mutually support.

I first heard this idea from Hank Green in those early days of You-Tube. He's a vlogger, educator, and entrepreneur who reached out to me after seeing some of my first videos. Hank was far more successful than I was, and I hoped he could tell me how to find shortcuts or big breaks, but he only affirmed that it was a gradual, community-focused climb. I was interested to hear this notion echoed nearly a decade later, the first time I worked with Dan Wilson, a wonderful songwriter with number one hits in his discography and Grammy awards on his shelf. And in the space between those two conversations, I had found this idea to be true for myself. Working with others in similar career stages builds long-lasting support that lifts everyone who makes meaningful contributions. A shout-out from a much more popular artist, or even a collaboration with one, is undoubtedly helpful, but it will more often lead to a short-term spike in attention rather than an overall buoying of one's station.

Of course, I try to approach it from all angles. While I most often work with others who share a similar audience size, I'm happy when I can connect with bigger creators. I also love being someone who can hand out a few spikes myself by collaborating with folks who have much smaller followings, and trying to host the occasional open, participatory project. Even before I had a career, I always thought that if I ever "made it" I'd want to bring up other artists with me. It overlaps with why I've always wanted to be open about my process. I'm here in this life to take music further in whatever way I can—sonically or culturally, opening people up to new sounds or perspectives, encouraging more people to make music themselves, or simply sharing some of the amazing talent I'm always stumbling across. I would love for everyone to hear what I hear. I would love for everyone to learn what I've learned and run with it in their own way. There's nothing more gratifying than knowing I've helped someone discover the joy of making music. There are people I've helped who now have more fans than I do, or who are thriving in careers as producers, recording engineers, or songwriters. Why would I ever want to close the door behind me?

SELF-REFLECTION

In what ways are you contributing to your artistic community? In what ways would you like to?

Who can you support by sharing knowledge, helping on a project, or telling others about their work? Bonus points: Is there a paying gig you can recommend them for?

Networking is a challenge for introverts, and believe it or not I'm one of the most introverted people you'll ever meet. Spending time with people quickly drains my energy. Being alone is when I come alive and thrive. (In extraordinarily rare cases, I connect with someone who *gives* me energy, get a taste of that extrovert life, and try so hard to become their best friend.)

I once spent ten days with no human contact, a self-imposed exile/creative retreat that I had craved for years. To ensure I would block out the time in my calendar, I booked a trip to Boston, where my friend Grant generously let me stay in an apartment he used for short-term rentals. We spent a day together after I arrived, and when we parted ways I sealed myself off. I didn't see or talk to anyone. I had ten days' worth of prepurchased food that I rationed out. I went outside only for the occasional walk. All I did every day was read, write, meditate, eat, exercise, and play music. I felt the most peace I've ever known. I wondered throughout this experience if I'd reach the depth of my loner nature and end up craving company, but I never did. At the end of the ten days I just wanted to keep living like that.

People are surprised to learn how much of a hermit I am if they get to know me through the internet first. In my videos I'm amped up, talkative, and often using my outdoor voice indoors. What you're seeing there is the most hyper, excitable sliver of myself, because I'm doing my favorite thing in the world—messing around with music and sharing what I find. It lights me up; I could do it forever. Most of the time, though, I exude no charisma at all. What I really am is a recluse—I love to hide away, forget about the world, and work on my projects. There's a part of me that loves to meet new people and loves to go to parties, and it comes out about twice a year. For the rest of the time, I may as well be on another planet.

So when I started being invited to industry events, whether on the music side or the YouTube side, I worked on a number of ways to hype myself up and build my stamina for extended social interaction. Some of these events would be low-key evenings held at bars in my hometown; other times I'd be flown a thousand miles to a convention of thirty thousand people, none of whom I'd ever met.

At the present stage in my career, I go to these events mainly if I know I'll have the opportunity to catch up with some long-distance friends. But in the early days, I recognized the importance of the networking opportunities, and I'd get out there and spend an exhausting three days smiling, shaking hands, and yelling above loud music. I was a small fish, but it didn't matter—at many of these events, all VIPs are lumped into one category with the same access to events and backstage areas, so I was there with my tiny channel, fringe content, and determination to have a good time.

For anyone who may have a similar introverted disposition, here are some things I found helpful. As I realized I needed to get better at being outgoing, I started playing some little games as I was going about my day. I called them "games" in an attempt to make them sound fun, when in fact they were just a series of uncomfortable activities. I would make eye contact with any and every stranger—at shops, on the bus, while passing on the street. If their eyes met mine, I had two goals: I had to give them a big smile, and I could only look away once they did. It was like a game of social interaction chicken. I played another "game" where I had to talk to at least one stranger every time I left the house, and it didn't count if they were an employee at a business I visited. Sometimes I'd manage to strike up a conversation, although often I would simply find something to compliment them on, but either way it was a continual reminder that most people are friendly. Lastly, the moment I saw an opportunity—a person across the room I wanted to meet or just someone I could try my conversation/compliment exercise with—I'd make myself do it within a count of three. It was good practice in taking action and removed almost all the anxiety about actually doing the thing. There was simply no time to worry about all the ways it could go wrong before I found myself actually engaging with this person and finding it was going just fine.

I came up with an opener that I used at conventions for about a year. I'd walk up to anyone, look into their eyes, smile, and excitedly say, "Can I meet you?"

It worked well for me. It was the tiniest bit funny—or awkward—in a disarming way. I like to imagine that for the more famous folks it was an easier engagement than the frequent requests for a photo or autograph. They could make it as small an interaction as they liked, and it would count as "meeting," and then they could be on their way without the need for any excuses or polite declining (or rude declining). No one ever responded to this line with anything but enthusiasm; I always got a big smile, and a "Yeah!" or "Of course!"

I distinctly recall using this line on both Hannah Hart and Link Neal (of Rhett and Link) when I found myself in the same room as them. Neither knew who I was, and I've since collaborated with them multiple times over the years. While our followings were of much different sizes, I was able to lend my musical skills to their projects, and, I hope, they saw that I was someone who loved the work and wasn't just trying to ride their coattails. I produced the music for a video that for many years was Rhett and Link's most viewed of all time, a "Nerd vs. Geek" rap battle, which has surpassed 50 million views.

"Can I meet you?" is not a bad line to use on anyone, VIP or not. It's direct. They'll probably be happy that someone is showing interest in them. Hopefully you have a good reason for wanting to meet them that you can also be direct about.

All of these things were ways to make it easier for me to get to know new people, and to spend large bouts of time in crowds of strangers. But I believe the most important thing is to focus on genuinely trying to connect with someone, and enjoying whatever time you have together. I don't know if I'll ever understand the approach of zipping around the room amassing contacts as quickly as possible, or the culture you find in some places where everyone's sizing each other up to see how useful someone might be to them. Focusing only on making a genuine connection means you'll find the people you'll love working with anyway—those you get along with and those who share your values—and there will always be natural opportunities to share what you can bring to the table. Business is a lower priority; I say this not as some life hack judo approach to getting better business thanks to your personality but because business actually is a lower priority, always, than being a kind, patient, and curious person.

# Chapter Seven

Until relatively recently, music existed only when conjured by someone in real time. One would hear it when listening to someone perform, or if you learned to play an instrument yourself. Now *recordings* are our main connection to music.

Though the formats shifted through the decades from vinyl to tape to compact disc, it was seen as a marker of success and legitimacy to have physical copies of one's music produced. By the 2000s this kind of manufacturing was within reach of the hobbyist, which put a dent in the prestige of having a physical record, but the next shift put the nails in the coffin. Music downloads took over, and very soon after that downloads were usurped by streaming. Few people care if you have a physical release anymore; most would rather not have a copy. Convenience has superseded everything: the specialness of a packaged physical artifact, the excitement of hunting for a rare track, even the actual sound quality of the music itself.

These changes all happened within a hundred years. Prior to 1925, sheet music sales surpassed those of record sales and were seen as the primary way to disseminate music. (It's interesting that in the age of sheet music's dominance, composers were and have remained celebrated, while in our era of recordings it's the performers who receive the most attention.)

People get very attached to the way things have "always" been done, and it's no different when it comes to music. We've only recently reached a point where musicians are focusing much more of their efforts online, and sometimes it seems as though one hundred people attending a club show is a more legitimate career marker than a hundred thousand people watching a video. When I decided to explore YouTube as my main outlet for releasing work, I felt I was playing catch-up to numerous creators who seemed comfortably established on the platform, with followings in the tens of thousands. At the same time, no musicians I personally knew were interested in this new avenue. Aiming for an online audience was seen as strange, counterintuitive, or even pointless. Most artists at this time did little on the internet besides set up a MySpace profile, whose primary purpose was to share a taste of their music with promoters for prospective gigs and to let fans know about those gigs. The ethos of the day was still to write and record an album, create music videos and tour as much as possible to promote it, and try to attract listeners and find favor with a record label so that you could repeat that cycle at a hopefully larger scale. (You would likely be going into debt at each step of this process as well.)

Once again, I relied on my instincts and openness. I tried to see things for what they truly were, or as close as possible to it, not clouded by preconceptions or expectations. I arrived at a number of conclusions that appeared logical to me. The more time I could spend making music, the better. Monetizing what I already wanted to create would allow me the most time for it. Going on tour, making music videos, and working with record labels were more often than not ways for artists to *lose* money. The point of all those efforts was to reach fans, to whom there was now a much more direct line. I had fun playing live, but it entailed a lot of repetition and wasted time—rehearsing, planning, traveling, setting up gear, and performing old songs over and over when I felt it would be more exciting to write new ones.

And so, tuned in to a platform where I could create on my own terms and at my then-favored breakneck pace, I leaned even more into a digital-first, social media–driven approach. Over the next couple of years, music videos fell out of favor with me. There were other formats to explore—ideas that could work only on YouTube, like remixing yesterday's viral video, or creating pieces that incorporated viewers' comments or media submissions. I performed live much less frequently, and when I did it was to support the YouTube channel. People would ask, "When's your next CD coming out?" and I'd enjoy telling them I'd never make another.

My audience grew haphazardly as I experimented with different kinds of videos, with no strategy beyond following what excited me at any given moment. It amounted to throwing everything at the wall to see what stuck, which, while inconsistent, revealed several compelling and repeatable video concepts. Viewers were interested in a series I titled *Double On Genre*, in which I would compose a song that combined two disparate styles of music, such as techno and polka. After "Pink Fluffy Unicorns," the next time I had a widely shared video was when I made music with the sounds of a thousand pairs of pants (a thrift store let me rent them for the day, charging by weight). While I had been incorporating everyday objects into my music for years, this was the first time I had created a piece using exclusively unorthodox sound sources, and it was the first time I had paired it with video. It was a winning combination, something novel and fun that was both visually and aurally captivating.

This was the point in my career when I felt I could shift to doing my own projects full-time. My income was derived from commission work, music downloads, and YouTube ad revenue. I thought it would be realistic to make the leap to let go of the commissions, at least for a period of time, and decided I would save enough money to take three months away from doing client work so that I could focus solely on developing the other two slices of the income pie: making music and videos.

Saving money is easier when you enjoy music more than anything else, your job doesn't involve interacting with other humans in a professional work environment, and you don't mind letting your social life fall by the wayside. You can cut out all entertainment, and most of your grooming, and still go through life just fine. I reverted to the routine of my earliest days trying to get my music career off the ground: no alcohol, no eating out, no movies, no new clothes, no new music gear, and (this one I do regret) I cut my own hair.

Weeks before my three-month focus period was due to start, life threw me a nice shiny curveball. Out of nowhere, Google, which now owned YouTube, offered me a job. Someone at the company had seen how I was able to build my channel (about forty thousand subscribers at this point) and thought that I would be a good fit for a new role they had envisioned, which involved weighing in on the development of new features as well as helping traditional industry figures establish themselves on the platform. No big deal—just give folks like Amy Poehler and Pharrell Williams some tips on getting their YouTube channels going.

It was a tantalizing offer. Google would find me a nice apartment in San Francisco, cover the costs of moving all my stuff, and pay me about $100,000 a year. This would immediately more than double my income. It was fun to think about possibly rubbing shoulders with some celebrities, and I was excited by the idea of helping to shape the platform I had grown to love—not just for how it had bolstered my own career but for what it represented: a direct connection between artist and audience, a level playing field for the arts. I thought it over at length. Maybe this was what all my messing around on the internet had been building toward—a cheat code to let me leapfrog over entry-level positions into a high-salaried "cool" job. I could work in a field I cared about and enjoy making music as a hobby, without any of the pressure of needing it to pay my bills. Or perhaps I could take the position for a couple of years, build up the resources to take even more time off, and have a much longer runway to try to get my YouTube channel off the ground. I went back and forth on what would be the wisest move. I suspected, however, that I wouldn't be able to escape the golden handcuffs, and I was more interested in forging my own path. Direct action toward my dreams *now* seemed to me more powerful than taking a roundabout in the name of becoming better prepared. No matter how things worked out, not taking a chance on myself would be the bigger regret. The moment I made my choice, I knew it was the right one. I needed to follow the path that allowed me to spend the most time creating music. I respectfully turned down Google's offer.

My three months without commissions turned into six months, and then into a year. Eventually I realized that I had crossed whatever line bounded the point between part-time and full-time creator. I was doing it. The months rolled along and I made my videos and released my music, gradually growing my audience, and finding out one day I'd surpassed one hundred thousand followers.

But for a long time I still cut my own hair.

Though I was working full-time on my own creative projects, it was not a smooth transition. Looking back, I have to laugh at how little strategy I had. All my plans could be summed up in a word: *more*. I tried to create more music and more videos and more types of both. There was no schedule and no road map; once again, I simply executed whichever of my ideas felt the most exciting and within reach. There was no consistency to my output, its performance, or my income. It worked out fine, but I later learned how much more effective I could have been with just a *little bit* of thought and commitment to an over-all plan. I imagine I wasn't alone in my erratic approach—it's easy to buy in to the idea of the artist as flighty and free, contemptuous of the calendar, ready to follow any whim. Some artists work well that way, and perhaps it works particularly well for those who are able to leave all their administrative and business affairs to others. When I went full-time I worked alone, and I didn't realize then that I was someone who thrived within structure.

These and many other lessons dawned on me as I worked to build my artist profile and my YouTube presence. I was forced to be resourceful. Previously I got things done under the pressure of being committed to a client project, which usually worked out to making one hundred to two hundred dollars for a day's work. After cutting out commissions, I relied entirely on royalty payments from my followers' engagement with my output: I was netting about seventy cents per song download and a fraction of a penny per YouTube view.

At the same time, I tried to be smart about harnessing support from fans. Sometimes if I used a unique item in a video that many people commented about, I'd auction it off. I also ended up putting together something akin to Patreon, the popular fan-funding platform, years before it existed: I encouraged people to sign up for a regular subscription of a few dollars a month, and in return I'd email them my tracks as they were released. Yes, I managed to get people to pay me to be on my mailing list. For dedicated fans it was a good deal. They would always be up to date with my releases, and in the pre-streaming era they got downloads of my growing body of work at a lower price than the official platforms offered. For me, it was a small but guaranteed chunk of monthly income.

Eventually, I took commissions again. It just seemed silly not to. Taking a few days away from my own projects could often earn me the same amount as everything I worked on for the rest of the month. Now that I'd been making a full-time living from my art alone, I was reconsidering a lot of my ideas about what an artist "should" be—some of which I didn't even realize I had. I woke up each day and dove into making stuff and eked out a living that way. Wasn't this how it was supposed to be? I bounced between projects capriciously, following wherever inspiration struck with no overarching plan—like a *real* artist does, right? I turned down any commercial work opportunities because . . . it proved my dedication to my art?

At a certain point I had to admit that surviving on my own creative work—while it was a wonderful privilege, and a personal goal achieved—did not have to mean anything in and of itself. I realized that many archetypal ideas about Real Artists conflicted with one another anyway. There's the picture of the Real Artist who's so consumed with their work that they don't spend time on anything else, letting their health and relationships suffer—I used to be this person. But so many creatives need time away from their art to let a problem percolate, to find new inspiration, and to live their lives. There's no doubt we believe someone is a Real Artist once they're well-known and earning a living from their work, but we also have the image of the Starving Artist, working low-stakes jobs in order to pay rent, creating what they can out of cheap or found materials in their free time. Supposedly a Real Artist would never sell out, allowing their work to be used to make money for a corporation, or compromising on their creations to cede to commercial interests. But isn't a record label a corporation? Wasn't a band's sound compromised to begin with when it could afford only a certain amount of studio time? Could a journalist writing a review accuse an artist of selling out when their own job was predicated on selling news subscriptions?

People use these ideas to tell stories, to others or to themselves, about how they think the world should be. But there are no rules and there is no "should." It's up to each individual. You decide what your art will be, and who you'll be as an artist.

As I made friends with people who worked in music, I found most of them tended to be more business oriented than I was. This was even the case for punk and indie bands who slept in their vans while on tour and made their own merch by hand (endless boxes of pinback buttons and screen-printed T-shirts). Albums had rollout plans. Photo shoots were planned weeks in advance. Revenue shares were cleanly delineated. Tour stops were heavily strategized—which stops would fall on weekends, what local connections could help with promotion or accommodations, which venues would take the smallest cut of merchandise sales, what driving distances were tolerable but also far enough that one show wouldn't cannibalize the audience from another. Per diems were strictly adhered to. Rehearsals occurred at regularly scheduled times. Roles were assigned for every logistical task. Press kits were put together and sent out. Everyone was thinking about their image.

"A band is a brand," a friend once said to me, and that simple phrase summed up the paradigm shift I was undergoing in my relationship with music creation. Listeners identify not solely with the art (sometimes not even *mostly* with the art) but with the *idea* of an artist and what they signify culturally, socially, and aesthetically. As someone who was culturally untethered but who had extremely broad musical tastes, I perhaps came later to this realization than many.

I emerged from a world of hobbyists, students, and fans, where it was fairly common to have discussions about so-called artistic integrity. As I met more working artists, this rarely came up—they would rather talk about what they were inspired to create and how they could make it successful. They would demonstrate a keen awareness of how they and their work were perceived by their audience, and where they might best meet, exceed, or subvert those expectations as they developed in their careers. This was counter to what my approach had been: chaotic, impulsive, and prone to sharp turns. At times I even enjoyed deliberately confusing my audience, curious how they would respond if I released, for instance, an aggressive rap over an experimental electronic beat as a follow-up to a heartfelt acoustic ballad. Having long ago left the confines of the genre box, I was still driven by some compulsion to try and pry it open for others. It did not make for good business strategy, and a more astute mind would have been able to anticipate exactly what happened, which was that most people who found me would soon be turned off, and my audience grew slowly and erratically as I held on to a small contingent of people already inclined toward eclectic tastes.

Thankfully, though, I *had* crossed the tipping point. I was cobbling together an income on my own creative projects alone, and the growth, however slow, trended upward overall.

## SELF-REFLECTION

Where are you in your creative journey? Maybe you've just begun exploring, or you're starting to find your voice, or you've been building an audience for a while. Maybe you're working for others but you'd rather be working for yourself.

Ask yourself, what will your next stage be? It's easy to dream about having it all and what it might be like to make it to the top, but what is the *very next achievable step up* from where you currently stand? And does that step move you in a direction that's in line with your artistic values?

# Chapter Eight

Nobody will believe this, as I broadcast myself to viewers across the world with well over $100,000 of music equipment in the background, but I'm a minimalist. Hah!

I try to convey that music creation is fun and accessible for everyone, and many of my videos feature me making music with only my phone, or only a single inanimate object as a sound source. However, I don't believe it's mutually exclusive to *also* enjoy gear—its tactile nature, its aesthetics, the inspiration and improved sound quality it can provide, or even the hunt for something rare and special. You don't need a lot of gear to make music. You also don't need to create and release polished tracks if you just like having a bit of gear to jam with. All the components of this equation can be enjoyed in their own right. I think the most important idea is that making art can and should be done with whatever you have. Creation is a story. It's the process of you working with, or pushing against, the limitations in your life to express yourself. Art is made by wrangling with your tangible reality, not by beaming fully formed pieces out of some perfect tool kit (spoiler alert: perfect tools don't exist).

My studio, where just about every available surface is covered in gear, is in stark contrast to my house, where—before Essa and I had kids anyway—people coming over for the first time would often ask if we'd just moved in. We don't hang art or decorate in any way besides having a few plants. Knickknacks are absolutely banned. There are no bookshelves; we just pass books on to others after finishing them.

We arrived at this less-attached approach to possessions when we spent a little over a year abroad, and in this time I realized I could create a tremendous amount (and sustain a career!) with no fixed workspace, and with so few tools they could comfortably fit in a backpack.

I'd been working from home for several years and it gave us the thought that we should take advantage of the flexibility. We'd live frugally for a while, save up some money, and then Essa would quit her job and we'd travel until either we felt like coming home or the money ran out. It would be a test of me working from the road—it wouldn't be strictly necessary as we could live off savings for a while, but it wouldn't hurt to have additional income, and it seemed wise to keep up the momentum I'd built. We were also going to see if it worked to have Essa take over some of my administrative tasks, because at that point I was still doing everything myself.

We gave ourselves a target of saving $10,000 each, which ended up taking a couple of years. I got lucky: I was a bit behind on my portion, and as Essa approached her finish line I landed a scoring gig for a commercial for a pizza chain—for $9,000.

Before leaving, we sold or gave away most of what we owned, leaving a few items in storage or with friends. Months into our trip, we didn't miss any of it. In fact, we continued shedding items from what we'd packed in favor of being lightweight. After playing a few shows that I'd booked in some of the countries we visited, I even sold some of the music gear I'd brought with me, and for much of the trip I was left with my most spartan setup yet: a laptop, a microphone, and an audio interface to connect them.

It was an incredible year. We boated in Cambodia, rode camels in Morocco, and drove almost the full length of New Zealand. In total, we ended up seeing fourteen countries in fourteen months, though we oscillated between quick stops where inside a week we'd cram in a lot of sightseeing and new food, and much longer stretches in places where we could relax and make friends with locals. I reached out to people I'd only ever collaborated with remotely on music or videos and they gave us free places to stay, in one case for three months in the Netherlands with a crew who have now become like extended family to us.

We opted not to have phone plans, picking up local SIM cards with just enough prepaid data to use our map and translation apps when needed. This was done out of frugality—it was cheaper than dealing with roaming rates—but it had the side effect of freeing us even more. While out and about, we had no reason to reach for our phones, so we'd take in more of what was around us and strike up conversations with strangers. And because we didn't have to answer to any schedule, life took on a spontaneous quality. When the person beside us at the bar in Melbourne told us about her comedy night, we actually went. When a viewer recognized me at an intersection in Tokyo, we joined her for karaoke. When we discovered that Salvador Dalí's childhood home was now a museum a couple of hours from where we were staying in Barcelona, we drove there.

I found that I was able to scratch the itch of music making quite well with my tiny setup. I'd build vocal booths out of bedding and couch cushions if I needed to, and almost everything else—even if it wasn't the ideal workflow—could be done with just my laptop. If I needed an instrument, I could usually rent one from a local music store. (Many people don't know that instrument rentals are surprisingly cheap—you can have a pretty nice guitar for a month for thirty dollars.)

It was still a bit of a bother to track down instruments, though, and this actually spurred my creativity and my career. *None* of my best performing work that year used a single traditional instrument. Making music with anything other than instruments became my calling card. While I had incorporated strange sound sources in my music for years, and even done a few videos using nothing but found sound, my nomadic year pushed me further in this direction. On my EP *Alloys*, the foundation of each song was created by twisting sounds from a YouTube video of a person welding steel drums. My next release, *Comet*, used *only* a single sound sample as every instrument—audio that the European Space Agency had just posted of oscillations coming from comet 67P/Churyumov-Gerasimenko. The sound, and its source, were so inspiring that I created the entire album in three weeks. Landing in another new city and searching for an idea for my next video, I simply recorded and made a beat from the chairs in the apartment we were staying in (only later did I realize the "musical chairs" pun). Trying to think of a creative way to promote a few shows I was about to play in Germany, I thought about covering a song by a German artist. Nena's "99 Red Balloons" came to mind, which I re-created by tapping, popping, and squeezing air out of red balloons. To close off the year, I recorded a medley of some of 2014's most popular songs using whatever I could find lying around—beer bottles, couch cushions, a frying pan, rubber bands, and more.

These videos garnered more and more views and soon attracted the attention of ad agencies. This had happened a couple times before with my earlier work. In fact, the music for the pizza commercial that had largely funded my travels was made using only pizza, pizza boxes, plates, and utensils. Now that I was creating this kind of video more often, similar opportunities popped up. A supermarket chain asked me to make music using produce. A restaurant chain asked me to make music with sounds from their kitchens. A car tire company asked me to make music with—what else?—tires. As they would often rely on my expertise in capturing the sounds, or in some cases even had me appear in the commercials, we now had a new (and highly specific) life hack for some of our travel expenses. I might be in Amsterdam at the moment, and an agency would want me in Los Angeles, so I'd head there, make a track with a frying pan and the new chili garlic shrimp dish that was being promoted, and then have the agency send me to Paris.

Besides the obvious benefit of landing more lucrative jobs more often, the frequency allowed me and Essa to learn a lot about the business.

Her simply being the main point of contact, a buffer between me and the client, created a more professional air that commanded better treatment compared to when people felt they were negotiating with a nerd making music in his bedroom. They also didn't care about any of the things that music producers care about—pristine sound quality, perfect mixes, natural-feeling transitions or endings—they were only after a specific feeling, and extremely quick turnaround times. It didn't matter if things ended abruptly or if the mix was rough; everything would be pushed underneath a voice-over anyway. I once did a revision that made it all the way to the final pass where I whistled the main jingle into my laptop microphone, in my hotel room, on the morning of the shoot for the commercial.

When I was flown around the world for these gigs, put up in nice hotels, and taken out for fancy dinners with large teams of people, Essa and I realized the budgets of these companies were gargantuan. For one job, when I wasn't able to travel to the other side of the world where the company was based, a studio was booked where I was staying and the company's whole team came to *me*. I was approaching the capacity of what I could take on, and we already knew we could live frugally—and also that these agencies didn't know anyone else they could call on to make music in this specific way—so we'd propose higher and higher rates without worrying if it meant we'd lose an occasional opportunity. In this way we quickly found the average upper limit of the fees for such work. All of a sudden, I could earn in a week what once took me a full year. It had been less than three years since the job offer from Google came in and I was already making much more than I would have there. Here was my runway.

Throughout this year of jet-setting, I'd continued to release music and publish YouTube videos in my haphazard way, made all the more erratic by the frequent travel. As we approached the one-year mark of our nomad lifestyle, we gave some thought to returning to Toronto and considered how we might reconstruct our normal life. We'd have an opportunity for a fresh start around the age of thirty. We'd return home but would need to find a new place to live—and have very little to move into it. We were both ready to return to stability and routine. I was ready to focus more deeply on my creative ideas. Essa, freed from the nine-to-five, decided to fully take over the business side of my work so I could focus more of my attention on music and videos. Here was my luck again. The person I'd already been married to for seven years had a natural talent for organization and strategic thinking, which was augmented by the fact that she'd studied law as an undergraduate. I suddenly had a business partner who was an astute negotiator, and I no longer needed to pay a lawyer to look over contracts.

Our travel experience had been amazing, and definitely one of the extremes anyone might expect to reach as far as work/life balance. Our schedule had been amorphous or nonexistent, and work was done in fits and bursts around the adventures we were having. It wasn't a sustainable long-term arrangement, and we knew we could impose more structure while retaining a lot of the openness. It had been a season in our life for exploration and recreation, but I had more I wanted to accomplish.

The turning point came for me on December 31, 2014. We celebrated New Year's Eve with new friends in Barcelona, enjoying a delicious meal and then spilling champagne in the streets as we joined the throng marching toward Plaça d'Espanya. Returning to our apartment in the early hours, I was buzzing with the fullness of life and the freedom you feel only when you've been out gallivanting an ocean away from your home. I checked my phone and saw that just that night my YouTube channel had surpassed two hundred thousand subscribers. If all this was possible with my disorganized, casual approach—all the fun, the travel, the audience, the income—what might happen if I really tried my best?

# Chapter Nine

A singular focus is powerful. I've always had broad interests and scattered attention, but with everything pointing to YouTube—all my experiences of the past several years, what had worked and what hadn't—soon after returning from our travels I gave myself a single goal: *get as many subscribers as possible.* I know it might seem like a superficial thing to focus on, but I felt it was the best *measurable* way to see whether I was making progress toward more meaningful but nebulous goals: growing an audience, building community, and sharing my music and ideas more widely.

During this period in my life, *everything* I did was based on achieving that goal. How I spent my time, which videos I made, and which opportunities I took—nothing was done unless I could clearly connect it to the aim of increasing the reach of my YouTube channel. I'd like to be able to say that this was only how I spent my "work" hours, but that wouldn't be true. I let my social life deteriorate again as I worked twelve- to eighteen-hour days, including weekends. If I did hang out with anyone, it would usually be another musician or YouTube creator for a couple of hours after we collaborated on something.

Previously I'd set goals for myself such as "make a living off of music," and I'd become accustomed to setting small goals for what I'd want to accomplish in a day or a week, but this was perhaps the first time I had a goal that was both large and concrete. It really drove home the fact that *concreteness* was key. Thinking or talking about a mission or a strategy will leave you with a vague sense of direction; putting it into clear-cut, measurable actions that you can take, metrics that you can quantify, or words that you can read back a year later (or, even, every morning before you start work) makes it a real and specific commitment.

My first real attempt at strategy came a couple of years before my nomadic adventure. I came up with this checklist and decided that any work I ever did had to check at least four of the following seven boxes.

☐ Passion

☐ Fulfillment

☐ Fun

☐ Money

☐ Content performance

☐ Audience growth

☐ Ease

The first three were personal.

*Passion.* Was I driven by a wholehearted belief?

*Fulfillment.* Did the endeavor fuel me?

(Note: There's a lot of overlap between passion and fulfillment but it's important to make the distinction. I'm passionate about music education, but because I do it at a remove—creating online videos and courses where I rarely ever see the blossoming of those who learn from me—the fulfillment is a shadow; I feel a bit of gratification only in knowing that I've made some kind of difference. Fulfillment in my working life tends to come from finishing a song or album.)

*Fun.* Hello, this should be on most lists. Almost any kind of list.

The next three items were business oriented.

*Money.* Kind of important. We aren't escaping capitalism anytime soon. (I'm fond of the story of a professor grading a paper that mentioned late-stage capitalism, circling "late-stage" and leaving the comment "Very optimistic!!!") I decided to aim high and treat money as a concrete goal, rather than what my former attitude had been toward it—some combination of "as long as I have enough to get by" and "being creative for a living is a privilege, so I shouldn't expect to make a lot." I didn't need to look at commissioned work as taking time away from my own pursuits; a gig that paid well *funded* my creative pursuits, buying me time to work on things that wouldn't necessarily be lucrative. At the same time, I was always considering how I could better monetize the things I was already creating for myself.

*Content performance.* It was clear that some types of videos performed better than others. Better-performing videos would be better for my career, and I decided I ought to make this a focus. If I had a sense that an idea would be more shareable or more compelling for people to click on, it was worth prioritizing. (Interestingly, as metrics for music performance were less easily accessible in this pre-streaming era, I didn't even consider aiming for a larger number of song downloads.)

*Audience growth.* Not all videos were equal. While some would be heavily searched or shared and might rack up a lot of views, these views might be from fleeting visitors who moved right on to the next piece of content. Other videos would drive a deeper engagement, leading people to comment, subscribe, visit my website, follow me on another platform, or participate in a project I was hosting. Ideally, I would be able to create videos that accomplished both, but I recognized that building an audience was a separate goal from having content that was widely viewed.

*Ease.* The wild card and, in this season of my life, often the deciding factor. Nothing should be done only for the reason that it's easy. But if a project ticked three of my other six boxes and could be completed without major challenges and/or in an extremely short amount of time, I decided it would be worth doing. This did mean that—while most of the time there was some overlap between personal and business boxes being checked—there would be times when I put a project away because it demanded too much of my time and energy, even if I fully believed in it and knew I'd have a great time doing it. It also meant that occasionally I would execute an idea I didn't particularly care for and didn't enjoy creating, but it would get views, increase my audience, and make money.

Eventually I honed my approach with a Venn diagram.

It was functionally the same as the checklist—I'd pursue projects if at least four of the circles overlapped. But it was refined significantly, and Venn diagrams are cooler to look at.

I'd rolled the previous categories of passion, fulfillment, and fun into one new category: *WHAT I WANT TO DO*. I'd added *WHAT I'M GOOD AT* as a qualifier—there were a lot of things I enjoyed creatively that I ultimately decided I should leave to those who could do them well. No one needs to hear the Andrew Huang country album or the Andrew Huang house/techno DJ set. This helped to narrow my focus (a little). And of course *MONEY* was still a consideration.

A fundamental change between the checklist and the Venn diagram was that instead of focusing on the outcomes of views and growth, I focused on two aspects of my videos that were under my control, and which could lead to those outcomes: trending topics and whether there was a style or format my audience had responded well to before. I had learned that, naturally, when creating on a platform that was also the world's second-largest search engine, any titles or keywords relating to something that was being heavily searched at any given moment could massively increase the reach of a new video. And for someone whose projects have always been all over the map, I was finally starting to see the benefits of focusing on repeatable formats.

One such format I named *Song Challenge*. I often experimented with working within creative constraints—it's just my idea of a good time—but the performance of my content with and without the framing of this format was like night and day. Looking back, it's easy to see why. Previously, each video was its own little island—I might cover a song in an unexpected genre or make music with garbage. Those two ideas don't have anything to do with each other. But *Song Challenge* positioned my videos as alluring questions for the audience—"Can a song be made with only two chords? With only bird sounds? In five languages?"—which I could answer in satisfying and entertaining ways. It also meant viewers had something to latch on to despite how different the music and videos would be each time. They would tune in for the challenge, the act of creation itself, even if they weren't interested in sampling, or music theory, or the song I was covering, or the weird genre I was exploring.

Eventually, I found the perfect center point of the Venn diagram, the format where all the flower petals converged. I would execute a creative musical challenge (*WHAT I WANT TO DO, WHAT'S WORKED WELL BEFORE*) using unorthodox sound sources instead of instruments (*WHAT I'M GOOD AT*) to cover a currently popular song (*WHAT'S TRENDING*)—and this would always get a huge number of views (*WHAT MAKES MONEY*). The meta-humor angle to this format that made it particularly shareable was that I would cover songs using items mentioned in or related to the lyrics. "Hotline Bling" was performed with phone sounds. "I Can't Feel My Face" was re-created with dental equipment. "24K Magic" was played on twenty-four carrots (yes, I carved carrot whistles for that one). Each of those was an easily communicated and absolutely ridiculous concept that intrigued sometimes millions of internet denizens and rode the waves of those song titles as search terms.

By the time I decided to focus entirely on YouTube, this Venn diagram had become a part of my soul. I rarely ever thought of it or referred to it; it was like an automatic filter for every idea I had and every opportunity that came my way. With the tenets of my strategy established, I created a system to deal with the details: a gigantic spreadsheet.

I love spreadsheets. I've used them for all kinds of things, like tracking my sleep, figuring out my budget, organizing video shoots, or making a custom, sortable to-do list. Creating a spreadsheet for my YouTube plans was probably the main thing—besides doing the work itself—that propelled my channel during its fastest period of growth.

The sheet evolved over time, but its function was always to determine my work priorities. Every single idea I wanted to enact got a row (there were hundreds) and the columns helped me sort out which would be the next idea to execute. At one point I ranked each idea based on how difficult it would be; later I changed that to an estimate of how much time it would take to complete. There were also columns for organizational details that would allow me to be more efficient through batch work—for instance, if multiple videos needed props sourced, locations scouted, or a particular camera or audio setup. (If you're interested in exploring the spreadsheet approach for your work, visit andrewhuang .com/makeyourownrules to access some templates I've created for you.)

I committed to a rigorous two-video-per-week schedule. I would publish something new on YouTube every Monday and Thursday. I knew it would be manageable—just. I had seen in my own viewing habits how much more regularly I would check in on a YouTube channel I liked if it had a clear posting schedule, and I sought to create that same audience relationship for myself. I wanted people to know they could depend on there being new videos at certain times, and to look forward to them. I wanted my channel to become a part of their lives, a viewing habit like any TV show.

With the schedule in place, it was simply a matter of consulting my spreadsheet every few days, and I had a simple rule for determining which idea I should tackle next: I picked the easiest one. This was how

I kept up with such a frequent video release schedule for so long. With the exception of a few bigger ideas that excited me, or time-sensitive projects that would occasionally come up—something for a sponsor, or deciding to cover a song that had just come out—my guiding principle was to prioritize whichever video idea would take the least amount of time and stress.

I'd never before or since had only one goal in life, nor worked as hard. In the next eighteen months my channel grew by one million subscribers.

With focus and consistency in my life at last, I soon noticed progress in just about every area. My thought about viewing habits proved to be true: I communicated clearly and often that I would publish a video every Monday and Thursday, even putting it in my YouTube and social media banners, and many viewers let me know they looked forward to seeing what I put out as soon as it was posted. The videos themselves improved a lot as I was getting constant practice at creating them. Editing, storytelling, lighting, even things like coming up with good thumbnail ideas—each of these was a skill that improved with regular application in real projects. The increased number of videos meant that there were more overall that had a shareable quality to them, which provided extra opportunities for my audience to grow through word of mouth or the many content-aggregating websites, which were in their final golden days.

The performance of the videos was stronger and more consistent than it had ever been before, which I attribute to the combination of all of the above, but also because every new piece of content was another shot at reaching new viewers through new topics and search terms, as well as an extra chance that YouTube's algorithm would recommend something of mine on its homepage, sidebar, or as the video that automatically played after the one just watched. To a large degree, it was a numbers game; assuming fairly consistent quality, you would have to churn out a huge amount of content for the quantity to become a detriment—videos cannibalizing views from other videos—rather than a benefit.

However, the algorithm soon took over everything. It happened on YouTube and on every other major online content platform. A tipping point was crossed where human recommendations could not compete with those generated via machine learning. The platforms and all the data they'd gathered on you—your search terms, viewing habits, and the accounts you interacted with—could now determine and serve the content that would be the most tantalizing for specifically *you*, with the aim, of course, of keeping you on the platform for as long as possible (to serve you the highest number of ads).

In another stroke of luck, I was in the thick of my most prolific period when one of the most noticeable shifts in the algorithm occurred. I've spoken about this with creators who were active at this time who had similar experiences. In the latter half of 2016, YouTube's algorithm made sudden leaps in specificity. Before, it was advanced enough to know the general topics you were interested in and the channels you spent the most time with, but it would still typically recommend only videos that were already highly viewed. Your feed would be populated with content from the most well-established channels and the viral videos of the week, making for a rich-get-richer ecosystem that benefited only a relatively small pool of creators who had the broadest appeal. But all of a sudden, those channels started being recommended less, and YouTube users' feeds became more individualized than they'd ever been. Now you might be served a video with only a hundred views if YouTube was certain it matched a niche interest of yours. It didn't matter if your hobbies were far outside the mainstream. YouTube knew, and it could give you the best new video about 3D puzzles or decorating cakes.

It was a boon for smaller creators who were creating consistent, high-quality content. Where once the algorithm used the popularity of a video to determine whether it would be worth putting in front of you, it now seemed to know what you wanted better than you did. It knew what kind of videos would be irresistible, would keep you watching longer, and would impel you to watch another once you were done. For music nerds in 2016, those videos were the ones on my channel.

# BRANDING

*You create your brand with what you put out into the world, whether you're intentional about it or not. So you might as well be intentional about it.*

I came across this sentiment by chance in some corner of the internet where I was looking for something entirely different, as it usually goes with me. Having arrived at a point in my life where I was actually ready to focus and be consistent with my content, it was the perfect time to receive this pointed lesson about branding. It completely turned around my former stance on it—that branding was inauthentic by nature and motivated only by marketing efforts. My output had flown in the face of the simple idea of branding for years. My musical approach and mood changed with every album, and my videos went from music to skits to vlogs, from artistic to comedic, from high production value to phone video. An early version of my website even had a drop-down menu that let visitors choose its colors. I didn't want to be viewed as one thing: I wanted to be shapeshifting, indefinable, a chameleon.

It's funny how long you can circle around the same lesson. I recalled that friend who years ago had told me "a band is a brand" and realized that *of course* the artists I loved had been stylized and marketed in a purposeful way. I had seen how collecting disparate video concepts under the banner *Song Challenge* had propelled a certain segment of my content much further than the rest of it. Still, it was only after stumbling upon this stranger's thought about branding that I understood I could, and should, apply these principles more broadly. All the work I'd been sharing didn't add up to any kind of cohesive picture; for all but the most dedicated followers, my eclectic output caused confusion and uncertainty. There was a way to bring it all together and communicate it clearly. It wouldn't just be about creating repeatable video formats; *Andrew Huang* was now the brand. Andrew Huang: eclectic music enthusiast.

159

In the days before *Songs To Wear Pants To*, when I first started sharing my music online, I didn't connect it to my name or photos of me or any imagery at all. On a website with only text inside boxes, I shared links to MP3 files. This was my attempt at "making it all about the music." Of course, this isn't a particularly unique approach. So my work—and that of anyone else who shared that stance—got lost in an unidentifiable sprawl. But branding doesn't diminish the music. Maybe it can if it becomes an outsize focus, but it can also enhance it. It can set up expectations, connect you to a wider story, and give listeners more to resonate with.

Where I'd once thought that branding was inauthentic and would make me *less* of myself—that it was about siphoning the most marketable parts of what I did to be packaged and ready for prospective consumers—I found that in fact it conveyed *more* of myself. "Weirdo being weird with music" was not just a convenient umbrella to bundle all my ideas under, it was the most core part of my creative self that I had named and was now emphasizing. Nearly everything I did flowed from that place. Identifying it for myself and for my audience amplified it and allowed them to latch on to so much more. Rather than limit my work, as I once thought it would, it allowed me to continue and even broaden what I was doing, while putting it in a more optimal context.

With a new focus to guide me, an idea I wanted to share could be given a slight rewording and have an added benefit: it would reinforce my personal brand and it would be made less generic. A song I was releasing could be shared in a light that focused on its creative peculiarities and reflected my exploratory spirit, rather than the much less interesting approach of trying to find some complementary imagery to slap beside an announcement.

The brand encouraged me to share more of myself, and as I shared more of myself, people connected with me much more deeply. What I'd previously been afraid to share, or simply thought less interesting, provided relational junctures for my audience. They weren't there only to see perfectly polished output, but to connect with another person. They were interested in seeing my growth and knowing my story. I could show my uncertainties, I could share my work in progress or the projects that failed, I could open up about my hearing loss, or my questions about what it means to be an artist, or even my struggle with branding itself. I'd get into some technical nerdery and excite my following of nerds. I'd talk about gender or expand the feminine side of my wardrobe and find acceptance with queer folks. Simply sharing more of my real self did as much for expanding my audience as any amount of following trends or applying marketing tips.

When I hadn't been thinking about branding, or when I'd been actively against branding, *that* was when my work was splintered and difficult to follow. Under the pretense of authenticity—doing whatever I felt like at any given time—I'd sowed fragmentation. I realized that I could never share *all* of myself (what a notion!) and so, no matter how I approached it, my audience would always be getting small slices here and there. Why not help people understand a bit better how these pieces fit together? And further, wasn't this kind of selective representation true of . . . everything? We show different facets of ourselves within different social circles and circumstances. Art itself is a selective process—all the editing and polishing, removing what's unnecessary. Why shouldn't our presentation and promotion of it be any less refined?

Branding is also not something you just turn on or off—it's a matter of degree, and you can be deliberate about how much you commodify yourself or your work. For some people, the preference is to become more of an entity or a company—they may remain faceless, take on a new name, and/or refrain from posting anything personal, confining themselves strictly to a branded voice and perspective. For me, this adds layers I don't want to contend with, but I have many creator friends who have specific guidelines for what they will and won't post. Their audiences have no idea that they're married, or have children, or live somewhere outside the United States. Some of them wear masks, or their content consists of demonstrations where you only need to see their hands. One of them has taken his online brand so far that he has someone on his team who is "trained in his voice" and whose job it is to respond to *every single person* who asks him a question on social media (and his follower count is in the millions).

Some people retain their apparent personhood but magnify it into a character, and at times I would find myself slipping into this—separating out the parts of myself that were camera-ready, or behaving the way I believed my audience would expect me to based on previously published videos. But becoming a character often means becoming simplified and rigid. It doesn't leave room for growth, and what doesn't grow dies. People get tired of something that never changes, that doesn't respond to an evolving world, and that seems calculated or artificial.

There's no doubt an even better branded version of myself could be put out there. I could reduce the number of genres and approaches I take with music to set and meet expectations better. There's no reason a YouTube channel should encompass music production tutorials, music theory explainers, gear demos, travel vlogs, and an original science fiction series, except that those are my interests. There's plenty of room for me to streamline, and I could achieve greater numeric success, but at some point on the way there I *would* cross that line I always feared—of being less of myself, of focusing on money or a follower count more than what I'm passionate about.

So there *is* a catch with branding. A brand is more effective the simpler it is, therefore, simpler things are easier to brand. This sugary drink is delicious. This phone is beautiful and easy to use. Things get tricky when you're a brand like Yamaha, a company that manufactures both pianos and motorcycles.

By primarily presenting myself as a musical explorer, I found a relatively simple way to brand something complicated (my smorgasbord of musical interests). But I was reluctant to become a fully brand-first entity; I still felt I should primarily exist online as simply *a person*, because I've never been able to let go of the idea that that's what it all boils down to. I'm a person who makes things and puts them online. I have good days and bad days. I have opinions. Perhaps it's so important to me that my public persona lines up with who I am because I spent so much of my life being unsure of myself, or feeling like I couldn't be myself.

In any case, I like that I can be straightforward and relatable. I like showing that I'm just like anyone else who might be interested in doing this. You could use the exact same tools or techniques I do. You certainly have little choice but to use the same platforms that I do. (This is an interesting thing about online-only creators—with the exception of anything they may have deleted, you can follow their exact trajectory post by post, seeing the response that everything had at different times. Most of the success any of us found in this domain was through figuring out the right things to post—what kind of content and brand worked. There are no backroom deals that land us ads in prime real estate, there is no payola to push us incessantly onto the airwaves, there are no power brokers with whom to find favor. We found things we wanted to share that resonated with others.)

I don't like the idea of seeing myself as an establishment, an enterprise, or a star. I still believe in a level playing field. You could make a video today that outperforms any of mine. Lots of people without audiences make incredible things all the time! All of this is why I often feature and collaborate with people who haven't built brands or followings themselves. I've done a decent job of packaging and communicating what I create, but I see all of us as the same thing: people making stuff.

But then, some might say that this ethos is part of my brand.

Online platforms change rapidly as they compete for people's time and attention. Content changes as trends come and go and as people get bored of formats they've seen before. Yet there are principles of good content creation and strategy that can be held on to no matter how things are shifting.

1. **Provide value.** No matter the platform, the topic, or the format, people who experience your work want something out of it. For those in the arts, your followers are likely after *entertainment* or *information*. They want to laugh, learn, or be inspired. The posts that serve only the creator—stroking their own ego or trying to promote something—tend to flop. Posts that best serve the audience always shine. If you have something you want to promote, it's possible to do so in ways that are valuable to your audience. Tutorials, free digital products, jokes, even sharing your struggles in the creative process: all of this provides something to connect to, instead of making people feel like they're doing you a favor by checking out your project.

2. **Use new features.** While a platform's algorithm will always be a black box, we know that they're trying to outdo competitors and improve their bottom line. Any major platform changes are made with these aims. When a new feature is introduced, you can be sure that it'll be favored by the algorithm for a period of time. A new video format, a new way to interact with followers, a feature that was blatantly stolen from another platform—if they're trying something new, they're going to push it hard for a while, and content that uses those features will surface more. There's a double benefit. Many people who consume but don't create will be exploring the new features, and the earlier you get in, the less competition your content will have for their attention.

**3. Aim to engage.** Basing work solely on what you think will be popular is a quick path to unfulfillment, but there are ways to do what *you* want while still attracting and connecting with folks on the other side of the screen. It's not about following trends, and it's not about being the best at something (though either of those things don't hurt). It's about structuring your content to generate and sustain interest and participation. Here are some techniques that help in this regard.

- Use visuals wherever possible. (See **Tools for Online Growth** on page 120 for more.)
- Front-load videos with the most compelling content—the visual or story element that's most likely to make people want to watch more.
- Videos with speaking should be captioned so they can serve those whose devices are muted and those who are hard of hearing.
- Ask questions that will start a conversation in the comments.
- Make a splash. People respond when something is particularly beautiful, impressive, funny, surprising, fascinating, the list goes on. What about your work can make the biggest impression? What can you do that few others can?

Algorithms are looking at data that can tell them what posts are keeping people on their platform—the number of comments, shares, likes, saves, or any other form of interaction with a post, as well as the amount of time people spend looking at it. So it's imperative to make content as interesting and concise as you can—and "concise" doesn't have to mean "short," but only what's necessary should be included.

# Chapter Ten

By the end of 2016, my YouTube channel's growth had exploded. Viewership and subscribership slowly increased with the changes in the algorithm, and suddenly, in December of that year, they spiked. In that month I received 13 million views, and over 150,000 people subscribed to my channel. With YouTube's click-through (the proportion of people who click to see a video when served the thumbnail) usually hovering around 5 percent, this means that YouTube had put my videos in people's feeds somewhere around 250 million times. And not just any people, but a viewer that YouTube thought would have an interest in my content.

I was spending almost every waking hour on these videos, but I was also in the right place at the best possible time. No ad campaign, talk-show appearance, radio station bribery, or tailored email blast was ever going to get me anywhere near this level of marketing value, and this had been absolutely free. If there was any lingering doubt about whether YouTube was where I should put my focus, it was obliterated. I was going to work my way through my spreadsheet of ideas, and I didn't have to concern myself much with promoting the videos—I just had to make the videos interesting. The algorithm was here.

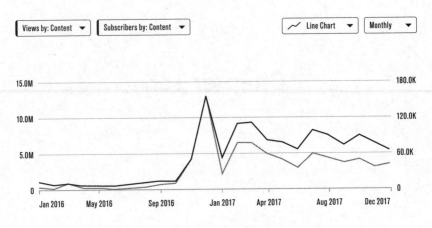

*Graph of views and subscribers by month, January 2016–December 2017.*

That December turned out to be the all-time high for my channel's reach, but as I continued with my regimented publishing schedule I settled into surprisingly consistent performance, with 5 to 10 million views and about fifty thousand new subscribers each month. The change of scale was bewildering. I remembered when "Pink Fluffy Unicorns" was viewed fifty thousand times in one day. Now if my channel got one hundred thousand views in one day, it was a low-performing day.

It was rewarding, challenging, energizing, draining, fun, and hard work. It was my entire life for two years. I can take no credit for the algorithm choosing to favor me at that time, but I worked night and day to take advantage of it. We were in a synergistic relationship. As YouTube amplified what I was creating, my continued output fed the algorithm, regularly giving it more that it would recommend to viewers because those viewers would engage with the content. There are all too many creators who have one piece of work go viral and are never able to find that reach again, or who come up with a format that's extremely popular for three months until nobody cares about it anymore. Luck can strike anyone, but well-directed work is necessary to sustain a career.

There's a common misconception about what makes "quality" content that actually has little to do with—or is even at odds with—what people will enjoy and want to watch. Professional lighting, swooping camera movement, a slickly edited intro with custom theme music—some creators focus on these kinds of things, and a lot of the time they aren't that important. As mentioned earlier, viewers are after entertainment or information, and if that core element is strong it hardly matters if something was filmed on your phone in a corner of your bedroom.

A creator I know started off aiming for these sorts of supposed markers of quality. Each video would begin with a long intro with flashy visuals and loud music and shots of him looking like a super-cool guy. Even in the body of his content, transitions between shots would be ornamented with quick camera moves and sound effects, and rather than getting right into the crux of his topic he would talk excitedly around it, making jokes and being a showman. The thing is, he was actually incredibly talented in his field, and people were watching because they were attracted to his talent. When he dialed back the video trickery and focused on showcasing what he was good at with directness and clarity, his viewership skyrocketed.

The flashiness, the effects, the jokes—none of these things are necessarily bad, and used well in some types of content they can be helpful. They can create excitement, reinforce branding, and be entertaining in themselves. But they should never be mistaken for what's actually important: delivering what viewers came for.

On the other side of the spectrum, I have a friend who creates tutorials who used to be entirely opposed to video editing. He's a respected expert in his niche and was always providing valuable information about advanced concepts that few other people would even wade near, but he didn't enjoy editing and wanted to save time, so he would simply publish the entirety of what he filmed. He did build a small following for these long, single-take lessons because the detail and creativity in what he was teaching was second to none. But when he eventually came around to the idea of editing, the performance of his content leapt up dramatically. Of course people wanted to learn the same thing in fifteen minutes rather than ninety. Of course they didn't want to wait around and watch as he prepared his next example. Previously, his videos were filled with pauses as he considered what to say next, and each of those pauses was an opportunity for a viewer to get bored and click away. Now, without the editing even approaching slickness, but simply condensing the content to only the useful information, tens of thousands more people were enjoying his work.

All of this assumes some flexibility in what you're creating. If you're committed to long-form, hand-animated tutorials with a square aspect ratio, you might find the odds stacked against you. But more likely, if that's the content you've been making, what's interesting to you is communicating and educating through compelling visuals. This can be done in myriad ways, and can evolve with platform changes and viewer interests, and doesn't have to completely overhaul your existing workflow. Long videos can be broken into bite-size chunks. Short videos can be strung together into compilations. Voice-overs or text can be added or removed. In YouTube's earlier days, when there was a culture of shorter videos and the demographics leaned heavily toward teenagers, I jump-cut through my video footage to create a relentless torrent of information and excitement. Now, with the platform having become a destination for longer, more relaxed viewing, and not just somewhere to alleviate boredom during a few spare minutes, I might shoot a very similar video but edit it with a more flowing, conversational pace. The core never changes, though—it's always about sharing my passion for music. Overall, it's not very different from music itself, where style, length, dynamics, and instrumentation all change, but at the heart of it, what most people resonate with is a good song.

## SHAKE UP YOUR CREATIVE ROUTINE

We all get stuck from time to time. Whether our output stops satisfying us, or the creative flow feels blocked, it's important to have tools available to help jog inspiration. Here are some I use often.

**Don't be yourself.** Deliberately try the opposite approach from the one you'd normally take. If you usually jump to hands-on experimentation and trial and error, see what happens if you dissect the work of someone you look up to, or try to make a detailed plan. If you're normally organized and methodical, inject a bit of chaos and spontaneity: press record and improvise; roll dice to make decisions; open a book to a random page and use a sentence your finger lands on as inspiration.

**Change the medium.** Produced a song on your computer? Try it out on acoustic guitar. Wrote a poem? Turn it into a personal essay. Exploring your work in a new context or format can widen its dimensions, even if you're just returning the work to its original state with some new ideas.

**Change the environment.** We can't help but respond to what's around us. Working in dark or light, in your bedroom or your kitchen, at a coffee shop or in the woods—all of this and more can affect our focus and our feelings. For example, focus can take many forms. You can be attuned in varying degrees to the details or to the big picture, to flaws or to momentum, to the texture of a piece or to the message it communicates. If you do your work in the same spot at the same general time of day, you may be limiting your perspective.

**Smash things together.** Whether it's old projects, unrelated concepts, or other people's ideas, see what happens when you combine two or more things that weren't intended to go together. Sometimes brilliant connections happen. I tag all my music projects by tempo so that if I'm feeling stuck I can see if another snippet in a similar range might add something. It doesn't always work, but sometimes it ends up as if the two pieces were always meant to fit together. My *Sonic Boom* series with Rob Scallon—where in each episode we explore a single musical instrument, concept, or challenge—seemed like an inevitability once we did it, but we needed more than a decade of friendship and collaboration to arrive at the format. It was only after an enormous amount of varied work together that all the pieces crystallized into place: our confidence in our chemistry, our trust in each other, our studio experience, the building of our teams, as well as the specific ideas we drew from—our shared love of certain shows and our other videos involving challenges or weird instruments that always performed well—which we eventually realized we could roll into a more unified and fun experience.

**Try a new technique.** I've been making music for almost my entire life and I've never gotten tired of trying new things—nor has it gotten any harder to find new things to try. Especially now with the internet, there's no shortage of people doing interesting things that I can be inspired by or even try to replicate. This might involve different approaches to writing, recording instruments, manipulating sounds, coming up with ideas, or any other part of the process. I find it fun to research creative studio tricks, usually in online forums, but it's also easy to find great articles and videos about artists or songs I love. (If you make music and want to cut right to the chase, visit andrewhuang.com/makeyourownrules, where I've compiled a heap of techniques and exercises you can try, along with other bonuses.) Having more techniques in your toolbox multiplies the possibilities of your creative expression. You're able to find more and better solutions to the challenges that come up as you create. You have more to draw on when things aren't working or when you're less inspired than usual, and with more sparks flying you'll find yourself in far fewer ruts.

Once you get into the minutiae of creation, you find there are lots of ways to do the same thing. Perhaps the exact details will differ, but the same aims can be achieved. In fact, the more I grow as an artist, and the more accomplished artists I work with, I find there's an inverse relationship between one's creative power and one's attachment to specifics. The more experienced you are, the less you worry about the importance of any one idea. You can try five ideas, get rid of them all, and come up with five more. Your work serves the bigger picture. It's rarely about a specific color or shape or melody; instead, you're responding to questions like "What needs to be communicated?" and "How should the energy flow?" and coming up with as many answers as you need to in order to find a great fit.

There's a balancing act between giving people what they want and giving them something novel. When you find something that works, there can be a tendency to latch on and repeat it. But evolution is necessary. Interest wanes over time as people "get it," and new ideas show up elsewhere that are more attractive. With my early work, I went too far in the other direction. I was so committed to novelty that I didn't give my audience any sense of a through line in my work. Indeed, the work was most successful when I found *some* expectations to frame it around—*Song Challenge* set people up for something peculiar but impressive; *Songs To Wear Pants To* had a cheeky humor most of the time. Having arrived at my understanding of branding, I was in a strong position to be able to find this balance. I simply had to ride the dial on my natural inclination to novelty.

My overall brand was set—here's this weird musician who will entertain and educate you. Every video had those elements—entertainment and information—but the blend wasn't always the same. I maintained a strong music production focus but could at times slip into content about music theory, songwriting, instruments, or the music industry, without it ever feeling out of place. I started various series to further focus some of these interests, such as *Weird Gear*, *Theory Thursday*, and *4 Producers 1 Sample*, which had no schedule of their own but were simply part of the rotating buffet of my channel's informative, musical fun.

I had learned my lesson early on: you have to bring the audience with you. Give them the satisfaction of seeing and feeling your evolution. A massive shock out of left field rarely has a positive impact; it usually confuses people and makes them long for more of the usual. And general inconsistency gives them very little to grow attached to. If you really want to throw a curveball, it should be a calculated one, anticipating how it could land given everything the audience already knows and expects of you. But those can't happen often, because they generate all-new expectations that you then have to work with.

I was in a great place. It was the only time in my life I had such a singular goal, and there was none of the usual existential questioning around what my direction should be or how I should be spending my time. I felt I was doing exactly what I should be doing. I continued adding ideas to my spreadsheet and working through the easiest ones—after all, I had only two or three days between each upload.

I didn't see it for far too long but, of course, always picking off the project that would take the least amount of time and stress had an inescapable downside. Gradually, the projects became increasingly time-consuming and stressful. Burnout was around the corner.

# PART THREE

# Money

# Chapter Eleven

Someone emailed me saying they had money that was owed to me. It seemed so much like a phishing scam that I ignored it until they followed up a second time. The company they worked for was in the business of collecting royalties for music played on satellite radio. I had never heard of this company before and had been under the impression that such royalties would fall under the umbrella of radio royalties in general, which were regularly being paid to me by the performing rights organization I was already registered with. With some research, I found that satellite plays were in fact a separate ordeal, and I handed over my mailing address. A week or two later, I opened my mailbox to find a check for a little over $40,000.

The music industry is a labyrinth of slivered revenue streams, and most musicians have to stitch together their livelihood from a variety of sources. There are few standards, and reporting can sometimes be opaque or nonexistent. I had forged ahead so independently—never working with an agent, manager, or label—that I missed a massive chunk of income. (I have since spoken with some industry veterans and confirmed that there are likely no other $40,000 checks waiting for me.) I still don't actually know who's been playing my music on the radio for the past decade, but thank you!

As every artist is unique, so is every creative career. I know people who are rich from royalties earned by writing songs for other artists, people with relatively little online traction who can still get a few hundred people to turn up to a show, people with barely any following whose music is being streamed millions of times every month, and people who are getting almost no streams but are supported by pay-what-you-want album sales from a small but dedicated community. We'd like to think there's some kind of sense to be made out of how people respond to music and how it can be monetized, but the audiences and business arrangements are as varied as the creators.

I once found myself envious of a friend who had five times as many monthly listeners as me. I made the assumption that he must be making five times as much in streaming royalties, and I dreamed of what life would be like with that much more passive income. The next time we talked shop, though, I learned that most of his streams came from one popular song he released a few years ago, and his audience hadn't latched on as much to his new material. A typical listener of mine would take in a few songs, so our actual streaming numbers were much closer than I would have guessed. I also hadn't taken into account that my friend was signed to a label, and it was taking a 50 percent cut. I had been completely wrong. *He* was making less money than *me*.

I don't think making money should be the focus of a creative pursuit—if you want to get rich, there are much more dependable routes than being an artist. But I believe it's worth being deliberate about business decisions as a creator, because the longer you can sustain a career, the more you can create. My approach won't be everybody's approach, but if I were to advise on career longevity, I would recommend two things:

1. Diversify your revenue streams.
2. As much as possible, know where your money is coming from.

Creativity, adaptability, and scale are paramount to making money as a creator. The online space is constantly shapeshifting, and the things that work best right now might be obsolete in five years. Being early to new trends is extremely advantageous; being the *only* one able to provide something desirable can be even more so. In one sense, scale is easier in a digital world—the same product can be sold ten times or ten thousand times without any practical change in overhead costs. At the same time, everyone is competing in the same pool—giant corporations, celebrities, local businesses, independent creators, and people who aren't trying to make money online at all—all these entities have access to the same platforms and are posting all the time. Standing out is the only way to make it.

What follows are six snapshots of how my income breakdown has looked at different points in my career, to show you how I evolved and adapted. It can't and isn't meant to be replicated exactly, but it may provide ideas for your own endeavors, as well as a glimpse at how variable, unbalanced, and chaotic one's revenue can be in a creative career.

## SEASON 1: EARLY DAYS

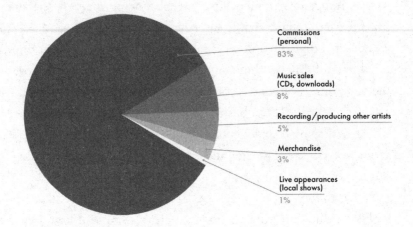

Commissions (personal) 83%

Music sales (CDs, downloads) 8%

Recording/producing other artists 5%

Merchandise 3%

Live appearances (local shows) 1%

In the couple of years after I started posting my eBay auctions, I survived only because of all those personal commissions. I created over a hundred songs a year for people's weddings, birthdays, and cats. That business brought a trickle of interest into what I was doing as an artist, and *Songs To Wear Pants To* itself developed its own following, but there simply wasn't the scale to make a living from selling CDs and T-shirts and playing shows. In essence, it was like I had a day job that supported my side hustle of trying to "make it" with my art—but it had the added benefit of helping me sharpen my musical skills.

These were also my final days of helping others with their records. That process was so rarely fulfilling for me—it usually felt much more technical than creative—that it wasn't worth pursuing further. My efforts often felt like a waste when many of these projects would never see the light of day.

This chart represents somewhere in the middle of this several-year period. In the very beginning my revenue was 100 percent commissions, and by the end I had developed my artist profile a bit more (mainly through trying to redirect *Songs To Wear Pants To* visitors to my other music) and was starting to experiment with YouTube.

## SEASON 2: "REAL ARTIST"

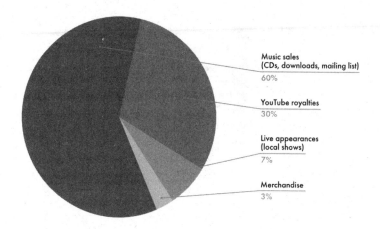

Music sales
(CDs, downloads, mailing list)
60%

YouTube royalties
30%

Live appearances
(local shows)
7%

Merchandise
3%

This is what it looked like the year I shunned all commission work.

I had built my artist and YouTube presence *just* to the point that I could scrape by without anything else, with a monthly income anywhere between a few hundred dollars and a few thousand dollars, depending on what I was releasing and how much it resonated.

This was also the period when I came up with my pay-to-subscribe mailing list where I would send out downloads of what I was creating. That was the only source of consistent income I had at the time, so I'm deeply grateful to the hundred or so superfans who supported me through this season. Platforms have since come into being that take a subscription-with-perks approach to providing creators with a dependable source of income (the largest of these being Patreon, which I've now moved to). I somehow managed to dream up and implement my own version of this a few years earlier, and it gave me a revenue stream that didn't exist for other musicians at the time.

Additionally, I played small local shows where between merch sales and my cut of the cover charge I might walk away with $100 on a good night. I probably could have looked at what was going well online and worked on strengthening it, but I wasn't thinking very strategically yet—I was simply taking every possible opportunity that related to creating and sharing my music.

## SEASON 3: EVEN SPLIT

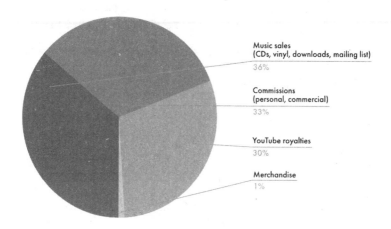

Music sales
(CDs, vinyl, downloads, mailing list)
36%

Commissions
(personal, commercial)
33%

YouTube royalties
30%

Merchandise
1%

When I came around to commission work again, I remember settling into feeling comfortable with three broad revenue streams that were very similar in size: commissions, music, and YouTube. Merchandise, for me, has always been a tiny sliver of the pie. During this period, with CDs and my only ever run of vinyl filed under "music sales," the majority of my merch was just T-shirts. Also, while I did perform live, I was experimenting with my first self-booked tours, meaning I was often not even breaking even—or the money I did make from a show would be from the CDs, vinyl, and T-shirts.

In this season I realized even more how good a thing I had with an online audience. The absolute best shows I ever played during this period were to about a hundred people, but often it was more like twenty to fifty, and I'd either lose money or walk away with just enough to drive to the next city and get a cheap place to sleep (or, sometimes, I would sleep in the car). I certainly didn't *profit* from it.

It's funny to realize that performing live, the prototypical musician's livelihood—the thing that was the most challenging, required the most logistics, and took me away from other work for days or weeks at a time—doesn't even make an appearance in my final income breakdown from this period. Ultimately, it also did the least for my career. The online approach was clearly working as I continued to release music and videos, and the subsidy of taking commission work again meant I could live comfortably. Though it wasn't always without financial worry, I remember being more balanced and stable during this time than I had been before.

## SEASON 4: COMMERCIAL WORK

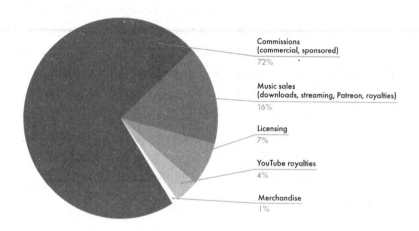

Commissions (commercial, sponsored) 72%

Music sales (downloads, streaming, Patreon, royalties) 16%

Licensing 7%

YouTube royalties 4%

Merchandise 1%

The most noticeable thing during this time period is how commercial work came in and absolutely dwarfed all my other revenue streams. You-Tube income didn't change much in this period, and music sales grew a bit, but the overall pie we're looking at is way bigger. Stumbling into this idea of making music with inanimate objects proved to be a massive boon and was what allowed me to pursue YouTube at full force once I came to that decision—because I could put virtually all my time into it.

I fully ditched physical music media, which I knew to be on its way out. Streaming was starting to encroach on download revenue, and was less profitable from the beginning, since a monthly subscription to a streaming service costs about the same amount as buying one album. But I replaced my mailing list with a Patreon presence and was able to attract a lot more supporters there, both because it was a more official-looking and established platform and because of the general growth of my audience.

In this period, I also stumbled into two new revenue streams. Through no doing of my own, I started getting a small amount of radio play, which resulted in actual payouts from the performing rights organization I'd signed up with long ago (because I learned somewhere that that's what you're supposed to do). I started licensing my music—allowing it to be used within others' media—for widely varying fees. I submitted my music to licensing companies, and was also approached for occasional licensing opportunities. This is always luck-of-the-draw—you simply have to have made something that someone else ends up hearing and deciding they'd like to use—but it's extra money for something you've already worked on that only involves reading and signing a contract. Also, since I created and released my music myself, I didn't need to consult anyone else about any of these opportunities, nor split the revenue.

Lastly, by making some T-shirts and hoodies available through an online print-to-order service, merchandise continued to hang in there at less than 1 percent.

## SEASON 5: LIVE & SPONSORED

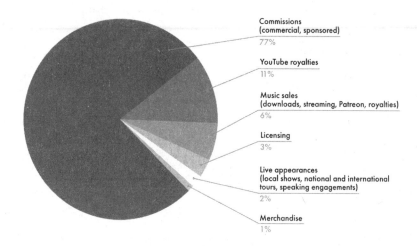

Commissions
(commercial, sponsored)
77%

YouTube royalties
11%

Music sales
(downloads, streaming, Patreon, royalties)
6%

Licensing
3%

Live appearances
(local shows, national and international
tours, speaking engagements)
2%

Merchandise
1%

As my YouTube channel grew, I received sponsorship opportunities, which would sometimes compare in value to my commercial work. This meant the commissions slice of the pie continued to overshadow all the others, and while the proportions harked back to my early days, it was very different from having a "day job" that supported the music career. These gigs would take a relatively small amount of my time and, in some cases, would help further my YouTube channel with compelling video concepts, like making music using candy. The income also allowed me to hire my brother-in-law, Phil, who—burnt out from the merciless demands of working as a commercial visual effects artist—was happy to have a role with reasonable hours where he would help with whatever I needed in the process of filming or editing.

This was a period when I *did* turn a profit with live appearances—mostly due to the benevolence of Hank Green. He invited me to be in his band for three tours; he also gave me an opening slot *and* he paid everyone on the team a much larger share of ticket profits than people in our positions would typically receive. Additionally, I found myself able to charge for speaking engagements now that my YouTube profile had risen. However, you can see that all of this—which, again, took a ton of logistics and travel time—still made up only 2 percent of the pie. On realizing this—and recognizing that being onstage was not at all a passion for me on the level of being in the studio—I stopped performing live altogether.

## SEASON 6: I'M A BUSINESS, MAN

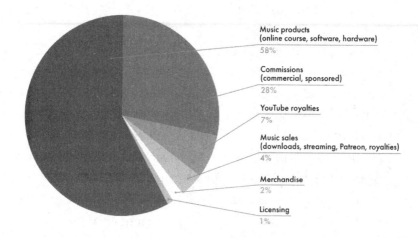

Music products
(online course, software, hardware)
58%

Commissions
(commercial, sponsored)
28%

YouTube royalties
7%

Music sales
(downloads, streaming, Patreon, royalties)
4%

Merchandise
2%

Licensing
1%

Here's where I've currently landed.

Revenue for recorded music is down—for everybody. Streaming has pushed other purchasable formats almost entirely away, so making money from recordings isn't dependable for anyone who isn't regularly getting millions of plays. Licensing is always hit or miss; the lack of consistency and wildly varying fees mean it can't be relied on for steady income. And as I'll get into later, I've made a deliberate choice to make less money from YouTube—so that I can be happier. But the products I've launched and the commissions I'm getting are going well, and I find I'm again in that bizarre place where I've invented a job for myself and am accessing revenue that's not even on other musicians' radars. It's allowed me to expand my team further: Sophie manages my social media, Marty is a music production and mixing assistant, Kyah provides additional video help, and Galen is a superstar who wears every hat that isn't assigned to someone else.

In the current season of my career, I've been enjoying developing products that contribute to other musicians' creative processes. I'm not interested in just slapping my name on someone else's work to make a quick buck; in each case, I've had a concept that I've found the right people to help bring to life. I'm poring over every detail as we brainstorm and design, I'm the most active tester, and I write a large portion of the manuals. Creating tools that help make music is now almost as much of a passion for me as creating music itself.

As usual, I've approached it from multiple angles—really, just following what I'm interested in, but it's led me to create tools that are compelling for very different markets. There are products for the software crowd and the hardware crowd, for people doing professional work and those who just like to jam, and there are affordable items that sell in large quantities alongside pricier boutique products with runs in the hundreds.

My app Flip Sampler was intended to be accessible; it's priced affordably and is one of the few full-fledged music creation apps available on both iOS and Android. My software plug-in Transit is similarly a powerful, professional tool at an accessible price point. It's been wonderful to see both being embraced by everyone from beginners to pros. On the other hand, my Eurorack module Ghost is the epitome of niche; hardware synth modules are expensive and manufactured in small batches for a very specific contingent of sound-making nerds.

My luck struck again when I created my online course. I'd wanted to put it together for years, but it was always a lower priority than getting the next video or album done. But I had a fan at an educational start-up called Monthly (now rebranded as Studio), and they approached me about creating the first course on their platform, offering to do all the heavy lifting of making my materials presentable, handling student sign-ups, and advertising. I took the risk, and it paid off lavishly for us both. Tens of thousands of students have taken the course and gotten a lot out of it—some have even been able to parlay the skills they picked up into careers as producers or engineers. And Studio is now one of the leading online learning platforms, with video classes from Charlie Puth, Idina Menzel, David Blaine, Mark Rober, Casey Neistat, and many others. Somehow my timing had once again worked out just right. When the world shut down in the wake of the COVID-19 pandemic, there was an online learning boom, and my course already had a proven track record while others who were interested in teaching music—with the internet as their only option now—were just starting to put their own courses together.

And in a twist of fate I never saw coming, my merch sales rose. This could only be attributed to First of October, my one-day-a-year band with Rob Scallon. Something we started as a joke—attempting to write and record an entire album in one day—created a superfandom within our audiences. Spending *one day* each year making an album together generates more sales than *five years'* worth of all my other merch sales. I don't know if there's a very actionable business takeaway from this. Artificial scarcity? Simply make a product that's a thousand times better than your other ones? What I do know from the responses we get to the First of October videos is that they make people *happy*. Many say it's their favorite thing either of us do. They rewatch the videos over and over. They cover the songs. The albums we make together land among listeners' most played music. The project just makes audiences feel great, and that's probably the ultimate thing. It's not about a product with the best features, or the promise of a problem being solved; it's just something that makes people love life a bit more.

# Chapter Twelve

A young boy sees that his neighbor's grass is overgrown. He knocks on their door and offers to mow it for ten dollars, which they happily agree to. It doesn't take him too long, so he tries again with the next unmown lawn down the street, whose owner is also glad to take him up on his offer.

Sensing an opportunity, he goes up and down his entire street, knocking on doors, speaking briefly with neighbors, making a map of who would like to have their grass cut regularly. It's far too much for him to do on his own—but he has a plan.

He reaches out to his friends to see who would be willing to mow a few lawns every Saturday for extra pocket money. He assigns addresses to those who are up for it, and soon a smooth operation is up and running. Most of the neighborhood's grass gets a weekly trim.

For each lawn, he pays the friend who mows it eight dollars, while he takes two dollars for organizing everything. In the end, he makes more than each individual who's out there pushing a lawn mower and sweating in the summer sun. He doesn't ever touch a lawn mower himself. He just walks up and down his street, collecting money.

I remember my dad relaying this story to me several times throughout my childhood as an example of working smarter rather than harder. It's simplistic, of course. Could this kid's young friends really be relied upon for a regular weekend work commitment? And where are all these lawn mowers coming from?

Regardless, it's what I remember of any business-related advice my dad tried to pass on to me, and in some way I'm sure it contributed to my entrepreneurial inclinations. I never did the lemonade stand or the paper route, but I was always coming up with some kind of outside-the-box childhood hustle. I enjoyed folding origami, and discovered that other students would pay me to make them paper "ninja stars," which could actually be whipped at their target with surprising accuracy. (My fifth-grade teacher eventually caught on and my business was shut down.) By high school, although I remained rather aloof, my musical activities became well-known enough that some classmates who aspired to rap superstardom would pay me to make beats for them. I even managed to sell a hundred copies of a self-made album, performing at every possible school function as well as playing the songs from my boom box during breaks and trying to make a sale from anyone within earshot.

I can't claim to be some kind of business tycoon, but I've often had decent enough instincts and I'm always ready to learn. I've shared about the luck I had, the skills I developed, and the hours I put in, but I had something else working in my favor: I was open to tackling commerce head-on, and with creativity, in a sea of musicians who weren't thinking about it, who were waiting for someone else to do it for them, or who actively avoided it.

I wrote earlier about my first encounters with working musicians who seemed much more business-minded than me—and at the time they were, especially in the worlds of recording and performing music. I was impressed by their organization, their attention to detail regarding their brand, and their knowledge of revenue streams, from touring to merchandise to royalties to grants. I learned a lot from them. As traditional avenues waned or dried up, the move to an online world was sluggish or even resisted by many in the industry, but I had been there early, experimenting with how my work could succeed in this immediate, hyperconnected, direct-to-fan space. While my friends in bands were driving huge distances to their tour stops and using the internet only to tell people about those tour stops, I was reaching more people, daily, just by clicking my mouse. While some musicians were telling me they cringed to even consider outright asking people to follow their accounts, my YouTube channel surpassed a million subscribers. Artists were hesitant to partner with brands for fear of "selling out," and I was doing five-figure deals with companies whose products I was already using anyway—and redirecting much of that income to create products of my own.

We're in a new age when everyone is expected to be online and active constantly, and when the promotional practices that work best are evolving rapidly. Artists are releasing music with pay-what-you-want schemes, dropping surprise albums with no warning to the usual press channels, eschewing albums altogether and putting out monthly singles, publishing weekly or daily videos about their work in the studio, livestreaming frequently or for astonishingly long stretches, and more. Few can get away with being quiet and enigmatic. Going off the radar for too long, you're likely to find yourself forgotten by a large portion of your audience. It's a rare artist that has the magnetism to be able to post once a year and have it be an *event*, or to disappear for years at a time and emerge with a masterpiece—the way it often used to be done. Social media not only has made the artist's online presence essential, it has made it personal. Artists are expected to be relatable, to show a bit (or a lot) of their "real" selves, and even to occasionally share photos or videos that were taken by themselves on their phones—or appear to have been, at least—just like any of us who are watching could do.

*Everyone* has to serve the algorithms. That means candid moments, talking to the camera, sharing quirky or inflammatory opinions, and making videos of themselves dancing, working out, trying on clothes, and eating. In the music industry, a curious new situation has emerged where major labels sometimes hold an album hostage, refusing to begin their part of the promotional cycle until the artists themselves have created enough organic stir on social media platforms (which they are often now contractually obligated to do). Few artists can ever focus solely on the music; there's constant pressure to produce *content*, and that works best when the artist is involved. A camera crew can follow you while you do your own thing, or a team of designers can churn out graphics for you, but nothing will be as powerful as your own personal touch. (It's telling, and kind of funny, that even some *billionaire* celebrities still resort to selfies for social media engagement.) Promotion depends more than ever on the artist. There's no more guise of musicians saying "I just make the music I like, and I hope other people like it, too" while a million-dollar marketing machine works behind them. By and large, the artists who find the most success now are those who own the fact that they want success, and work hard to get it.

Accepting that I was the best person to market myself had very little to do with my creative interests, and at times even slowed down those pursuits as I focused on business matters, but it was key to the flourishing of my career. It ultimately bought me vastly more time to create what I want. Early in my career, I thought that if I found the right agent or manager, they would be able to see the perfect avenue for my talents and guide me to massive success. I eventually realized that—of course—no one can know your path better than you, and no one will work harder for you than you will for yourself. (My own wife—who adores me, who wants nothing more for me than to see me successful and fulfilled, who eventually quit her job to spend years taking on every part of my business that she could, and who gets far more than a manager's share of my income—does not work as hard on Andrew Huang as I do. I don't think I would fare better with Ron from the talent agency.)

Putting my own time and effort into moving myself in the direction I believed in was always what led to the greatest results, however slowly and irregularly they came at first. We hear stories of artists with so much talent that rich, well-connected managers just had to swoop in and dedicate their lives to sharing it. If you do happen to have a world-class talent that can fit into a mass marketable package, then you might just look enough like dollar signs that you can attract dollars-motivated people who will give all they have to support you for as long as the dollars are flowing in. But even the megastars need to be involved in the marketing of their work—sometimes all-consumingly. You can champion your own work too.

There's a myth that art and business are separate affairs, or that they're each better suited to different types of people. I know too many musicians who avoid anything to do with either their finances or the promotion of their work because of this belief. I can share examples of three friends of mine.

**Friend #1.** A musical genius. I learn something with nearly every other sentence they utter. Their music is innovative and varied, and they experiment a lot—with different studio setups, with different ways to play shows, and with different collaborators. As such, most things about their career are inconsistent, including their income. They once told me, "I kind of love not knowing anything about the money. It's like a surprise what I'll have every month."

**Friend #2.** Well-known and respected in a popular subgenre. Plays huge shows regularly. Coproduced a song on a recent Justin Bieber album. When we last hung out, they had just wrapped a tour, and we were talking about synthesizers. They said they weren't sure if they could afford a particular one that cost under $1,000. I asked about their tour income—"Yeah, I don't really know what I'm getting." I asked about their Justin Bieber royalties—this was a year after that song was released: "I don't know if that's come in yet."

**Friend #3.** A creator of beautiful sounds who had a moment in the spotlight but decided it wasn't for them. A piece of theirs was sampled by a Top 40 record producer for a song for a major artist. Agreements were signed, and it all seemed aboveboard, but in several years they've never received a cent. They're not sure if they missed a step somewhere or misunderstood a contract, but at this point it's been so long they don't feel they can ask about it.

\*        \*        \*

Whether we're unsure, indifferent, or embracing ignorance, not paying attention to money as creators leaves us wide open to losing out on revenue we've already captured, if not actual exploitation by those who control the books. It also means we might put resources into things that don't make sense. If I weren't paying attention to my income I'd probably still be touring, because I enjoy it enough and it's widely viewed as one of the main ways artists can make money—though even that's started to change, with more consumption shifting online and a pandemic that amplified all the costs and uncertainties that touring brings with it. But being on top of tracking income and expenses (a habit I developed out of necessity when I was living frugally, had not developed any passive income streams yet, and had complicated tax filings as a self-employed person), I was able to look at my touring revenue and see clearly that it was a waste of my time. I could spend the same amount of time at home making a few great videos and pieces of music, and those would both earn me more and build my audience more. Or if I did just enough to make a similar amount as I would have on tour, I'd be able to take a week or two off!

There's a parallel viewpoint that permeates creative circles when it comes to promoting one's work: *I'm the artist—promotion should be someone else's job.* It is, of course, fantastic when a creator can focus solely on creating, and all the marketing and publicity can be handled by other dedicated people. But I believe promotion can be stronger when the creator is interested in being involved—how many times have we seen a painful interview where the artist clearly doesn't want to be there? And, in our online era, it has become both more necessary and more powerful to self-promote in the early stages of one's career. Companies and agents now look for followings as much as they do for talent—in some cases perhaps more so. But those kinds of entities are also less essential in a world where something you filmed on your phone in the morning can reach a million people by the afternoon.

It seems some creators feel that putting any of their time and energy into the business side of things will take away from their art. They need to be purely, one hundred percent focused on their craft. Their image of an artist is of someone who creates all the time, someone who is above business and administrative work (or simply bad at it because they're *so artistic*). I think that's nonsense. Every artist I know—from the hobbyists to the pros, from the amateurs to the savants—all make room for other interests and responsibilities. No one bats an eye at a musician who also loves fashion, or film, or sports, or who is a great cook, or who is a political activist. Yet with the exception of the uber-wealthy pop star class, there's a resistance to accepting musicians who embrace business. It has too many undertones of selling out.

I used to live in this mindset. *I'm an artist, not a marketer.* But as I dismantled all my inherited ideas about what an artist should be, I stepped outside of this one as well. I found that I enjoy a lot of the business aspects of my work, and I might even be good at it—or better than the average musician allows themselves to be, at any rate. I now encourage everyone to at least explore the business side for themselves, because it *will* be helpful. Maybe it's not for you, or you might be lucky enough to find a business partner who can take it off your plate. Maybe the three friends I mentioned above genuinely have not a single business bone in their bodies. But I think many more people do than have discovered it for themselves. In large part, I've made it as far as I have because I was open to the idea of engaging more with business endeavors in the first place—it was just extra fortunate that I ended up enjoying it. Not nearly as much as I enjoy making music, but enough that it helps me get results. The two can even create a healthy working rhythm. When my ears are fatigued after a long session, I'm still able to get through emails. After coming up with a week's worth of social media posts, I have an entirely different well of creativity that I tap into for writing songs. When I'm bored of refining a guitar pedal design, I'm more than happy to go and play an actual guitar.

Most working artists are not the artists of popular culture—the rich and famous who create only that which is fueled by inspiration and passion. Most working artists *work*. Even those who are established enough to make their living from a passion project usually take on some extracurriculars, because creative career income is never entirely consistent. I know popular musicians with critically acclaimed albums who still score films, video games, or commercials. I'm friends with some well-exhibited painters who still take commissions for corporate illustration or restaurant murals. The ideal is for the gigs to grow as you grow. In a jagged but ultimately upward spiral, you search for opportunities that are just a little bit bigger than what you've done before. But how do you get started in the first place?

1. **Portfolio.** You need to have a representative collection of work before people will trust you with high-paying or high-stakes projects, and building a portfolio almost always begins with the opportunities that present themselves as favors for friends and family, or connections that are made in your network after you've let your skills be known. In the early stages of taking on commission work, you probably can't afford to say no. But even if you can, I believe a lot can be gained from doing the "low quality" jobs—the things that aren't prestigious, or don't align with your brand or your interests. Even—in the *very* beginning—the things that don't pay well or at all. (An unfortunate reality of creative work: because parts of it are more enjoyable than, say, accounting, there are tons of people willing to do free or low-compensation work in hopes of getting out of their jobs in, say, accounting.) The absolute best way to build a body of work, however, is just making things up for yourself to do. Post something you've worked on every week and very soon you'll have a consistent feed that demonstrates your

abilities and range. You could do something that pays tribute to other artists you admire, or try your own take on a recognizable piece within your field. You could set challenges for yourself, limiting your time or materials for a project. All of this is great practice for your creative muscles and expands the size and scope of your portfolio with regularity.

2. **Submission opportunities.** Be on the lookout for companies or events that are openly receiving work for consideration. An early win for me was submitting a piece for a theme song competition hosted by a duct tape company; I walked away with the second-place prize of $1,500 (and a lot of duct tape). Another time, I stumbled across a post from a credit card company whose idea for a brand awareness campaign was to support three lucky Canadians in their visions for "inspired interactive urban environments." My pitch for a sound installation ended up being selected, and the piece—an ambient musical work that visitors could shape through interactive touch screens—was hosted at the Four Seasons Centre for the Performing Arts in Toronto. As part of the deal, the company brought in Emily Haines of the band Metric to help me develop and promote the idea. Also, they gave me $10,000.

3. **Online presence and outreach.** It can be a good idea to curate your work on a website, where you're able to present yourself exactly as you think best, organize your work in a way that makes sense for prospective clients, and share any information you think they might need. But often, a strong social media presence is more than enough, and it's definitely more important in terms of reaching people. If you're in touch with even a small community online, I've found that many people—especially other artists—are very supportive of "open for commissions!" posts and will help to spread the word. Make these posts visually attractive, list the things

you're available to do, and provide one good contact method. If you can find a way to make the post itself creative and fun, and something that showcases your talents, even better. You can also approach from the opposite direction and look for the people who are hiring. Search "call for artists" on your social media platform of choice and sort by latest. Try different searches, customized to what you do, and maybe add keywords. For example: "call for digital artists," "call for artists nyc," "paid music opportunity," and so on. The possibilities for connection on social media are staggering, and that applies equally to finding an audience, finding collaborators, and finding good work!

When it comes to artists doing work for hire, I know far too many who are too timid to follow up with clients who've forgotten (or "forgotten") to pay them. Some artists are even too shy to bill people in the first place! As a project draws to a close, they wait for an invitation to send an invoice that sometimes never comes—or, worse, when approached for a project, they don't broach the topic of payment at all, and find themselves working pro bono by default. It's not entirely their fault; there's a pervasive misconception about artists that they're happy just to be doing work they enjoy, or that some amount of "exposure" on offer is more than enough compensation. But it's all the more reason that creatives need to advocate for our worth and be firm about it. Easier said than done when you're starting out and every opportunity seems like a chance to further your career, I know. But look at it from the other direction. If you're working on something that is not compensating you fairly, then you're losing ground. Your time and energy are going into something that's setting you back rather than moving you forward.

Determining the value of your work can be challenging, as every project is unique, every industry is different, and creativity in general is impossible to quantify—but it's essential to believe in your value and to continually refine what makes sense to charge for what you can offer.

**Your starting point.** Make a rough estimate (and usually a slight *over*estimate) of the time a project will take, and the hourly or daily rate you'd effectively be making. Get in contact with others doing similar work to ask questions if that would help. A good rule of thumb is if you're consistently being turned away after the fee discussion, you're probably asking for too much, while if people tend to accept your rate without the slightest attempt at negotiation, you can probably charge more.

**Navigate negotiation.** The golden rule in negotiation is not to fight for a larger share of the pie but to work together to make a bigger pie.

Look for any of the ways that a client's goals are aligned with yours. Think of every possible extra offering you have on hand that helps you by helping them. Show that you have their interests in mind. At the same time, remember that most people don't come out of the gate with their best possible offer, so ask questions and see where they might be flexible, and you may find yourself able to improve on a deal—even one you were already happy to accept.

I now find myself on the other side of the equation when I hire others to help with my albums, videos, or product launches. Sometimes I'll send a preliminary message just asking if they'd be interested in a project, and they respond ready to collaborate purely for the love of it. That level of passion isn't a bad thing, but it's a bit funny following up to let them know I actually want to pay them $2,000 for something they were willing to do for free, and it makes me wonder how many paying opportunities they may have missed out on for lack of asking. You don't have to come right out with a fee schedule and start listing your payment methods; even a simple "Is there a budget?" moves the conversation in the right direction.

**Know when to say no.** Always be ready to walk away. Whichever side is more attached to the deal has less negotiating power, and as much as you're hopefully trying to work together to create a mutually beneficial arrangement, sometimes things just don't line up. My deep wish is that you'll be approached with exciting, inspiring, lucrative projects, but they can't all be like that. Sometimes you're just producing a thing that other people want so you can make ends meet. There's no shame in that. *Mozart* did that. It still allows you to deepen your craft and maybe even make discoveries that become useful in your personal work. Sometimes, a project won't pay what you would normally get, but it'll be an opportunity worth taking anyway—a chance to learn from someone wiser, or to travel somewhere amazing, or to fulfill a childhood dream. I once licensed a piece of music to a major motion picture for a paltry sum, because as much as we discussed it they wouldn't budge. But it was a live-action remake of a cartoon franchise I loved as a kid, and so where

I normally would have walked, I accepted an embarrassingly low offer because being a part of this movie made my inner child happy. In the end, it turned out terribly and bombed at the box office. But, just for me, I love that I got to contribute something to that franchise's universe.

No gig is perfect, but when it's questionable from the outset, you might want to walk away. If they don't seem to respect what you do, walk away. In any situation besides a desperate season where my bank balance was negative or I had zero work prospects on the horizon, I've regretted any job that I took reluctantly, or anything I took out of guilt that I should feel grateful just to have opportunities as a freelancer. In my early years, in moments when my income was iffy, I found myself saying yes to things that were completely outside any of my personal or professional goals—doing foley for an indie film, or helping an acquaintance's kid record cover songs. This was not how I should've been spending my time. Whether it was way too little money, or something I did only for the money but didn't enjoy, it was never worth it to take on any of these projects. If the food and rent that month didn't depend on it, it would always have been better to put my time and energy elsewhere—into my own projects, into anything not work-related to replenish myself, or, at the very least, to have the opening in case a better offer came in. We are creatives! We don't just trade our time for subsistence, *we shape reality*. We bring beauty into the world that didn't exist before. We turn nothing into something. It behooves us to concentrate our efforts as much as possible on the things that only we can do.

I got pretty good at saying no; it was crucial for carving a purposeful path for myself. Everything you say *yes* to is a *no* to something else. When I started to build momentum for my own projects, it was hard to break the habit of taking on minor client work. I had become so used to taking everything that came my way because my income had been so unpredictable from month to month, and I was eating into time that should have gone into the music and videos that were now starting to make money for me. For a long time, as a daily reminder, I had a large sign above my workspace that simply read **NO.** I started to take longer to respond to offers of work. Rather than jump in with the excitement of a paying gig (and sometimes, let's be real, the validation of feeling valued), I would let a message sit for a day so I could think over what it would actually mean for my time, my energy, the development of my skills, the advancement of my brand, and my relationship with the client—and, most of all, what it would take time and energy away from. This breathing room usually had the effect of lessening the luster of a proposal and helping me to weigh its pros and cons more clearly. With more difficult decisions, I always found it helpful to meditate on them. Even as little as three to five minutes sitting comfortably with my eyes closed, turning over the facets of an offer—this was often enough to arrive at a decision I could feel fully confident in. Those three to five minutes in some cases could save me days or weeks of detours and stress.

Once I was established enough that I didn't feel the pressure to take on every opportunity that came my way, I learned something that proved to be a beneficial shift in perspective. Given the importance of what we say *yes* and *no* to, it's helpful to exaggerate how we express them. *No* isn't just *no*, it's *absolutely not*. And *yes* isn't good enough. If something is worth doing it should be a *HELL YES!*

In the period immediately following my channel's explosion with the algorithm, YouTube was working out incredibly well for me, but for most people it was still nowhere near being considered part of the mainstream. For a couple of years, everyone's question for me—whether it was a journalist, a music industry contact, or someone I met at a party—was "You can make money from YouTube?" It was clear that outside my bubble of YouTube associates, I was still early to this game. Now, just a few years on from then, we've seen online creators saturate every possible market, and, according to numerous studies, "YouTuber" is the number one choice when today's children are asked what they want to be when they grow up.

During the years when I'd felt the pull toward the platform, I'd had to shake a lot of ideas about what it was supposed to look like to have a music career. Accordingly, I let go of a lot of the activities I used to engage in, even those that made up my livelihood. DJing, recording and producing for other artists, releasing physical albums, performing live—none of these things were in line with the direction I was headed or the way I wished to spend my time. I loved working in my home studio, creating and exploring music, and being able to share my ideas and discoveries with anyone else who might find them interesting. YouTube allowed me to do exactly that with my career, and I was fortunate to have reached a scale where it was no longer necessary for me to do those other things to sustain it.

I also let go of many things that I wanted to do. I used to enjoy gardening, drawing, cooking, chess, video games . . . there was no room for hobbies anymore. I gradually streamlined my life to direct all my energy at creating a great music channel, and I happened to reach that point *right before* a seismic shift in the way that smaller but active channels were recommended on YouTube.

## STREAMLINING

There are a few principles that work together to create a powerful focus, though they require some discernment because they sound as if they're at odds with one another.

> Do what you want to do.
> Don't do what you want to do.
> Do what you don't want to do.
> Don't do what you don't want to do.

Let me explain.

1. **Do what you want to do.** I know it's not often possible to simply do exactly what you want, but it's worth working toward. I can't tell you how many people I've seen ignoring the art they're dying to make because they think they have to follow today's trends, or who could be sharing their beautiful voice with the world if they embraced social media instead of waiting to find a manager or record deal. If the way things are usually done line up with what you want to do, that's amazing—consider yourself lucky. But when they don't, take every opportunity to break from the mold. Paths exist outside the traditional ones; you just might not have found them yet. Maybe no one has, and you'll be the first.

2. **Don't do what you want to do.** There are many things that we want to do—even very good things—that will ultimately take away from our larger goals. Spending less time on the enjoyable or even rewarding but less important things in life gives you more time to put into your truest aspirations.

   Put it mathematically: Say you spend an hour a day on something you like, but that doesn't move the needle on your goals. Maybe it's

211

gardening, maybe it's watching TV. Perhaps an hour a day doesn't seem like much, but assuming you sleep six to eight hours a night, you're spending more than 5 percent of your waking life on that thing. Put another way, you're spending three hundred and sixty-five hours a year on that thing. Three hundred and sixty-five hours divided by sixteen waking hours a day is *twenty-three days!* That's roughly how many weekdays there are in a month. Imagine having a month off work every year to dedicate to your creative goals.

Of course, a single hour is harder to work with than a nice long stretch of the day. Anything worth pursuing will likely need other, bigger windows of time for deeper work. But there are many things that can be done in an hour. You can practice a technique. You can generate several ideas to experiment with, or flesh out an idea you came up with last time you brainstormed. An hour, approached with urgency and intent, can force you to be bold. It's natural to wonder what you could possibly achieve in an hour, but take it as a challenge, or gamify it. *How many iterations can I come up with for an idea I'm stuck on? Can I make something in the next hour, however small, that I'd be proud to share?*

I'll also note that there are things not worth giving up. If yoga is your best de-stressing activity, if pottery gives you a joy you feel nowhere else, then these are healthy things that will make you feel the best you can. When I was in my period of extreme streamlining, I still made time for reading books and exercising. But I was willing to give up all my other hobbies and entertainment to take my music and videos further. It's not always easy—but if it's any consolation, unless you've reached nirvana and conquered all desire, life is too short to do everything you want to do anyway. Be deliberate with the time you have.

3. **Do what you don't want to do.** This might be the most important one, and it applies on both the business and the creative sides. There are always boring and unglamorous things that need

doing—sorting through vocal takes, syncing up video clips, responding to emails. There will be many times when it's more attractive to take a snack break, scroll through social media, or get started on a new creative idea. But the boring things are needed as much as the exciting ones.

When Essa and I were traveling, we would sometimes rent cheap accommodations where our host would be sharing the living space with us. After hearing about my presence on You-Tube, one such host shared an idea he had for a channel. I've heard a *lot* of content ideas over the years, and this was at least a 9 out of 10—something I'd never seen done before, which had the potential for massive appeal, and which was a perfect mix of two different areas where he had passion, knowledge, and skill. I was hustling particularly hard at that moment, trying out a temporary *daily* video publishing schedule while flying around for a busy commercial season, and the juxtaposition could not have been greater when I asked what was stopping him from getting his channel going: "I'm waiting till I meet someone who'd want to edit the videos for me." I wouldn't be surprised to learn if he's made no more progress toward that channel since our conversation ten years ago.

There will be times when you don't even want to do the thing you want to do! Setting up will feel like a hurdle, the blank canvas will be too daunting, or you'll be afraid to fail. Many people wait until inspiration strikes or they're in the right mood before starting on their creative work. Those can be the most enjoyable times to work, but other useful times include: any other times. A regular creative practice yields so much more than a flurry of activity whenever you happen to feel like it. And you may find that it doesn't actually take much—trying a new chord, writing two lines, throwing some color on the canvas—to get you to a place where you *do* feel like it. It's harder to start than to keep going.

4. **Don't do what you don't want to do.** This is another one that's not always possible, but well worth considering wherever you can. If there's some part of your process you absolutely don't want to do, can you outsource it? Can you barter with another creative to help each other in complementary areas?

I've always embraced the DIY ethos—realizing that to get my musical ideas out it would be more effective if I picked up a handful of additional skills like mixing, mastering, filming, and video editing. For some circumstances, it may be better to procure outside help. Even now, having developed proficiency in those areas and even enjoying them for the most part, it's a better use of my time to do what I'm best at—music creation—and hire others to help with everything else when possible.

Of course, all of this presumes you want to barrel full force toward a single shiny point on the horizon, demolishing every obstacle and leaving no potential untapped. "Hustle culture" has been embraced by many and is often celebrated; there's also considerable backlash against it. For me, the answer, as usual, is that both are valid. It's entirely dependent on what you want out of life. I respect those who wake up before sunrise and put in an eighteen-hour day trying to move the needle on their ambitions. I've been there. I have no regrets about spending a portion of my life that way. I also think it's wonderful when people are confident that they don't need to chase anything, when they can enjoy their gifts without feeling any need to commodify them. I've been there too. I've stepped back for certain seasons (admittedly much shorter ones) and created for nothing but the joy of it. Sharing none of it and documenting none of it. Just letting the music happen as it disappears into the air. Being content with little and working hard toward something big are not mutually exclusive. The world might tell you that only one of them is right, but what matters is which one—or what point along the spectrum between them—is right for you.

I find myself in the middle now. I never again want to hustle as hard as I did in my early thirties. But I loved that season in my life, and it brought me to where I am now—a season I also love, where I have the freedom to do even more of what I want.

Something that went hand in hand with streamlining my life was an attitude I always seem to have had, but which went into overdrive when I had my single giant goal to march toward: I channeled everything, whether positive or negative, into that goal.

Every success energized me, and every failure was a chance to learn. Either one was an opportunity to create content. I was sharing my process, and my audience resonated with the results, whether I ended up with something impressive or had simply given a challenging idea my best shot. Each piece of feedback fueled me. Positive comments encouraged me to keep going. Negative ones didn't get me down—I would just work that much harder to prove myself. (I'm not saying this is healthy . . . but it did give me productive results for a period of time. More on external validation later.)

I would do the same thing when looking at my channel's performance.

"This video is doing super well—I'm going to make a bunch more this month and they're going to be awesome!"

"This video is doing terribly—I'm going to make a bunch more this month and they're going to be awesome!"

Yes, some people have described me as an optimist. But I don't know any other way to live. Thinking that things won't go well doesn't really soften the disappointment when they don't. If anything, it makes it more *likely* that they won't go well. I'm going to keep tornadoing through life with a tune on my lips and a skip in my step, riding every wave that'll have me and turning every obstacle into an opportunity to grow.

Good work doesn't succeed on its own. We'd love to have a meritocracy, and many people might believe we do—the hard work paying off, the adulation and riches reaching those who deserve it most—but it's not the case. In music, there are flashes when movements center themselves around discovery—websites pop up that reflect a social media feed where all the posts are people's original songs, venues host events and foster communities that show up for new, unheard, or experimental music. But in large part the success of a piece of music (the way it's typically measured, anyway—with numbers) is a product of a thousand forces, both calculated and unintentional, that are separate from the actual sound waves reaching actual ears. It is, after all, a *product* that we're measuring when we speak about success—not the music itself but the commodity of it. A song might give people hope or a new perspective, it might inspire a million kids to start playing guitar, it might even deter someone from self-harm. These are undervalued merits; they're not ticket sales, streaming numbers, or sync placements. There are no dollar signs attached to them.

I'd like to think most of us believe art has intrinsic value that has nothing to do with how well it might perform in a marketplace. But I'm also not such a purist that I would ignore the realities of the benefits of commercial success and the ways we can optimize conditions for it. That's not to say that the art itself needs to change, though I would argue that capitalism and commodification shape what artists create far more than anyone wants to admit, and I'll examine that in a bit.

An avalanche of machinations work together to produce anything that resembles success in music. The way you look (or the way you hide) has to fit with the way you sound. The way you sound has to fit with the way people feel about you. The way you sound has to interest enough other people to begin with. Someone has to believe in you enough to invest in promoting you, or you have to find ways within your means to promote yourself. And when success is measured in numbers, it will always be advantageous to simply do the thing that larger numbers of people are interested in. A D-list pop singer is always going to be more popular than the world's biggest noise artist.

I've had to confront this time and again; my career has been a microcosm for these principles. Having worked with many people, in many genres, with many release strategies, for two prolific decades' worth of singles and albums, I can tell you that the music was more successful when it had:

1. **More promotion.**
2. **Better promotion.**
3. **An audience that's easy to reach.**

Let's take each in turn.

1. **More promotion.** There have been a few times when I've attempted to post a video every single day for a month. It started as a challenge that some creators undertook once a year, back in the early days when YouTube was just for fun. I also embarked on a couple of similar attempts later on, as a strategic experiment, once "daily vlogging" was starting to establish itself as a format. Whenever I did this, I was only thinking about my YouTube goals: have fun and grow the channel.

   One of these bouts of daily posting happened to coincide with a new album I was releasing, *Lip Bomb*. It was not any more or less special than my previous albums—I had the same level of excitement about it, and I had worked on it as hard as I usually did. I wouldn't have said the music was any better or worse than anything else in my catalog at the time. It was the next set of songs I happened to finish among my growing heap of projects. But because I'd committed myself to a month of daily videos, much of the content became about the album. I made several quick music videos for songs that I otherwise never would have. I filmed myself drawing the cover art. I got a new piece of music gear and used it to create a live performance of one of the songs. One day, when I was out of time or at a loss for what to make, I simply talked to the camera about some of the challenges I encountered creating the merchandise around the album.

In my innocence, I didn't even consider any of this to be promotion. It was art and/or content that I was making because I had committed to an arbitrary challenge intended to make me create more, just to see what would happen. I enjoy challenges for making me both start and finish a number of interesting ideas that I otherwise wouldn't have executed. This time, in addition to that, I happened to do the best album promotion I'd ever done. Far more people bought the merch and the album (this was back in the download days) than any of my previous releases. The results were immediate, but they also had a lasting effect. *Lip Bomb* was talked about within my community for much longer than a release normally would be. A larger than usual proportion of songs from it would be cited as listeners' favorites for years. Again, I didn't feel this album was any different in quality from what I'd put out before, but I'd given it a lot more exposure. And, perhaps, by inadvertently investing more in its success, I had made it appear more special to some of my listeners.

I felt a bit silly that, as is so often the case, I had to learn lessons that in hindsight seem logical or even obvious by stumbling into them. In any case, I had now registered some of the absolute basics about marketing: Promotion works. You should do it. Do more of it than you think you should. People need to be made aware of your product, and they need to be reminded of it multiple times.

2. **Better promotion.** Quantity is one part of the promotion equation, and the other, of course, is quality. You could run an expensive ad campaign to have your album art and a snippet of the lead single

show up in a lot of people's feeds, and it would almost certainly have less impact than making one really funny video that features the song—even one you film yourself with your phone. It's not bad to approach promotion in some of the standard ways—people need to be shown your work, and sometimes they just need a nudge. But when you're able to make promotional material fun and exciting in its own right, you'll probably get a more enthusiastic response.

We're in the grip of a smart device era, where people's idle attention falls on a small handful of media platforms. Succeeding on those platforms is crucial to succeeding in general. Print and television advertising value are in sharp decline. People read on their phones and watch shows online. People who *do* watch television are likely on their phones during ad breaks. I can't help but imagine that billboards and posters are also probably losing whatever effectiveness they once had; everyone outside is on their phones, too.

I'm regularly hired to create music or video for ad campaigns—even for corporations with massive budgets, even for Fortune 500 companies launching a new product—where the entire campaign happens on two or three social media platforms. The most potent promotion now happens on social media, and your posts are in competition with everyone else's. Algorithms elevate posts that keep people's attention and suppress those that don't generate engagement. It's an arms race to create content that grabs the broadest audience and holds them for as long as possible. (It's easy to view that cynically, or hopelessly, and social media addiction is a very real issue. But social media itself isn't something I can outright vilify. These platforms have delivered tremendous power to ordinary people who use it for social and political change, sharing knowledge, building relationships, and . . . promoting their latest single.)

In an endless, captivating feed, how do you stand out in the noise? It goes back to entertainment and information—skewing toward the former. What can you create that people will get something out of, even if it's in the name of promoting your work? Are there lessons or stories you can share? Is there a joke or a skit you can make around it? Did you capture anything behind the scenes that might be funny or is an interesting look at what you do?

*The creative process.*

You're always doing indirect promotion on social media if your posts are compelling. Some days I'll grow by hundreds of followers because I've shared a resonant opinion or created a relatable meme. These are shared by some of my followers, or pushed outside my usual circle by the algorithms, bringing new people to check out what I'm up to. It's very "trickle down," but you'll probably notice that creators are more generally active on social media when they're promoting new work. (You can always just tack a promotional line or link onto the end of an otherwise unrelated post, but this *will* curb its performance significantly.)

Sometimes—often, even—promotional content outperforms the art itself. I used to find this disheartening, but it makes perfect sense—it's a by-product of everything we share now having myriad performance measurements attached to it. Nothing has a one hundred percent conversion rate; promotion by nature needs to reach much further than the product it promotes. You've seen more movie trailers than movies and read more headlines than articles. My YouTube thumbnails are seen by twenty times as many people as watch the videos—that doesn't mean I'm primarily a thumbnail creator.

I once posted a short clip on social media of me playing a drum with a cucumber. It was a snippet of an actual recording I was doing for an album; I had recently had the idea that cucumbers could provide a different tone on hi-hats than drumsticks and used them on a couple of songs. The total combined streams of the thirteen tracks on that album are now at about five hundred thousand, while the cucumber video's views are approaching one million. It's fine. The comparison between these numbers isn't meaningful. It's a funny seven-second clip compared to a full album. People being mildly entertained for seven seconds (or perhaps inspired to play instruments with cucumbers) is totally different from people taking in several crafted, emotional pieces of music.

3. **An audience that's easy to reach.** It makes sense, doesn't it? Given the choice between an audience that's easy to reach and an audience that's hard to reach, which is more likely to lead to greater success for a creative work?

So what makes an audience easy to reach? It's not just one thing—it's everything that contributes to a project being easier to find and define, more widely understood and accepted, and having a head start in the game of anybody giving it a chance at all. It's about a work's cultural context, the expectations of fans and passersby, and the appeal of the product itself.

An audience is great if they're already there. If you've built a following—however you've done it—your new work has a better shot than your earlier work. An experimental noise track I put at the end of an experimental noise album today will get more plays than a beautiful ballad I wrote when I was just beginning my career, simply because of how many more people are currently curious about my work.

If you're just starting out, there are audiences out there to tap into. If what you do slots into an existing scene—contemporary jazz, speed painting, classic video games—then there's a community you can invest in, there are peers to build relationships with, and there are established events to take part in.

You also don't have to link your entire identity to a particular scene but can make points of connection where you choose. When my friend Madilyn Bailey (American singer-songwriter, musician, and fellow YouTube creator) shared her strategy with me, I was floored by its ingenious simplicity. She creates a cover version of *every* song that hits the top spot on the Billboard Hot 100. It means she's always creating something that's relevant, heavily searched for, and interesting to a huge amount of people. For years she's regularly created pieces that are perfect for some of the biggest audiences in existence; as of this writing, her YouTube channel is approaching ten million subscribers. It works terrifically for her as a pop artist, but covering a popular song in an unexpected genre can be equally engaging. For Madilyn, it doesn't hurt that she's beautiful and sings incredibly, but at the same time, how many beautiful singers have we all come across? Strong promotion is one of the main ways that anyone will have a shot at building a career.

If you're a true original, it might help you to stand out, but equally it might give you no footing; listeners won't know where you're coming from, and other artists may think you don't belong with them. You can take an inverse approach to what Madilyn has done—rather than create material that serves the broadest audiences, amplify a slice of what you're already doing to make it a focal point for a niche. Maybe your highly original music incorporates a lot of a certain instrument; you can build interest within the community of people who are super into banjoleles or modular synths. Maybe you have a personal aesthetic that's easy to identify with and the angle is that people won't believe such incongruous music is coming from a goth kid/hippie/cat lady/guy who wears fedoras.

What's the quickest way to make an audience bigger? Add a second one. Collaboration is a timeless key to growth (not even just audience-wise but in terms of your abilities as an artist). Musicians are always writing together, touring together, releasing songs together, remixing each other, and telling their followings about each other. Few things are more powerful than finding others at a similar stage in their careers and supporting each other.

Lastly, if your work leaps out at people, they won't be able to help getting deeply involved with it—coming back to it repeatedly, sharing it, discussing it, and creating their own content around it. Yes, the tip is *make things that people love*. The reality is that some things are much more attractive to larger numbers of people. Although I love and work hard on and release tons of different music, and promote all of it as best I can, the experimental stuff performs the worst and the poppy stuff performs the best. Music that's catchy, singable, not overly complex or abrasive, not so short that it's unsatisfying but not so long that it challenges a listener's patience, music that fits well in a playlist—it's much easier for this type of material to rise to the top.

There's always a touch of mystery—no one can predict a hit with certainty, and there are many left-field artists who gain popularity. There's also something to be said for how much one element can compensate for another. A lot of simply passable, mediocre offerings can sometimes be marketed into the mainstream, and some off-kilter but special work can transcend humble beginnings and spread like wildfire as it inspires grassroots support. Overall, though, creations will have an easier time succeeding if they're easier to understand.

Of course, the takeaway here isn't that mass-appeal, lowest-common-denominator material is the best thing to strive for. It's that there are audiences for just about anything you want to make, and there's a lot within your power you can do to optimize your reach. Mastery of technology and engagement with online communities are more important than they ever have been to a thriving creative career.

If this sounds like too much marketing talk, I completely understand. I used to shun such thinking because I thought it would take away from my music. It took me a long time to consider how it could *add* to my music—or how, in ways I wasn't paying attention to, it already was.

There are a lot of common missteps artists make regarding self-promotion online (and I speak from experience with all of them).

**Doing too little.** Too many people who do promotion for themselves don't do it nearly enough. When marketing my online course, we found that a conversion from a casual follower to a course enrollee tended to take around *twelve* ad impressions. Promoting music should be easier than that since checking out music is a much smaller commitment than taking a course behind a paywall, but anyone who's done any promo will tell you how challenging it can be to even get people to click a link.

**Not having a strategy.** On the flip side, you could do a ton of promotion, but without some planning it's easy for your efforts to fall short. Just as important as the promotional content itself is the timing and variety of posts. When you're launching a project, figure out how and when it would be compelling to start building awareness, and how and when you can continue reminding people of the project once it's out in the world. Think of what kind of posts might work on every platform you use. Consider the variety of angles you can take: direct or mysterious, grand or sincere, moody or fun . . . Each endeavor may need a different approach. Would behind-the-scenes content work better prerelease, after people have already taken in the work, or perhaps not at all? Can you collaborate with others to help spread the word? Should there be hints and drips of intrigue, or will you favor a big, sudden bombardment? It's exciting to share about an upcoming project, but be mindful about how often you go there—it's possible to take the wind out of your own sails. (It's also possible that it's more exciting for you than for anyone else.) Work out a schedule of what you'll post when; fans and followers appreciate a release with well-considered timing. No one wants the anticlimax of waiting around forever or wondering whether a project got scrapped. Perhaps you'll want to go the route of the surprise release, which is becoming increasingly common in our age of instant gratification; why waste social capital on hype when it can be used to direct people to the product when it's already available?

**Feeling guilt, shame, or discomfort about it.** Some creators have a hard time with self-promotion when it feels like bragging or showing off. And maybe it is if your approach is *Hey, look at me, I hope you think I'm amazing, and I'd love to make some money off you!*—which I hope it's not. But if you fear that's how it comes across, try reframing. Your art is a gift to you, and it can be a gift to others as well. Maybe your perspective can be one of contribution and connection: *I came up with something here that brought me joy, or helped me heal—maybe it can do that for you too.* Promotional devices are uncomfortable to some—residues of the perception of selling out, I would guess. For instance, I know a lot of people who refuse to mention their merch when they're onstage, or who never want to ask people to subscribe to their YouTube channels. I'm sorry, but get over it. If you don't want people to buy your merch or subscribe to your channel, then by all means keep it far from their thoughts. But if you do want those things, be straightforward about it. No one will think less of you, other than maybe some other artist who also hates talking about merch and subscribing. Don't allow preconceived notions to deter you from sharing your art and reaching more people.

**Being boring.** Some forms of promotion are zero fun—such as asking people to click on something, or sharing a poster that's mostly text. Posters, in general, don't have very high engagement; if you're going to use one, incorporate some mind-bending visuals to at least get people to stop scrolling for two seconds. Putting creativity into the promotional material will always get better results. It also makes it more fun for you as the creator. Don't fall into the trap of thinking promotion can't be creative, artistic, or personality-driven.

**Not doing it at all.** As mentioned, some creators don't promote in general. They feel the work should be dropped into the world and encounter whomever it may (which is often no one). They believe their art's merit alone should determine its success. Perhaps that's how it *should* be, but it isn't. "If you build it, they will come" is *not* good business advice—it's a misquote of Kevin Costner's character in *Field of Dreams*, a 1989 movie about ghosts who play baseball.

I understand the hang-ups about self-promotion. It can seem narcissistic, uncomfortable, or simply isn't what you're interested in spending time on. But it's essential to getting a career off the ground and keeping it afloat. It may not be your favorite activity, but it can often be turned into something fun. And it doesn't make you any less of an artist.

If you're this far into the book, you probably have a project you're working on that you'd like to share with the world. Here's how I think about making a launch successful. Disclaimer: I will say that even after all these years I don't nail this every time—too many work projects overlap, or other things come up in life that prevent my full attention going into a release plan. Not to mention that we all sometimes make something that just doesn't connect with as many people. But in an ideal scenario, I do all of the following to try to give a new endeavor its best legs to stand on.

**Deadlines.** Determine the date your project will be *finished* and the date it will be *released*. You could decide either one of these first but, no matter what, they are contingent upon each other. You'll need the space to know that your work is truly done—no more final tweaks!—and some amount of time to do all your prerelease preparations. (If you're ever able to have your project completely finished before setting your release date, you'll be working in luxury.)

**Prerelease preparations.** This might include creating and posting content, planning events, manufacturing physical merchandise, and contacting others to help you get the word out. There's no limit to how far you can take this—indeed, some companies have multiple teams dedicated to these tasks, and the stage between *release ready* and *actual release* can stretch for months. Think about what's realistic for you to take on that will have a measurable impact. You may want to get ideas from artists you admire. How did they share their most recent work? What did you feel was successful about it?

**Schedule.** Work backward from the promotional ideas you want to execute. What needs to be posted before launch, on launch day, and after launch? Put every item in your calendar. How long will each take to create? Give it your best estimate and then add 20 percent more time as a buffer—that's the period you have to prepare everything.

**Actually do it.** Break down the steps you need to take for each part of your promotional plan. Get any materials you'll need and contact anyone who can help. See if there's work that can be batched together. If you've done the previous three steps, you have your game plan and your due dates. Block off specific hours to do the work and make this thing happen.

# Chapter Thirteen

Does money taint an artist's integrity? Only if it compromises your values. I have no problem making music for a candy commercial. I eat candy. When I've been approached by casinos and cigarette companies, though, I don't even begin to hear them out. I have a friend who has a vision board posted in her front hall, and on it are items like "Platinum record" and "Win Grammy for Album of the Year"—not an approach that I would take, but for her, with a world-class voice and a love of pop music and culture, it's an authentic pursuit.

But money *will* change your art.

A lot of things can happen when you start monetizing a creative passion. If you can afford more time to create or better equipment, that can improve the quality of what you make. But just as easily it can make things worse. You have more time to second-guess yourself, or to explore superfluous tangents. You might polish and perfect all the personality right out of a piece.

Your relationship with creating might change once it becomes a source of income. What once was enjoyable and fulfilling might become a chore. Finishing a project might feel more like a technical exercise than a creative exploration. Performing every night could drain all the specialness and spontaneity out of the experience. Spending more time on your craft can raise your standards, meaning everything takes more work than it previously did to be satisfactory. And of course, when you start to pay your bills with your art, it will inevitably lead to thoughts about what you could do differently to be able to pay more of those bills.

Many artists find it difficult to untangle ideas about what makes "good" and "successful" art. If a piece is less popular with your audience than usual, does that alone mean it's bad? (I would say no, of course not.) If you're inspired by a new creative direction but know that it has less commercial appeal, then which has more integrity: exploring it on your own, and only putting out more of what you know your audience will love, or bringing this new work to release, regardless of who it might alienate? I don't think there's a simple answer. I don't think we need to put a value judgment on whether an artist creates truly for themselves or with an audience in mind.

I discovered a deeper truth to this when I no longer needed to make money. I don't mean that I fully disconnected my music making from considerations of how to monetize it, although that happened as well. I mean I made an enormous amount of money and could have stopped working for several years if I wanted to. There were a couple of years when, financially speaking, I had a tremendous run. The products I released were performing beyond all my expectations. I was being approached constantly for lucrative advertising work—either scoring commercials or appearing in them. Many of these didn't need to go on my YouTube channel, but if they did, I could charge a premium thanks to the size of my audience. And at the same time my own creative work was at a peak: the massive number of views, the growing radio royalties, the licensing opportunities. Essa and I found ourselves sitting on an eye-popping bank balance, not needing to answer to anyone or anything, and I would walk into my beautiful studio and feel absolutely lost. I had to confront the fundamental motives for every creative act I engaged in. How much of what I did was for myself or for other people? For enjoyment or for survival? For money or validation or even to distract myself from dark thoughts? I could enjoy total freedom for a long time, and it was debilitating. I'd have fun playing my instruments, and feel no compulsion to develop my ideas into polished pieces. Why should I work on the parts of the process that I didn't enjoy? Why should I do anything challenging? The freedom to do anything made me call *everything* into question. Why was I editing a video when it was a beautiful sunny day out? Why was I optimizing my studio layout when I could be drinking a cocktail on a beach? And, if all I did was have fun noodling on my instruments and not actually finishing any projects, why did that feel like such a waste?

I had to admit to myself that I had been far more externally motivated than I would have previously conceded. The need to make a living motivated me. Growing an audience motivated me. Feedback on my work motivated me. Expanding the ways people thought about and worked with music motivated me. These were not at odds with my internal motivations of enjoyment and exploration. They worked together.

Needing to make money had affected what, how, and how much I created; now, not needing to make money was affecting it. I had dreamed of the freedom I now had, and discovered when I attained it that I needed to rewire how I operated and why. Doing whatever I felt like in the moment *seemed* to be the purest version of a creative life, but all it led to were insular days of noisemaking and puttering around with gear. It was alarming to think about what it would be like to not finish and release any more music, or to not be on YouTube anymore. There's fulfillment and enjoyment in making public-facing work as well, and yes, it's inextricable from capitalist systems, and yes, it takes work to see it through. I had separated creative output from the commercial expectations of how and why it should be made; now I had to separate my financial situation from the expectations of what people who've "made it" are supposed to do. I'm the kind of person who would rather be optimizing my studio layout than drinking a cocktail on a beach. Maybe being that kind of person is what helped me find success in the first place! Freedom in life is not the freedom to move through it with ease and pleasure, it's the freedom to choose to do what's meaningful to you.

Ultimately, I thought about the music I loved. What if history's great musicians didn't seek out a musical livelihood or an audience? How lifeless would the world be without the sounds of Radiohead, Prince,

Kate Bush, Joni Mitchell, Stevie Wonder, the Beach Boys, the Beatles, Ella Fitzgerald, Louis Armstrong, Debussy, Chopin, and Beethoven? Exploring and enjoying their gifts for themselves was only one part of the equation; refining and sharing their work was just as important.

We can acknowledge the presence and power of extrinsic and capitalist forces without letting them overwhelm us. Depending on our goals, we all have some degree of freedom in choosing how much we create for others and create for money. I don't begrudge those who use it as their drive to create, any more than I would those who shun public or commercial aspirations altogether. It's up to each of us to work out the right balance. Don't worry about whether money will taint your art. It already has.

In the end, for me it was a short-lived struggle, because Essa and I spent all the money on cars and jewelry. Just kidding. But we did spend a lot of it. We paid off the rest of our mortgage. We took care of some of our family who had precarious housing situations. And we invested some of the funds back into our business: hiring people, developing new products and video formats, and focusing more on what I wanted to do rather than taking on quite so many commercial gigs. Prosperity was an amazing thing to achieve, but it was not the end—now we had capital we could use to bring bigger dreams to life.

Also, I bought a lot of synthesizers.

There's no such thing as artistic purity.

Some people think a work of art comes out of a perfectly inspired vision channeled from a higher realm—and parts of the process do occasionally seem like that. But everything is affected by the granular realities of the lives we each live: a news headline that inspires an idea, a vintage instrument found in a thrift store, a deadline in a week or in three months or not having one at all. Brains are dynamic and reactive; what you come up with and how you interact with creative tools and collaborators can change if you listen to something different on the way to work, if you slept one less hour, or if a friend calls you with good news. Looming large over most of this is the money we have—or don't have—and our relationship to it. We don't always want to admit it, but market forces are hiding in just about every nook and cranny, doing wonderful and terrible things.

It's impossible to avoid the effects of capitalism on our creative impulses and output. Its values are deeply ingrained in us. Society is entirely structured around the idea (and, for most, the necessity) of earning your survival through productivity; of course it's going to have massive impacts on what and how we create. It's important to acknowledge and examine these effects, because beyond changing *what* we create they change how we *feel* about what we create, and how we feel about ourselves.

I'll provide an example. How long should a piece of music be? It can be any length a musician would like, of course, but once recording came into the picture there was a hard cutoff. In the early days of commercially available recordings, phonograph discs were limited to two or three minutes per side. With the technology of the time, record grooves could only be so close before audio quality dropped, and records needed to be a manageable size to be shipped to and bought by people who could bring them home. Companies produced 7- to 12-inch discs, and musicians shortened songs to under three minutes. Then there were generations of kids who grew up with songs under three minutes as a native form—not a concession made for the recorded version of a piece but the natural duration to work with when composing.

Another example of commercialism's effect on music is *mastering*, the final step in the process by which recorded music is prepared for the listening public. Mastering engineers use techniques to balance the tones and volumes of songs so they flow well throughout their duration, as well as in the course of an album they're a part of, and finally so that they're suitable for the different formats in which the music will eventually be housed. What this means is that just about every published recording is a compromise. A song is polished to sound the best it can *within the range of possibilities that will maintain a cohesive experience within the medium.* Songs are shaped for commercial standards and consumption.

Thanks to loudness standards in online streaming, we've recently left a decades-long period referred to in the music industry as "the loudness wars." There's a psychoacoustic phenomenon that leads us to feel that louder songs are better, and thus people scanning through radio stations tend to choose the louder one to listen to. Tricks and techniques were developed to master songs as loud as possible. Eventually it was common practice for a song to be pushed as close as it could be to the volume limit at all times, resulting in wave forms that have come to be known as "sausages"—no discernible peaks or valleys, just blobs of unrelenting loudness. This led to music that was lacking in dynamics and fatiguing to listen to. Decades' worth of music was made to sound worse in order to make it louder, and it was made louder in order to compete commercially. In our new streaming paradigm, it's the production and arrangement that are being affected. Landing on popular curated playlists is so key to success that many artists not only shape their sound to be more suitable for specific niches, they also know that they have to structure their songs so that the first few seconds will be enticing to the tastemakers of their subgenre.

There are countless examples of our drive to extract profit overriding the integrity of art, and it's wise to be wary of it. But it's possible to recognize that art has benefited from it as well. Huge swaths of music, movies, and other forms that are loved by millions were created with commercial aims. Works of pure passion don't always escape capitalism, either. If the artist needs help bringing their vision to life, it needs to be paid for, and the size of the budget will certainly affect the outcome of a project. As one example: I'm not alone in considering the Beach Boys' *Pet Sounds* one of the greatest albums ever made; its sublime pop symphonies came out of Brian Wilson being granted complete creative freedom by his record label, and in the end it required about seventy people to create and cost a then unprecedented $70,000 (over $650,000 in 2023 dollars). How did he find himself in such a luxurious position? Well, in the preceding four years, the Beach Boys had released *ten* tremendously successful studio albums. Wilson had earned this opportunity by generating monumental profits for Capitol Records, and this allowed him to make incredible music that would otherwise have been impossible to bring to life.

Despite the limitations of the early technology, I think most would agree that recording has been a good thing for music as a whole. It's allowed new work to be heard around the world, it's preserved beautiful voices that are no longer with us, and it's become an art form unto itself. All of this began with the phonograph—an invention that came out of Thomas Edison's industrial research lab, which he was able to establish only after making a vast sum from selling the rights to some of his developments in telegraph technology. His company's innovations were possible only because he and his team were able to accumulate capital through the monetization of their creativity.

I don't mean to defend or commend two rather problematic systems— capitalism and the music industry—but I think it's important to recognize their complexities. As capitalism spurs the adoption of various music innovations, our relationship to music is affected. Recording allows us to be able to enjoy it more easily and passively. Electric amplification allows us to put on concerts of a scale that would be unfathomable a century ago, with crowds gathering in the hundreds of thousands and a whole culture evolving around music festivals. Advancements in digital audio have made music production more accessible than ever before, and provided artists much more power and control over sound manipulation—to the degree that they've led to a baseline increase in the general listener's expectations of audio quality, mixing polish, and even how in-tune singers should be.

Digital audio has also changed our music experience. With streaming, there's no excitement of bringing a record back from the shop. Albums are less important than before; listeners build their own experiences à la carte with playlists. As I watch my kids get obsessed with individual songs and want to hear them thirty times in a row, I wonder how that experience has been different for the last few generations: pressing the repeat button; trying to rewind the tape to the right spot; lifting and moving the turntable needle back; waiting to hear something on the radio again. Does music become less special as innovations make it more ubiquitous and convenient?

With streaming making music so accessible, both in how instantly searchable it is and how little it costs to enjoy, music has become in some ways devalued. The direct negative impact on artists' incomes is the most visible result, and this has rightly received a lot of attention. I believe there's a fairer model for the division of streaming revenues, and I think streaming subscriptions in general should cost more. But I'm open to the idea that I could be wrong. It's great that for a monthly fee lower than the cost of a take-out meal, anyone with internet access can explore a library of music that spans countless cultures and just about every recorded era. A beautiful cross-pollination of genres has been accelerating rapidly in recent years. Would this have been the case without instantaneous access to what artists around the world are creating?

The benefits of digital media and the internet for small artists cannot be denied. It might be the worst time since the recording industry began to make money from music, but it's the best time *in history* to be an artist. We've never before had such a plethora of relatively accessible tools and resources to help you learn, execute, and share your craft—or to monetize it. Decouple ideas of monetary value from the creative output itself, and there are avenues that weren't even dreamed about a generation ago—the immediacy of fan-funding and sharing online, the creation of digital products, the possibility of remote events, the ease of promotion. It's not that there's a certain way that things should be and that we've fallen far from it; we're in the next stage in the evolution of what music means to people and what it means to be an artist. Musicians used to perform to make money; then they performed to promote an album to make money; now they have much more freedom in how much and how often they want to release their work. While making music is their primary draw, they use it to bring people into what it is that actually earns them a living—and this is more varied than ever, with fan clubs, merchandise, sample packs, brand partnerships, livestreaming, online classes, private tutoring, and maybe some performing still, too.

I might even question the monetary value that used to be placed on music. On the one hand, transcendent music that changed lives and culture and history deserves to be exalted. It *can't* be valued—it's worth too much, certainly much more than twenty dollars a copy. On the other hand, the concept of physical artifacts that contain recorded music has been with us for only about a century—why should it be the benchmark? It's a blink of an eye in a history of music that dates back, based on the earliest discovered instruments, more than forty thousand years. (If you're curious as to what those instruments were: bone flutes. Flutes made of bones.) When you break down the retail price of physical albums in their golden age, most of the money didn't go to the artists but to manufacturers, distributors, stores, and record companies. So was spending twenty dollars on a life-changing album in my teens an amazing bargain? Or was I getting ripped off, because the music had almost as little value as it does today, and I was actually paying for plastic, gas, a brick-and-mortar shop's expenses, and a record executive's drinks?

Financial value has shifted away from recorded music, to be sure—but maybe the freedom listeners now have in accessing music is the trade-off for the freedom musicians have in sharing their work. It's a challenge, and the major labels still have major advantages, but sustaining an independent music career is far more within reach than ever before. We can connect to our audiences directly, and they can support us directly—just in ways that aren't about paying to hear a recording.

There's another business model we can look at: YouTube. Audiences stream videos on demand, and they either pay a subscription fee or endure the ads. In contrast to most music streaming services' 30 percent cut of revenue, YouTube takes *45 percent*. And YouTube's rates per stream, while they fluctuate a lot more than streaming services' rates because of the variety of ad types, tend to be lower. But YouTube creators aren't protesting in front of YouTube headquarters about this. It's not a great injustice. They don't feel they're being stolen from. It's the accepted revenue share. And culturally there's an expectation that a YouTube video should be free. It doesn't matter if it's three hours long, highly educational, and took more work and resources to create than a song. There's an expectation of access. It's not a reflection of its value. The value is up to the consumer—they're choosing what to spend their time on, and they know what they get out of it. It might be ten minutes of distraction, it might be a piece of knowledge that brings them to a new level in their career, it might be something they regret clicking on within five seconds.

When you compare anything solely by monetary value you run into absurdities. A drink at a music festival can cost as much as an album. The ticket price is likely to be significantly higher. Even a band's T-shirt can cost more than an album (if they're even still making physical albums). But if a band is making more money from their merch than from their music, we still consider them a band—not a T-shirt retailer. The money is not and probably never has been a reflection of value; it's always about what products are more attractive and have better margins, and what systems are in place that recognize and remunerate artists for their work.

Almost all value resides in the music—people buy merch or tickets only if they love the music. What will keep shifting is how we capture that value.

Money as the sole marker of value is the capitalist mindset. It's the corporation that tries to expand its profit margins and market share as much as possible, and makes its bottom line the top priority. Art doesn't work like that. You can't churn it out like a product on an assembly line. You don't get a bonus if your work makes someone feel like they're not alone. You can't put a price on a song that sparks a revolution.

I'm all for artists making money, and I absolutely support the push for better streaming royalties. I do believe a career in music is worth pursuing, but preconceived notions of what that looks like may be far different from reality. If recorded music continues to be cherished and passionately supported I will celebrate. If it turns out that this business model was a blip in history I won't be surprised. Either way music's importance and ability to influence us will remain. Our relationship with music evolves with culture and technology, but music bringing joy to people's lives will not change. It's the religious service filled with voices, the hobbyist learning to play a song they love, the parent singing a lullaby to their child. Music is much, much bigger than the music industry.

# PART FOUR

# Authenticity

# Chapter Fourteen

A little girl wakes up. She climbs out of bed—a wooden platform she shares with her brother, uncle, and grandmother. They don't have electricity, running water, a shower, or a toilet; she sets off for the nearby stream where a few families in the village share two outhouses. Bamboo shoots and tropical trees loom above. The air is thick and hot. She brings a large stick in case she needs to fend off the pigs and dogs.

Her parents exhort her to work hard, but school in this region only fills four hours of the day, leaving plenty of time for a free-roaming childhood. She runs barefoot around the village, playing games with other kids. Her toys are stones and old food tins. She steals her parents' matches and sets fire to twigs.

When she's nine years old, she sees two schoolmates playing the piano and insists on learning from their teacher. In one year, her skill surpasses theirs; in four, she's reached the sixth-grade piano syllabus. Around this time, her family moves from the rural village to a middle-class neighborhood, where one day, a pastor hears her playing and asks her to be the pianist at his church. She learns every hymn in the book.

Her father is politically active. He joins Singapore's main opposition party, whose anticolonial cause eventually leads to some of his colleagues being imprisoned without trial. He flees to England, where his daughter later joins him. Under pressure from him, and also realizing she may not be willing to endure the long hours of practice, she sets aside her dream of becoming a concert pianist to study medicine.

There's an unofficial quota at this time that fewer than a quarter of medical students can be women. Galvanized by the discrimination, she eliminates her social life in favor of receiving extra tuition and mock exams from her teachers, even at their homes on weekends. She earns a place at Manchester University with a government grant covering her tuition and living expenses.

She's a doctor by the age of twenty-three. Drawn to pediatrics, she spends much of her career treating emergencies at birth, doing everything she can for newborns who otherwise wouldn't make it—and who sometimes still don't. Her days swing through emotional and psychological extremes: the joy of new life, the loss of a child.

She gives birth to me. In many ways, she is a parent the way her parents were: demanding of hard work but allowing exploration, a complicated blend of supportive and domineering. I am, of course, like her as a child: reckless, always trying something new, and in love with music.

She tells me her story when I'm young, and sometimes she talks about her work, and I'm reminded often of what's important in life and how precious it is. But I still feel young and selfish and invincible, and I don't completely put it together until much later: She would treat a preterm infant who might be beyond resuscitation, and then come home and make dinner. She would watch new parents hold their child for the first and only time, and then drive me to a piano lesson. While I was in the basement focusing obsessively on the guitar, she was out there on a mission to *save lives*.

As I grew up, I better appreciated the realities of her story, and its lessons are never far from my mind now. Life is fleeting. Joy is precious. So much of what's highly sought after in our culture is revealed to be utterly superficial when juxtaposed with these simple reminders of what's important. This perspective has been a grounding point many times in my life—I know that things could have been very different. I could have had *nothing*, so I choose to be grateful for *everything*. I'm compelled to do what's true to me because I know how short life is and how rare it is to have that chance in the first place. I recognize how often I'm faced with a choice between what others value and what I value, between what the world expects and what's right for me. If there's one thing I hope to impart, it's this: Whenever we have the opportunity, why choose anything besides pursuing our fullest selves?

- ☑ Anxiety

- ☑ Detachment

- ☑ Listlessness

- ☑ Low mood

- ☑ Difficulty concentrating

- ☑ Lack of creativity

- ☑ Fatigue

- ☑ Negative attitude

- ☑ Lack of commitment

- ☑ Absenteeism

- ☐ Job turnover

- ☑ Quickness to anger

- ☑ Cynicism

- ☑ Emotional numbness

- ☐ Headaches

- ☐ Generalized aches

- ☑ Muscle tension

- ☐ Gastrointestinal disorders

- ☐ Hypertension

- ☑ Difficulty sleeping

- ☐ Susceptibility to illness

- ☑ Frustration

- ☑ Exhaustion

- ☑ Loss of purpose

Having eighteen out of twenty-four signs of burnout was probably a good indication of burnout. It was hard to notice because of how gradually it happened, and also because there were still many pockets of excitement in my work. But after eating, sleeping, and breathing YouTube for almost two years straight, I was exhausted; I often dreaded even the thought of turning on my camera. These feelings had started about one year in and had only grown in severity. The more time went by, the more I questioned the meaning and value of my work. My guiding ambitions were losing their luster. Much of the work I once loved started to feel like work I didn't want to be doing. If this wasn't burnout, I was certainly heading there quickly.

When I surpassed a million subscribers in 2017, YouTube threw me a party. The company covered all the costs, from the event space to the catering staff. There was a photo booth, a nail-painting station, an open bar, and only my favorite foods were served. I invited about a hundred friends and family members, and there was also a portion of the evening that was open to fans. I was amazed that many old friends I hadn't seen in years showed up, some driving in from out of town—it seemed as if they thought this was more important a milestone than I did. It was a memorable night—everybody was celebrating me. I was presented with my gold million-subscriber plaque, everyone laughed at my jokes, and there was a huge tray of cupcakes with my face on them.

By the end of the night I was already thinking about the diamond plaque: ten million subscribers. Spending the evening with these people was wonderful—besides my wedding, it was the greatest number of my loved ones ever gathered in one place. But when the buzz of the party wore off I was left with only the feeling of having reached a million followers, which was: not much. It was like checking an item off my to-do list. *Good, that's taken care of, what's next?* Maybe I'd anticipated the achievement for so long that I'd already worn out my excitement. Maybe part of me can't help but see almost everything as arbitrary—a million doesn't really mean anything, but it's the first seven-digit number when you count in base ten, so here we were. Or, maybe, I had become so achievement-oriented that nothing was ever going to satisfy me. I didn't feel good about my channel if it was simply growing—it had to be *accelerating* at a rapid pace. I was only ever looking ahead and above, thinking about everything I had yet to do or everyone who had already done more than me.

But if a million wasn't enough, ten million wouldn't be the answer. Achieving more and more was not going to be the path to contentment. I was approaching a fork in the road, and that night was the clearest I'd yet seen it: one direction that would see me hustling harder and harder, clinging to this ideal of continual explosive growth, and another where I could recalibrate priorities around what was most important to me. Putting everything I had into YouTube had been the right thing to do for a certain period in my life, and that time was now over. I was moving into a new stage, and what was once authentic to me had shifted.

I'd been under the not uncommon impression that achievement was a destination, and once you'd reached it you were all set. Park the space-ship and throw a tarp over it, you'll never need to move again. I wonder if it's actually like that for anyone, because I keep finding that there's no landing and settling anywhere—not for long, anyway. It's always a balancing act. You find what works, you improve on it however you can, and you run with it until it's time for something else. You could be doing exactly what you want to be doing, exactly the way you want to do it, and a year later you might have gotten bored or discovered new things. The world will have changed around you, and you'll respond to that somehow.

I started to internalize these ideas but continued barreling ahead at my breakneck pace. But my two-videos-per-week publishing schedule was sustainable only as long as I could comfortably create a video every three to four days (and that already involved working through the weekend). In the beginning, this was *just* manageable, but I wasn't coming up with new quick and easy ideas at the same rate that I was executing them. My ideas got more ambitious and more complex. Rather than focusing only on the surface-level fun of a musical instrument or technique, I was interested in diving deeper. I started my *4 Producers* video series, which entails wrangling a lot of filming and music production from three other artists. (Common mark of a great musician: they can be rhythmically accurate within a few milliseconds yet miss a deadline by months!) I was also striving for higher standards of music and video production. As I developed as a producer, there was so much more I wanted to put into my craft. On the video side, while I still didn't care for flashiness for its own sake, I was always adding to my tool kit of techniques that helped drive higher audience retention, such as a well-placed sound effect, B-roll shot, or additional camera angle. The time needed to create my work was ballooning, and even after hiring two video editors we were barely keeping up. On top of that, the more successful my channel became, the more I was approached for opportunities that were good for my brand—invitations to travel, speak, perform, and collaborate—yet impeded the work I needed to do in order to have a worthwhile brand to begin with: making great music and videos. Worst of all, I realized, creating music was what I truly enjoyed doing, and the proportion of my time I could spend on it was continually shrinking.

It reached a point of absurdity when a company offered me a $50,000 sponsorship fee to create a video that would have been perfect for my channel, and everything in me was repelled by it. It was a version of a video format I'd found success with many times, but I realized I was sick of it. It would have meant a few weeks of overstretched days, and I found I wasn't willing to sacrifice my health and sleep to make a video I didn't want to make. I know what you're thinking—who wouldn't burn the candle at both ends for a few weeks for $50,000? As an isolated offer, it was of course enticing, but it came on the back of months of swelling fatigue and dread. It was just a bigger version of everything I had been going through. Every day, week, and month, there was some kind of reasoning with myself to stay up later, work harder, reach the next milestone, and postpone taking the break I'd needed for a year. There was money to be made, accolades to receive, and dreams to achieve. For two years I had barely spent time with nonindustry friends. I never took a day off—the weekend being another arbitrary human construction I disregarded—and the idea of a vacation was always put off because my calendar was continuously replenishing itself with projects. I was eating poorly, drinking more, and losing sleep. I was stressed about the details of producing each video, the performance of each video, and getting each one done on time. Now I was stressing over the ultimate first-world problem: looking at a $50,000 deal and knowing that either accepting or rejecting it would feel like the wrong decision. Taking it would deplete me and pull me further away from both much-needed rest and projects I actually cared about. But turning it down would be wasteful. I'd be dismissing a sum that for most people would be life-changing.

Going against every reflex I had developed as a freelancer, I said no to this offer that only a few months earlier would have been a slam dunk. I was at a turning point—in multiple ways. I wanted to go in a different direction with my channel, and I was well past the point of needing to stop working eighty to a hundred hours a week. Such was the acceleration of my career that I realized I suddenly had too many amazing opportunities: Not only should I be turning down projects I didn't want to do but I also had to say no to things I would have *loved* to do, things that five years earlier would have been career defining, beyond anything I had dreamed about as a kid. If I didn't, I would just keep running myself into the ground until I wasn't able to give any more at all.

It was my obscene privilege to be able to turn down the opportunity to make so much money because now I had more than enough. It wasn't a moral issue—like promoting cigarettes or gambling—where I would have felt I was compromising my integrity. That would have made the decision much easier. It was a company I'd have no qualms about supporting, but a video idea I was creatively bored by, and it came at the most overworked time in my life. Everyone I've shared this story with has thought I made the wrong choice. But I have no regrets about it.

Some would say this was a matter of scaling my business—that the additional revenue should pay for more hired help that would allow me to expand my operation, put out even more content, and take on any lucrative project that came my way. That's certainly possible to a degree, and I've been happy to hand off many tasks to others. But I'm not that kind of business. As a creator, I'm always working with a finite resource: myself. There are only so many songs I can produce and videos I can appear in. I've envisioned a large-scale expansion in a hundred different ways. Others could conceptualize and script my videos or ghostwrite my music. I could start a label or a collective and produce other artists' work. I could focus on only my highest-earning products and make as many apps and online courses as possible. I could work on only super-high-performing video formats and lie back as my soul drains from my body. There's no version of me that owns a juggernaut company while also being able to spend most of my time either in the studio or with my family. I fully accept the fact that there's a certain size my business and audience can't grow beyond if I want to continue to do what's authentic to me, and if I want to have even a glimmer of this thing I've heard of called "work/life balance."

With these realities in mind, I began deliberately decelerating my audience growth and making less money. The most painful irony wasn't that I had achieved a success that now threatened to cannibalize itself—it was that the stress and exhaustion had been my own doing. No one but me had decided what I was going to create, how frequently I would share it, how active I would be on social media, what production values I'd hold myself to, or how much of my life I would spend in front of my computer. The hundred-hour workweek was a treadmill I'd built myself and willingly hopped on. What had started as an exciting pursuit had become a trap; I thought I had found freedom but I was bound by ambition. While I'd sidestepped many of the preconceived notions about a music career, I was still in the grip of something that went much deeper. Everything always pointed to *more*. More money, more views, more followers, more clout . . . Anything that was good was never good enough. It had to be the biggest version of itself. It should reach ever more people. It should be better than everything else in its space. In an always-online, hyperconnected world, turning off at any point felt like a concession. I could get more out of my business the more I put into it—every ounce of energy could be used toward it. More content would mean more growth and more income, and wasn't this my dream? Wouldn't I be robbing myself to put in anything less than every last drop?

A dream, inherently, is a falsehood. It's not real, and it's not colored in with many details. I kept climbing higher and higher, dreaming bigger and bigger, hoping to find something that would tell me I'd finally *done it*—whatever "it" was. But there was nothing like that. The place where I felt real satisfaction, wholeness, and joy was the same place I'd been visiting since I was a child: that haven where time stood still as I lost myself in creativity. I thought again of my mother's story and recognized the imbalance of my values; I was prioritizing external rewards to the point where it was costing me my joy and taking time from what I loved. Awards, applause, reaching an audience, checks with lots of zeroes—all these things were great, but none of them compared with a moment in creative flow, something I'd had even as a toddler scribbling in crayon on the kitchen floor.

## PROMPTS ON PERSPECTIVE

Here are questions I've asked myself when I needed to jolt my perspective away from an irrational quest for fame or riches.

**Is there a numerical goal?** Is there a specific number—of followers, of streams per month, of dollars in your bank account—that when reached would flip a switch and you'd suddenly be satisfied forever?

**What does that number mean?** Would the same number of followers you currently have be enough if everyone else had fewer—if you were actually number one? Is it a number that's important or is it being ahead of others? And how far ahead of everyone else would you have to be in order to feel comfortable in your position?

**Who do you want in your audience?** Do you care which million people follow you, or just that they add up to a million? Does it make a difference to you if they're all suburban moms, or kids in STEM programs, or retired DJs? Billions of humans who are no longer alive will never know your work—a lot of them may have enjoyed it. Is it disappointing that they're out of your reach?

**What does it all mean for your day-to-day?** Everything about your life stays the same, but you have a different number of followers. Picture your exact same activities and your everyday feelings but underneath your name on the internet there's a 500, or a 10M, or a 37K, or a zero. What connection do you believe exists between that number and the coffee in your mug, the guitar strings against your fingertips, the friend across the table?

**Is it as important as the work?** A genie can grant you as large a following or bank balance as you like—you pick the number!—but only if you give up your art for a career you don't enjoy. Maybe you're a celebrity lawyer, or you win hot-dog-eating contests. Do you accept?

**Is recognition more important than impact?** What if the genie grants you an inverse relationship between your reach and your fame? The more people your work reaches, the more anonymous you become. Would you want your work to touch more lives at the cost of your being celebrated?

**Can you acknowledge that the work we deem worthy of glorification is skewed?** Do you know who farmed your food or designed your phone? Do you know the doctor who delivered you? Probably not. But how many actors and musicians can you recognize in a split second?

**A perspective on fame and validation.** You suddenly find yourself in an alternate reality where, somehow, no one is able to perceive anyone else's status or accomplishments. Does it change your values or how you feel about yourself? Does it change what you do with your life? Do you want to do what's important to you, or do you just want other people to think you're important?

**Do you *really* want people to know *you*?** If recognition is important to you, how deep does it go? Do you want people to know everything? Your regrets and insecurities? There are ways that being vulnerable can be good and helpful, but we often paint over what we don't want others to see. When we're overly concerned with status, we're not in competition to be the best; we're in competition to create the best virtual persona. Are you hoping that if you convince enough people you're good, it will mean you're actually good?

I can't pretend to be a master of calm—stress and frustration still find me, I still bite off more than I can chew, and work/life balance continues to be a tightrope walk. But I can at least share the things that help me remain on the path that's right for me, and that keep me a comfortable distance from burnout even in the busiest seasons.

**Gratitude.** I began a daily gratitude practice. I tried a few methods, but the one that stuck was writing down three things I was thankful for each day. It's hard to believe you don't have enough when you pay attention to everything you do have. Being alive is tremendous; feeling the air outside and being able to take in a deep breath of it. Time with loved ones, an inspiring song, a delicious meal . . . most of us experience beautiful gifts each day and forget to pay attention to them. To some degree, we have to ignore a lot of astounding beauty in order to function—we have to attend to our responsibilities and plan for the future. But it can be amazing when you have the chance to open up and tune in to the experience of the moment in front of you. I can become fully absorbed by the sound of the wind moving through the leaves, how light refracts through my drinking glass, or the contours of a crumpled-up tissue. Tasting a raspberry becomes nearly a spiritual experience. And there are so many more wonderful and more meaningful things that happen to me each day. When I remember how much there is to be thankful for, I end up approaching my life with a clearer perspective and deeper intentionality. I make better decisions, I feel more fulfilled, and I have a more intimate sense of what's right for me.

**Commitment.** When I was in single-focus mode with YouTube it made things a lot easier. Everything could be measured against what seemed to be the best move for growing a channel about exploring music. As I felt my interests shifting toward a wider range of pursuits, I had to get more specific about what I was trying to accomplish. I had to think about what was realistic to achieve if I was going to aim for more than one target. I wanted to explore more niche topics—how could I still make them appealing to the audience I'd built, and bring as many of them as I could with me in a way that made sense? I wanted to help others make music not only through sharing information but also by creating tools—who were the best partners for this, and how much time would it take? Previously I could just waltz onward with a mindset of *grow the channel*—I'd never set a target of how many views or followers I should reach or by when. My new goals required more planning and attention. It was imperative to write them down, commit to time frames for various stages of completion, and check in regularly to see whether I was on track, whether anything had changed, or if I needed to adjust.

**Acceptance.** We all have to contend with reality. We have limited time, every action has consequences, and not all endeavors are equal. Pushing yourself super hard can produce more results in the short term, but it will take a toll on your mental and physical health. Balance looks different for everyone, but we all do need to find it and try to maintain it. There will be boundaries that aren't possible to cross. We live in a fantastically interconnected era, where it's easier to reach people than ever before, but it's also easy to fall into thinking that the perfect combination of text, sound, and visuals could unlock fame and fortune for anyone. To an extent, that's truer than it ever has been, but there are still a finite number of people on the planet with their own specific interests. Some topics inherently have more allure than others. I have some of the most viewed music production content in the world, and it will never be able to compare with the top channels that focus on cars, computers, or comedy. I also know I would have a much harder time building an audience if my passion was creating videos about model trains or fountain pens. If a part of our dreams is predicated on external outcomes, it's highly likely that there will be compromises, in our processes or in our products, that we'll have to accept.

In the very early days of my career—probably within the first year or two of my website existing—I received an email from a fan where one line jumped out at me: "I really appreciate that you clearly just make your own rules for life." I felt a deep resonance with this: that was indeed what I had been doing, but no one had ever so succinctly reflected it back to me. This stranger saw me better than I saw myself, just from following what and how I created. Now, having it plainly identified, I was able to embrace it. It wasn't just that I'd rejected a lot of things I didn't connect with, and I wasn't living in some chaotic state of untethered free-for-all. I had made my own rules. I had been deliberate and thoughtful about choosing my own values and ways of doing things. I marched to the beat of my own drum—but there was definitely a beat.

There's good reason for there to be rules—or at least guidelines—and not total "freedom." Whenever I throw myself into the seductive arms of freedom, it only encourages me to give in to my worst impulses. I let myself be lazy. I turn out subpar material or I don't even work at all. I cop out at the first sign of a challenge. A bit of structure and discipline propels me to the life I really want, one that fulfills me and provides something of value to others. And the truth is, if you're not consciously following any rules in your life, it's probably an indication that there are lots of rules you're following *unconsciously*. How many of your choices, habits, and aspirations come from the conventional ideas found in your culture or your upbringing? How much is your behavior motivated by a fear of what others will think of you? Maybe a lot of the traditional rules work just fine. But when they don't, you can make your own.

The rules can be big or small, can last for many years or just a season, and they can apply to anything. They can be as specific as setting a time that you will work, or as broad as prioritizing creative freedom over commercial viability. And, as any artist knows, rules can always be broken. The game can be changed. Use what works until it doesn't, and then find the next methods you can adopt. We go through a lot of change in life, and we all come from different contexts. My rules won't be yours, and these rules aren't hard and fast. It's about finding a good match between who you are right now (and who you want to become!) and the possible perspectives or approaches available to you. Are you the kind of person who needs motivation to work or permission to take a break? Does starting a new project energize you or intimidate you? Maybe you're someone for whom these things change from season to season, or even day to day. Can you learn to identify what you need in each moment to be most effective for you and your goals?

When you're deep in your work, you'll likely need to change things up depending on whether you're brainstorming, experimenting, crafting, polishing, or publishing. For example, you may need to set boundaries that keep you from distraction, or schedule specific times for open play. You may need to limit the number of parties you go to, or force yourself to get out of the house. You may need to delay a reward until you've finished editing a certain amount of video or writing a certain number of pages.

We can also examine ourselves more broadly. Are you in a place of growth and expansion, or recharging and rest? Are you exploring and learning, broadening the net of your inspiration, or are you zeroing in on a fine point that you're currently passionate about? Openness lets you see the whole field; purpose helps you clear your path.

From a young age, I was attracted to musicians who explored new frontiers, who showed me that there's infinitely more out there, and that dividing lines are almost always human-made. Genres and instruments can be mixed willy-nilly. Unintentional and everyday sounds can be elevated to artistic splendor. People can compose in conjunction with machines, or even let the technology take over. Just about every artistic boundary can be blurred or broken. You don't have to stay in one lane. Exploring music as a child, its open-endedness affirmed my innate curiosity and creativity, and my relationship with it eventually blossomed into the openness with which I live my life.

Music will teach you a lot about life if you let it. Life itself *is* music. Our planet circles the sun with more precise timing than that of any drummer. Events build together toward moments of impact that resonate out over what comes after them. Even the material things we use every day are not inert; looking closely enough we find that the very atoms that make them up are always vibrating, and do so at specific frequencies.

Everything I've learned about music has deepened and augmented my experience of life. Silence is important just as taking breaks is important. Harmony is the way we work together, make space for each other, and lean on each other's strengths. What about priorities? The notes you don't play are as important as the ones you do. And relationships: How can you respond to someone if you don't listen?

Music taught me to be bold. What an odd thing to pursue, making sounds. Many don't consider music a respectable aspiration until you've somehow "made it," and even then, it's not a "real job." But here was something I felt was so worth investing in that I forged ahead regardless of the consequences to my status, social life, or employability. It was only through boldness that I could make it work—taking action, believing in my own ideas, and doing things in ways that no one else was. In most areas I tend to buck against tradition, classification, and set understandings. It's not for its own sake, and there are many ways where I simply slot in with what is typical and expected, but I am usually keenly aware of what does and doesn't work for me. I think most of us probably are; I just had the experience of standing out in too many ways as a kid that I realized very early it would be futile for me to attempt to fit in, as much as I sometimes would have liked to. Music brought this out even further, because all the giants I adored were people who did something that had never been done before. Music taught me that you have to be true to yourself even if you're the only one who gets you. It's funny that originality is celebrated in the arts, while elsewhere we fear stepping out of line or appearing different from the norm. But doing things the usual way gets the usual results. Original thinking is the only thing that ever changes the world.

The openness I tuned in to through music eventually spread to every area of my life—the clothes I wore, the schedule I kept, the dreams I dreamt, and how I defined myself . . . none of it had to be dictated by any particular expectation. I would always find my way to what was right for me. Of course, I was particularly privileged that my eBay song commission idea worked when I was nineteen, and so I never had to join the traditional workforce. But I'd always had a particular stubbornness about doing what I wanted even if the world shunned it, laughed at me, or didn't understand. It started with small things. As a kid, some girls painted my nails, I liked how it looked, and it simply became something I did despite the comments and looks from people at school and my mom's not-at-all-veiled horror. Eventually I started doing things like walking around public places pointing a camera at myself, or abstaining from drugs and alcohol at the prime irresponsible partying age of twenty-two. I wasn't seeking attention or trying to provoke anyone. I was just doing what I felt drawn to do.

Where I'm most grateful for this openness is in regard to my gender and sexuality—which, perhaps due to how we tend to deal with these things, took the longest time for me to come to terms with, well into my adult life. I had always struggled with feeling a little different. Not tremendously different from how I was "supposed" to feel, but definitely different enough to be confused. Why did some traditionally feminine expressions of gender feel right to me? What did it mean that I sometimes found myself attracted to people who presented as male or androgynous? I envied both the straight, cisgender people in my life who never seemed to need to think about these things, as well as my queer friends who had come out after finding an identity that was fully them. I was constantly questioning myself, trying to find a label that would fit—or, worse, thinking that there must be something wrong with me. Only through spending years in the openness and diversity of music did I eventually find the answer: there doesn't have to be an answer. You can accept and even embrace the ambiguities and the multitudes. I was living and working in this beautiful medium where I had found means to be outside of and in between genres and creative approaches. I did what I wanted without calling myself a musician or producer or content creator or businessperson. After years of anxiety, dread, and therapy, it suddenly clicked that there was nothing stopping me from bringing that perspective to my identity as well.

Language and labels are only necessary when they're helpful; they can often limit our understanding of ourselves and of the world. They can limit our potential. I realized there didn't need to be any kind of name or marker for who I was. That would only be for the benefit of other people; I didn't have to provide that for them. I didn't have to be anything. I could just be.

It surprised me how suddenly this understanding came to me. I still remember the exact moment: a quiet evening at home, the sweater I was wearing, my wife reading on the couch beside me. And in the space of a thought, that part of me was at peace. In the coming seasons, as that perspective gently seeped deeper and deeper inside, even more worlds of possibility opened up for me—not in the way that more options make a decision harder, but in the sense that I had found a freedom that allowed me to choose *exactly* what was right for me. I had shed layers of other people's rules, and only my own remained.

SELF-REFLECTION: ART & IDENTITY

How has your art, or the art you consume, influenced how you do or don't identify? Do you see a pattern with how you view yourself and how you view creative work?

When I knew I couldn't continue producing work at the pace I'd set for myself, I took a short break and returned with no posting schedule at all. The effects were immediate. Views dropped and subscriber growth ground nearly to a halt. I was seeing the flip side of unwavering consistency. When you stop feeding new material into the machine you get swallowed up. When you take up less room, there's a sea of content that will rush into the space you've left.

For the most part, I was okay with it. I knew this was the right decision, and I was enjoying being able to approach work at a more relaxing pace. I was excited about what I was creating now. I was happy to leave behind some formats I'd repeated many times. Though there was still plenty of life in concepts such as using inanimate objects to cover popular songs, they no longer held any creative interest or challenge for me. (Once, succumbing to insecurity, or perhaps it was covetousness— thinking maybe I *could* have it all—I resurrected the inanimate object cover song. I used a few metal rings of different sizes to play "7 Rings" by Ariana Grande. I even had my friend Grant take on a lot of the music and video production in an attempt to see if this was an area where the operation could be scaled up. The video got 2 million views, I didn't enjoy working on any part of it, and I never touched that concept again.)

There was a freedom in building an online presence and business around my passion. I got to spend all my time on things I believed in, and a good amount of it on things I enjoyed. But past a certain level of success, there was a much greater freedom in *not worrying about being more successful.*

When TikTok became an undeniable social media competitor, establishing a presence there seemed like a necessary business move. I used everything I learned through YouTube—working out engaging formats, providing value to viewers, posting regularly (in this case *daily*)—and went from zero to a hundred thousand followers in one month. But I didn't enjoy working on such short-form content, or at such a hectic pace, so I stopped. I'll create in that format when I have a fun idea or something I want to share, but that experience proved to me even more that I just wasn't interested in focusing on growth anymore. It was perfectly fine not to be on every platform or jump on every trend.

As I crossed paths with musicians with increasing degrees of industry success, I felt at odds with that lifestyle. I sensed an almost compulsive level of ambition in some of them, the familiar sense that nothing would ever be enough. I didn't want to be the person who had every minute of my day booked. I didn't want to be the person who found out about a work mix-up while hanging out with friends and made an angry call to his manager right then and there—at one a.m., while the rest of us awkwardly drifted to other parts of his swimming pool. I didn't want to be the artist who, in my first conversation with him, managed to complain that he was worth only $20 million when a similar artist from his scene had made $40 million.

As I wrestled with questions about how to be truer to my values, I discovered a strange silver lining to my hearing loss: I always know if I'm making music for public consumption or just for me. My ears are messed up; I need to bring in a lot more bass and treble to get close to hearing what I want to hear—so anytime I'm crafting music for others to listen to, *I have to make it sound worse to me*. At every step along the way, I'm acutely aware of whether I'm polishing something up to be shared or just enjoying it for myself. It eradicates the confusion I used to have, and that I know many artists share, about why we create, who it's for, and what's authentic. Am I working on this for the fun of it and the love of it, or am I seeking validation, acceptance, fame, status, or money? It might be a mixture of any of these things; it might change from time to time or from project to project. Having clarity about your intentions allows you to best move forward.

Barring commission work, I always start out creating for myself, and then, sometimes, there comes a point where I feel what I'm developing could be more widely enjoyed. (Or I think it's something I'd like to challenge other people's ears and brains with.) That's when I know things will face outward, when I'll want the ideas to be the best possible versions of themselves so I can most effectively communicate what I want to communicate. Let me make it as great as I can for others, because music is one of the most exciting things in life and I'd love for my songs to delight others the way so many songs have delighted me.

If that point doesn't come, or if it comes and then goes, then there's no pressure. I'm back to doing my hobby instead of my job. I'm back to enjoyment, or I'm ready to let it go and move on to the next idea. My hearing loss has given me an overactive barometer for what's release-worthy or just a jam, what's work and what's play. I now know without a doubt when I've been externally focused for too long and haven't taken the time to recharge, explore, and do music just for fun. It creates a boundary for me between the sacredness of the creative act and the choice to commodify it. Because of my hearing loss, I know I'll never slip into the trap of absorbing the whole of my creative passion into business endeavors and losing the joy. (Also, people compare me to Beethoven sometimes. I'll take it.)

My new goals have little to do with money or fame, numbers or clout, achievement or traditional success. I hope to maintain those things enough that I can spend as much time as possible with my greater aims: pushing forward the evolution of music, and enjoying myself while doing it. I want to make sounds and share ideas and design tools that eke out new possibilities in music and open creative doors for others. These things are harder to measure than a follower count, but infinitely more satisfying to pursue. Saying *no* takes on a different dimension when traditional measures of success are low priority. I've surprised myself sometimes with how little allure I feel for opportunities that I know many people, including myself a few years ago, would jump at. A representative for South Korean music sensations BTS invited me to submit beats, but theirs is not the type of music I feel particularly called to create, as much as I enjoy listening to it. Lauryn Hill was interested in having me produce new versions of her songs to be performed on tour, but it was a sizable time commitment that would have taken me away from my own work. There are so many wonderful opportunities like this that I *could* do—but I'm already doing exactly what I want. I know most people see it as less legitimate, but I'm so happy—and so grateful—that I can just experiment in my studio, on my own schedule, and share my discoveries as I release songs, videos, and music tools. Traditional industry paradigms are less enticing to me now; the only part of me that wants to seize those opportunities is the ghost of my younger self. It's the part that wants to focus more on the length of my list of accomplishments than on the accomplishments themselves. It's the part that wants to be seen as a "real" musician, even though the work that would best engender that perception would be far less authentic to me. It's my ego wanting a boost, despite already being beyond the capacity to take in all the kudos from my existing audience. It's my greed fueling a desire for more money and influence, even though I already have more than I ever dared to believe possible.

Picasso is quoted as saying "It took me four years to paint like Raphael, but a lifetime to paint like a child." I've seen many meanings attributed to these words—that children are spontaneous, or fearless, or express themselves without a filter, or aren't influenced by other artists. I'll offer an interpretation that occurred to me when I stumbled across a coffee-table book about his final years, filled with photos of him and paintings he did at that time. They were strewn all around him and leaned up against every wall, most of them looking unfinished, with large areas of the canvas left blank, and sometimes only a single color used to make a few crude strokes. In these works, I didn't see anything particularly inspiring or skillful. But what I did see was someone who truly didn't care. He held the foremost place in the world of art; he had no need to prove anything. He had no more need to concern himself with quality, value, or legacy. I saw someone who enjoyed the process—wholly—and didn't need it to be anything more. Maybe I'm wrong. But I arrive at places like that sometimes when I'm creating, when it's not about anything at all except the magic of the moment, and that is no less valid than creating work of great quality or reach.

I don't mean to disparage the idea of work created for public consumption. The reason why any of us have such a feast of amazing creations to enjoy is because other people wanted to share what they had inside them. It's not a bad thing to want to reach people.

I've gotten better at maintaining a balance between the inward and the outward, the passion and the business, the work life and the personal life—and it is *balance*. It's not something you find once and then never touch again. It's not something you set and forget but a constant act. It requires presence and care—otherwise you fall off the tightrope. I've tried a lot of things: coasting without a plan, outsourcing, dipping back into high-frequency publishing, stopping for varying lengths of time, and even coming up with formats that require less planning, filming, or editing. What's working right now is to have a *massive* amount of structure. That structure includes unstructured time—playtime is the most important time of all—but I have to have a solid frame in place for my days, weeks, and months, otherwise I know the balance falls apart. I have very specific hours each day for work and family, which Essa and I settled on within the first few months of having our firstborn, and the schedule has held up quite well for a couple of years. In work life, every task, project, and goal is written down (in spreadsheets, naturally). And on a larger scale, time is booked for rest or special projects that shake things up—a family trip, or someone from out of town staying for a few days of flurried creative activity. The schedule is not inflexible, but it's always the guide. It bends a bit as needed, but prevents me from going off the rails.

Significantly, my structure is all internally focused. It's about making the conditions right for my workflow and my mental health. I don't have a video schedule, I don't aim to release a certain number of songs or products each year, there's no amount of money I hope to make or milestone I want to pass by any date. As long as I accept that I can't do everything, I have the luxury of letting everything take the time it needs.

## SELF-REFLECTION: VALUES & GOALS

Write two lists: one for your top five core values as a creator, the other for the top five goals you're currently working toward.

| Values | Goals |
|---|---|
|  |  |
|  |  |
|  |  |
|  |  |
|  |  |

When you consider these lists side by side, which values are reflected in which goals? Is every value represented? Do you have goals that are not connected to *any* values?

We don't always have the luxury of pursuing exactly what we want the way we want, but it's beneficial to examine how well our values are aligned with what we're currently placing importance on in our work. Looking at these lists, are there any goals you'd want to add, adjust, or remove? What can you change or reenvision here that will help you show up every day as the artist and person you want to be?

ronically, and with my unceasing luck, stepping back from the You-Tube cash cow put me on the path to making more money than ever before. It opened up the space for me to explore some bigger ideas that I'd never been able to focus on previously, leading to the creation of a number of products such as my app Flip Sampler and my online music production course. Even the new and much more niche branches of my content about advanced production techniques or modular synthesis eventually led to lucrative partnerships with companies that make music software and hardware.

This didn't happen immediately, of course, and there were a couple of years I spent slowly disentangling the parts of myself that had become skewed to seek out validation from how fast my channel grew, the views that my videos got, or my earning power. Many viewers drifted away, some taking the time to let me know that what I was creating no longer spoke to them. I had formerly placed much more focus on entertainment, and when I did create educational videos they were aimed at being digestible by beginners or in some cases even people with no music experience at all. But I was ready to start tackling more advanced topics; I didn't want to limit the explorations on my channel to things accessible only to the layperson. This caused my audience engagement to take an even sharper plunge than my drastically reduced publishing schedule. I was suddenly targeting a much smaller potential audience.

An astute interviewer once observed that it seemed as if, after I hit a million subscribers, I took an abrupt turn away from the broadly appealing content I'd been making, and counterintuitively started broaching narrower and more technical subject matter. He was exactly right. The one-million-subscriber milestone is held up high by viewers, creators, and YouTube representatives alike; when I reached it and found that the fulfillment it offered was so fleeting, it made me almost apathetic about audience growth. Funnily enough, this did eventually lead me toward a greater sense of contentment, because I was able to confirm for myself that this achievement didn't have any inherent meaning to me. Everything about its value comes from outside—from people tapping a button on your social media profile, or from others seeing how many people have tapped a button on your social media profile. The only thing you should need in order to value yourself is yourself.

I have the good fortune of being surrounded by level-headed, self-assured people. Those in my family and on my team know what they want in life, and prestige has no allure for them. They do their best work in a normal amount of hours and are grateful to spend the rest of their time with loved ones or on hobbies. I seem to be moving closer to their level of contentedness. It took me years to see the paradox in our circle. Here I was with thousands of people telling me that I was amazing and that they loved my work, and I was the most insecure of the lot. I always fell into questioning whether I was doing things the right way. Whatever I did was never enough. A childhood of ostracization had simultaneously given me the grit to stand out and a deep need to prove myself. To top it all off, I had chosen an occupational field where you're not considered successful unless you've reached tremendous heights of fame.

For most of human history we could only compare ourselves against others in our community. Now, we're all aware of hundreds of the top performers in the world in any given field, as well as many of those who came after video and audio recording technology who were so great that they have endured beyond their deaths. This only exacerbates the working artist's plight. From early on, you feel like you're in competition with not only your local scene but the entire world. If you think in terms of winning and losing, you can't ever be happy. There's room for only one at the top.

Many end up chasing status because they're trying to fill some bottomless pit inside themselves, and the thing with bottomless pits is: there's no bottom, they can't be filled. I've found there's no correlation between anyone's stature in the industry and their sense of satisfaction.

Real success is not about how you measure up against others, it's something each of us has to define for ourselves in alignment with our values.

It's a continual cycle of learning for me, reminding myself that the world's values are not mine. It's only about following joy and inspiration as I try to push music forward.

## SOCIAL MEDIA BALANCE

My phone reports that this week I spent less than twenty-five minutes a day on social media. This is down from what used to be *hours*. Most of us know how easy it is to pop into social media for what we think will be a couple of minutes, and then emerge in a daze an hour later. When being online is a large part of your job, social media can have an even stronger draw; it's hard to ignore the benefits of being active on all the popular platforms.

Embarrassingly, and perhaps tellingly, here's the thing I've been most reluctant to share in this book: most of the time, someone else posts on social media for me. My social media manager, Sophie, has been working with me for a few years, and has probably done as much for my mental health as any therapy, meditation, or vacation. She sees all the music and videos I'm planning in a shared calendar. Anytime I finish a project I fire it off to her—sometimes it's ready to go for social media, sometimes it's something she'll edit appropriately. We meet for an hour every Wednesday to sort out what will be posted in the coming week. Everything is still what I want to say and share—here's me desperately trying to convince you it's authentic and not some kind of corporate machinery—I just don't have to think about posting at the optimal time, or formatting media properly, or tracking down tags (another set of things you mistakenly think will take only a couple of minutes). Preparing posts in batches is key, and it's a luxury to be able to employ someone to organize and execute the bulk of the work. If I could go back in time, I would have prioritized that expense over any gear upgrade.

Occasionally I'll create a spontaneous post, and replies to comments still come directly from me. That's where most of those twenty-five minutes go. I'll open my social media a couple of times a day—and occasionally get pulled into a bit of scrolling—but by and large I just try to read and respond to a few comments, because sometimes people have good questions, and I want to let people know I appreciate their support.

Before I worked with Sophie, I tried a few things to mitigate my social media use. I tried the feature on my phone that blocks certain apps at certain times. I would leave my phone in another room before I sat down to work. I deleted apps so that my phone would be able to access social media platforms only through its web browser—a clunkier and less enjoyable experience. These approaches would help to some degree, but nothing ever felt as good as taking time off of social media completely, which I very occasionally do for a few days or a week at a time. I experience a palpable added mental clarity when there's no social media in my life at all. There really is an inverse proportional relationship between time spent on social media and the quality of your mental health. Even without the unavoidable envy and outrage it surfaces in us, the little interruptions to our day—*to our lives*—are more potent than we like to admit. What would we be thinking and feeling and doing without the constant detours and numbings of social media?

There's a part of me that almost feels shameful about having a social media manager, as if I'm supposed to be a *very online person* because *very online people* are the folks my business benefits from the most. I used to worry about whether it was hypocritical of me to generate so much content and then engage so little with what else was out there. But I don't care anymore. I'm doing things the way it works for me and the way I want. No one would give a hard-core touring musician flak for performing three hundred concerts a year but attending only five as an audience member. I create much more than I consume—and as necessary as social media is to my career, being away from it makes me better at my actual job. It's also not that I look down on social media; I love it—maybe a little too much! That's what got me so far down this path in the first place. But I recognize that the majority of it is junk food. I'm going to moderate my consumption.

Is this necessary at all? Wouldn't I be truer to myself if I just wasn't on social media at all because I've recognized that it chips away at my contentment? Well, I do still believe that social media is the best avenue for sharing work and ideas as an independent creator. (Also, internet humor has given me a few of the best laughs of my life.) I do want to have an active presence on social media, and I also want to minimize how much it needs to touch my fingertips or enter my eyes. I think I've gotten as close to that dream as I can at the moment.

Thanks, Sophie!

## SELF-REFLECTION: SOCIAL MEDIA

As a creator, it's important to examine how your art relates to the way you use social media. Are you using it to promote your work or find collaborators? Do you draw inspiration from it, and, if so, is it worth the distraction and discontentment that are hard to avoid? While these platforms provide tools that can elevate and expand your reach, there are downsides to keep in mind and hopefully mitigate. It can be helpful to do a social media audit from time to time to consider whether you could reshape your engagement with these platforms in ways that would better serve your personal and creative aims. Ask yourself:

- Are there accounts worth unfollowing or muting?
- Should you limit your social media use to certain times of day, or a certain total amount of time?
- Can you compartmentalize your personal and your work-related social media use?
- Are there platforms you want to leave altogether?

In the bell curve of your audience, you're almost always hearing from the very edges of the bell.

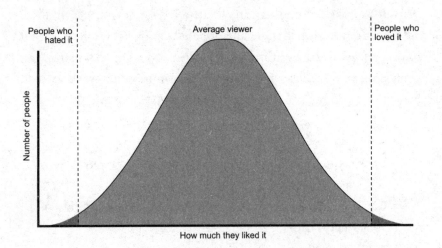

Engagement on social media—interaction in the form of a comment, like, share, etc.—is usually under 5 percent, and very often not even 1 percent. So if a thousand people see something you've posted, you should expect to see fewer than ten comments. This all means that the average person in your audience does not leave a comment, so when someone does, they're often compelled by a stronger than average response to your work. They were so touched, inspired, entertained, offended, or disgusted that they wanted to let you know about it. And *that* means every comment *must* be taken with a grain of salt—especially the salty ones. You equally cannot pay heed to the people calling you an unparalleled genius or an embarrassing failure.

If there's one thing I've learned from the micron of fame I've experienced it's that you really do have to live your life for yourself. I think we all understand on some level that it's healthier not to care what other people think of you; time and again I've been shown this in full force by having thousands of people tell me their thoughts about me and my work. At the extreme ends of that bell curve, I've discovered, almost every possible opinion exists.

Sometimes I notice exact opposite reactions to the same song, video, or social media post. When I knew I would be writing this book, I began collecting some of these conflicting couplets. Keep in mind, these aren't just random comments that happen to disagree with each other. Every one of these was found beneath the same post as its partner—they show different people responding to the *same piece of media*.

| | |
|---|---|
| You have the voice of an angel! | His singing is soooo bad |
| I need to know what fuzz pedal was used!! I love that tone!! | Your guitar tone is awful 😆 |
| Andrew has got to be the most genuine creator out there. | I can't stand how fake this guy is. |
| This video was packed with so many helpful insights! | Typical vlogger. Takes 15 minutes to say what he could in 1. |
| You are a creative GENIUS. I wish I had an ounce of your talent! | What a hack. |

And my personal favorite:

| | |
|---|---|
| His eyes are too close together. | His eyes are too far apart. |

Beauty is in the eye of the beholder. Everything else is also in the eye of the beholder. (And my eyes, I assume, must be the perfect distance apart.)

Who *should* you listen to? Yourself, with occasional input from someone you trust. A bit of sage advice or constructive criticism from someone who knows your field and knows *you* is worth the world. A stranger taking ten seconds to type something negative about you is near meaningless. You don't know where they're coming from. How they respond to you or your work is much more about them than it is about you. Assumptions and miscategorizations run rampant in our daily interactions in general; this is only exacerbated by the complications of online communication. Look at any post with an active comment thread and you'll see the polarization, the misinterpretation, and probably a number of comments that you yourself are unsure how to make sense of. A significant portion of the people who come across a piece of content *will* receive some unintended message or feeling—or bring so much of their own baggage with them that they can't see much of anything else. When it comes to people who waste the precious moments of their lives typing out nastiness to send to people they don't know, they're always going to find something to lash out at. You just happened to be in their feed that day. When you get a negative comment on the internet, take those words and picture them coming from a thirteen-year-old boy who just crawled out of a garbage can to grumble at you. That's how much weight you need to give to that kind of comment.

Giving credence to any feedback from strangers, the good or the bad, is another way we fall into acting (or not acting) based on external values. If you're trying to prove yourself, you'll never run out of people to prove yourself to. If you need validation from outside yourself, you'll never stop needing it. If you give in to fear about how others will respond to you or your work, it might protect you from some discouragement or disappointment, but it will also definitely prevent you from fully flourishing in the way that only you can.

Sometimes people ask me how to get over the fear of putting yourself out there. They're worried about what people might think or say, that their work isn't as good as they hope it is, or that who they are is too weird or different to be accepted. Maybe I got a head start on thickening my skin because I was unavoidably, visibly different from the kids I grew up with. But it's more than that as well. I do sometimes still fear what people will think of me or say about me. The greater fear, though, is imagining spending a lifetime not being true to myself.

## SELF-REFLECTION: EXTERNAL FEEDBACK

Being affected by extreme comments is a pretty universal experience. How much importance do you tend to place on outside criticism? Have you ever found yourself altering actions, intentions, motivations, or hopes based on outside feedback or pressure? In those moments, it's best to remind yourself that you know what's right for you better than anyone else. Refer back to the core values you laid out on page 270. Can any of those help bring you back toward your purpose, joy, and authenticity?

# Chapter Fifteen

I'd barely pulled away from arrivals at Pearson Airport when my friend Bill, who I'd just picked up, started looking through his phone for a contact.

"Hey, while I'm here, would you want to meet up with Joel?"

A few artists have reached such heights in the industry that everyone who is remotely involved in any electronic music scene, whether they know them personally or not, uses just their first names with no need for clarification. There's Sonny, there's Wes, and there's Joel.

"He says we can come over tonight."

Bill goes by Mr. Bill, and his music is some of the most exciting I've ever heard. He's a producer's producer. He knows every trick in the book—he invented quite a few of them—and whatever anyone else can do, he can do it a bit tighter, with greater risks taken yet with more compelling results. I remember discovering him on SoundCloud when his tracks were averaging five thousand plays and feeling like he was making what I wished I could be making (and what I still wish I could be making). We ended up chatting a few years later, after both our profiles had risen. I was surprised he knew of me, actually. He was one of the first people who was finding success with a more traditional music career—touring, DJing, album release cycles—who enjoyed and respected the YouTube–heavy approach I was taking.

When one of his tours had a finishing stop in Pennsylvania, we agreed
he should take the short flight to Toronto afterward so we could finally
meet in person and collaborate. So I woke up one morning thinking I
was just going to pick up the legendary Mr. Bill from the airport, only
to find myself that evening en route to meet a whole other legend.

It was a long ride beyond the outskirts of Toronto. Far enough that all
metropolitan apparatus had dissolved behind us, we rarely saw another
car, and the next intersection was never visible from the one we had
just passed.

In this area, you can find a turn that brings you to a set of wrought-
iron gates, beyond which a comically long driveway leads to a three-
garage castle. And if you step between the stone columns that bookend
its enormous front entrance and ring the doorbell, the doors will inch
open and he'll be standing in front of you: Deadmau5.

I've never been one to deify celebrities. Even as a kid, as much as I would obsess over various musicians, I kept in mind that they were just people. They had to eat and sleep and bathe. They wrote songs with the same twelve notes as the rest of us.

My mom laid the groundwork for this outlook when I first started listening to music that wasn't what she'd introduced me to. You know—music made in the same decade we were living in. "These stars are just people who got lucky one time," I remember her saying. "If you can get a lot of attention once, people will pay attention to the next thing you do. And anyway, a lot of these rich and famous people aren't very happy." Mom never treated anyone differently based on status, nor did she ever expect special treatment. Even at the end of her career, as head of neonatology at her hospital, she was still regularly cleaning the staff room microwave on her breaks.

I never picked up the microwave-cleaning habit, but giving everyone the same shake stuck with me. Of course, if someone's highly regarded in their field and their work has resonated with you, it's exciting if you have a chance to connect with them. But from a young age, I didn't look up to the musicians whose work I loved—I looked across. I thought of us as equals. (As a young person there was likely also a mix of arrogance and naivete here.) By the same token, there's no looking down. No one is beneath me because of—what? The quality of their artistic output? The number of people who clicked "follow" on their profile on a platform that none of us even like all that much?

It's why I've loved bringing my community into my videos, whether it's featuring them and their work, or incorporating the ideas and sounds they offer me into mine. Some of the folks I've featured on *4 Producers 1 Sample* had fewer than a thousand followers when I asked them to be on the show. I just wanted them there because I loved their work.

We've all seen huge acts tank after a string of successes. With incredible talent, virtually unlimited budgets, top-tier collaborators, slick videos, and even payola, sometimes artists still produce flops. And just as readily, fourteen-year-olds with pirated music software on decrepit computers will create absolute bangers. So I try not to succumb to the luster that fame confers on the individuals in its grasp. Fame is an indicator that you have people's attention, probably thanks to a good deal of luck. It doesn't intrinsically mean you're more talented or harder-working than anyone else.

It's hard for our brains to understand scale, and so a lot of us still tend to think of mainstream celebrities whose faces are plastered everywhere as "famous" and everyone else as small potatoes. But in our siloed social media bubbles, we're creating every conceivable size of following, in ways that usually don't involve any of Hollywood's machinery, and if you're not part of a given silo then you probably don't know it exists. Every few days I discover someone with a homegrown following exceeding a hundred thousand or an artist I've never heard of before who has millions of monthly listeners.

With the size of my following, "fame" means I can securely make a living as an artist while only being recognized a couple times a month when I'm out and about, almost always by a lovely person with whom I can enjoy a quick chat. But there are also interactions that give me pause, like people who write to me daily or figure out my phone number and call me. On one tour, a fan followed me and my friends after a show for several blocks, hoping to hang out, and when we told him it wasn't appropriate, he tried to guilt trip me into letting him stay in my hotel room because he'd supposedly come to the show from out of town with no plan for how to get home. And none of this compares to the stories I hear from my female friends who are in the public eye: stalking, harassment, doxing, death threats.

I feel a lot of discomfort about the hierarchies that fame creates. You see it at every event—the bigger artists, the smaller artists, the inner circles, the event staff, the fans; the assistants who linger in the group but are never brought into the conversation; the eyes that glaze over when the person you just met at the industry mixer realizes they're much more "important" than you.

It's unfortunate that fame can reduce our humanity on either side of the equation. The ultra-famous are so constantly vexed by fans and the media that they can't interact with them as real people, and they themselves have to be so on guard that they're prevented, in some ways— despite all the wealth and privilege—from living a full life, from having innocent encounters or genuine relationships.

At first I thought Joel was eyeing me suspiciously—and I wouldn't blame him; to him I was just a hanger-on of Bill's he knew nothing about. We stepped inside onto white marble floors and met Joel's wife and some out-of-town friends who were staying with them. A part of me hoped we'd see this night turn into a rager, but we kicked things off by standing around the kitchen counter making small talk and drinking water.

"All right, well I guess I should give you the tour, huh?"

We wove through the mansion and saw the home theater, the custom gaming setup, a casual row of luxury cars in the garage that somehow seemed bigger inside than out. But of course we were most excited about his studio: a high-ceilinged room wrapped in acoustic panels, with a wall-to-wall synth collection sprawled across neatly organized shelves and racks. After Bill and I let out our involuntary fawning noises, Joel blasted a couple of tracks, including one of Bill's that his label was about to put out, through his massive speakers.

And then there was the taxidermy room. Between the kitchen and the front foyer, under an ornate chandelier, was a tableau of a safari. A giraffe loomed over the staircase. A bearskin rug (bear head still on it) sat atop a hide from some other even larger animal. In one corner there was a moose, in mid-stride, wearing a top hat. Various skeletons, skulls, antlers, and tusks adorned every surface.

We cautiously walked around and asked questions. Joel ended up going on about the flak he got for it online. People thought he was some kind of trophy-hunting villain, when actually these taxidermized specimens died naturally and a large portion of the exorbitant sums he paid for them went to wildlife conservation efforts. He reached over to a corner of the room and picked up what I thought was a baseball bat in the dim lighting. As he brought it closer I realized it was shaped more like a sword, but thicker, and it was made of a chalky white material.

"Check this out," he said, grinning. "You know what this is?"

We didn't.

"This is a whale's penis bone."

Everyone laughed, and we took turns holding the penis bone.

How much of wanting to make our mark is based in ego?

For me, it used to be a lot. Driven by a need to prove myself, I wanted to show the culture that was unaccepting of me all my life that I was worthy. I wanted to be special and I wanted people to know it. I looked up at the greats and wanted my art—and my name—to be as timeless as theirs. As my musical interests expanded, I wanted to excel at all of it, and I wanted people to see what I was capable of creating without outside help. Parts of this were virtuous—I wanted to break boundaries and arouse more open-mindedness, and I liked being an example of hard work. But much of it was just a self-centered cry: *Look at me, aren't I talented? Aren't I great?*

That ego drive has subsided, in part with age, in part with already having proven myself to some degree, and in part from seeing the futility of focusing on proving myself at all. I'll do the work I feel called to do, but it's not up to me to judge it, and it's okay not to be recognized for it. I used to get frustrated if someone executed an idea that I'd also had—maybe their success could have been mine! Now, I welcome when that happens. *The idea is out there—wonderful. And I didn't have to work on it at all!*

The hearing loss also contributed to this. There was no pretending to myself that I would reach anywhere near the heights of the world's finest sonic craftspeople. I have some of the worst-performing ears in the industry, missing swaths of frequencies and with often unreliable volume. It forced me to come to terms with not aiming to be the best, but doing what I was particularly suited to do.

One night at Joel's house erased any lingering doubt that I should be doing what works for me and not hustling toward the highest heights. I can't speak to how he feels about his situation—it might be perfect for him; he has a natural talent, works hard, and creates music that millions love. But even with my extreme introversion, I couldn't see myself enjoying being forced by fame to live in such isolation. The clincher, though, was something he said when he gave us the tour of his studio. "I haven't been in here in like three months." For months, the demands on his time to tour and run his label and attend to other business ventures had been too great to work on new music. Again, maybe this works for him. When Bill and I woke up the following morning, Joel was already in his office, making tweaks to the programming of his show's accompanying visuals. He's involved in many more aspects of the industry than I care to be, and also makes time for playing video games and driving race cars (both of which he is also annoyingly talented at). But walking around inside the world of someone who had made it in all the ways I had been brought up to desire only created a greater contrast to the goals and values I'd discovered for myself, and reinforced my determination to pursue them in my own way.

## SELF-REFLECTION: ANALYZING THE DATA

We're surrounded by numbers. Almost everything we put online has metrics attached to it: impressions, views, likes, comments, shares, saves, streams, earnings, watch time, demographics. It's not a bad thing to analyze any of these to see if there are connections between what you're creating and how it performs. Any successful business is probably doing exactly that. But sometimes our hearts go against the data. I've heard from hundreds of creators who feel that the work they're proudest of, or that they'd like to do more of, is not what's most popular with their audiences. What's most meaningful to them is not aligned with what gets the most engagement or makes the most money.

If you're feeling the pull to take things in a different direction, whether it's about work/life balance or remaining authentic, it can be scary to do something you know could jeopardize what you've built. It seems to defy common sense to look at a bunch of numbers that indicate success and then choose to do things that will lower those numbers. But what about the data you're not looking at? While your feelings about your work aren't exactly quantifiable, there are ways you can gauge whether you're on a good path. How many hours in your creative practice were enjoyable or tedious? How many days did you move the needle on a passion project? In the content you've published, what's the ratio of items you *loved* making, as opposed to ones you thought you should?

You can also measure many things in your life that might give an indication of your mental, physical, and emotional health: hours slept, friends seen, alcohol consumed, time spent outdoors, time spent on social media. What about the number of workouts, meditations, journal entries, baths? How many days did you practice gratitude? How often do you laugh?

It's worth periodically taking stock of the ways you're measuring your success. It doesn't matter how many metrics you have at hand—if you're not looking at the right ones for *you*, it's easy to be led astray.

I was the worst musician in my school.

Not in high school. (I crushed it in high school.) But when I was accepted into a postsecondary music program, I was suddenly and exclusively surrounded by other kids who were great at music in high school. Almost all my classmates had phenomenal talent, or tremendous dedication to their craft, or both, and I (much as I do now) flitted between a wide range of usually experimental and exploratory interests. It was fortunate I'd applied to York for classical composition—the only music program offered by the school at that time that didn't require a live audition on an instrument—because the dexterity and expression in my playing was far behind that of my peers. I was in my second year of study when my hearing issues began, knocking my abilities even further back. In high school, my talents in music made me believe I had something special; in university, I was intimidated by how good everyone else was.

But I was unconventional, and the ways I was different proved to be my greatest strengths. Most students had gone through some formal music theory education, but few had elected to do their own independent learning beyond that, or internalized the principles outside the context of their chosen instrument. After an aptitude test at the beginning of my freshman year, I was one of only two students to be exempted from the core music theory curriculum. Waves of students poured in and out of the always-booked practice rooms I never even entered. I would instead be in a deserted section of the library, seeking out documentaries and recordings of early electronic music, building an understanding of a hugely consequential slice of music history that is rarely taught in schools. And while I could never hold a candle to my fellow students in performance, few at the time were interested in creating music with a computer. I began to carve out the music production career that eventually led me to a sizable audience and lots of commercial work, while their opportunities were—and, in some cases, still are—limited to playing cover songs on pub nights.

I've learned to lean hard on certain weaknesses. Many things I once considered flaws or disadvantages about myself I've been able to use to my benefit. I'm not saying that I don't work to better myself, and certainly I have natural tendencies that don't serve me as well as others might. But if something that's atypical or unorthodox comes naturally to you, finding a way to work *with* it rather than *against* it can suddenly make things a lot easier. From that place of profound openness, many supposed weaknesses can be viewed as *excelling* at something we don't normally consider. The greater the weakness, the better you are at its counterpart! Do I overthink things and obsess over details? Yes, often. But that's the same part of me that's allowed me to iterate prolifically on ideas and execute them with precision. Am I a naturally gifted vocalist? No—and folks in my audience remind me of this nearly every time I incorporate my singing in a project. But I've seen a tendency in many musicians with beautiful voices to rely heavily or even exclusively on them, and it can limit them in other ways. I think the development of a lot of my musical skills and knowledge came in part because I was compelled to work harder on elements that didn't have to do with my physical capabilities. As I've gotten to know other successful artists and creators, I've found that this strength/weakness paradox is quite common. For example, the front man of a popular band, who was eventually prevented from touring due to health issues, pivoted and became an in-demand songwriter, working daily with A-list artists from his home. A YouTube creator struggling with attention deficit disorder learned to collaborate and delegate, enabling him to create more, better, and higher-performing content than he ever could have alone. Go with the flow wherever you can, and let the motion and momentum that are already in place work *for* you.

When it comes to branding, too, incorporating more of yourself, even the "flawed" parts, is much more powerful than trying to wedge yourself into the shape that somebody else decided was acceptable.

People respond to the openness and confidence—as well as the vulnerability—of someone who is unapologetically themself. The more I leaned into my quirks, the more people connected with my work. So many things about my brand are at odds with how a musician would normally go about things. There's no mystique—I'm in my home studio showing you the exact settings on my gear and the attempted ideas that didn't work out. I'm *not cool*; I'm a huge nerd—but there's a place for someone like me, who gets excited about learning music theory and loves reading synthesizer manuals. Cultivating an air of mystery or keeping a composed, detached distance never worked for me—because it's *not* me. And I think people can usually tell. I need to be the wide-eyed weirdo with the high-pitched laugh, running around a studio blathering about a C6/9 chord or the feedback loop I've created with a motorized reverb pedal.

Who are you?

SELF-REFLECTION: REDIRECTING WEAKNESS

Think of some things about yourself you tend to view as shortcomings or disadvantages. Can you instead see them in a positive light? Take a moment to recognize ways they may have helped you in the past, or could in the future if directed the right way. What are three things you might consider weaknesses that could be turned into strengths?

| Something I consider a weakness | How can this trait serve my goals? |
| --- | --- |
|  |  |
|  |  |
|  |  |

I've spent a lot of time thinking about authenticity. I spent my childhood as an outsider looking in on a culture where I couldn't belong, which frequently made me question what was natural and what was learned. Then, as an adult, I found myself with a following on social media, where "authenticity" is touted as the most crucial precept. You need to be real on these platforms in order to maintain trust and credibility with your followers. There's a lot of backlash against social media as nothing but a highlights reel. Countless stories have come out about people being caught displaying fabricated lives as they attempt to build a lifestyle following and attract sponsors beyond their worth. A service even exists where you can pay by the hour to take selfies on a set designed to look like the cabin of a private jet. In an age of corporate-owned media and constant advertising, people are hungrier than ever for what is real—or at least feels like it is.

Authenticity, of course, was important in the arts long before social media. The sense that a performance comes from a "real" place gives a much stronger foothold for an audience's emotional connection to a piece. When a public figure turns out to be quite different in private than the persona they convey to the outside world, their admirers may feel betrayed. It calls into question what they thought they related to—not a person but a construction. A product. And though we understand in many ways that art is a product—we paid for the ticket or the sub-scription or the box set—we feel it's something more than that as well. It ministers to us about the human condition, and can have a powerful effect on our thoughts and emotions. When something speaks to us intimately or has a profound impact on our lives, a lot of the wind is taken out of the sails if we discover it was a commercial contrivance or had no real roots in its author's lived experience.

But what are art and performance, anyway, if not fabrications? The line between authentic and inauthentic can shift wildly depending on the parameters we put around it. Is the song an artist sings for the thousandth time as authentic as it was when they first wrote it twenty years prior? Is it more authentic to capture a single live performance, or to create an edit of multiple takes that presents an idea at its best? Can any performance that's been rehearsed be authentic, or is that only possible with pure and unself-conscious improvisation? In all cases, we're creating something that wouldn't exist otherwise, something extraneous to the natural order of things, but which gives us pleasure, comfort, or even a glimpse of the divine.

When I first began taking music production seriously, I aimed for what I thought was an honest approach, documenting pieces with min-imal studio trickery or postproduction work. In my mind, it was a little too "fake" to dramatically alter a recording through extensive editing and effects. My perspective quickly shifted when I heard an analogy from a production veteran: "We're not making home movies, we're making *movies.*" The authenticity wasn't to be found in a lack of fabrication; it was about putting your heart and soul into forging something *transcendent*, bottling something real and deeply human in your work that could leave an imprint on others.

There are conflicting layers to authenticity as well. It's a gross over-simplification to think that we each have one way we *really* are and the rest must be somehow put on. We're constantly making choices between opposing but equally honest parts of ourselves: to eat healthily or to enjoy a treat, to look sharp and presentable or to lounge around in sweats, to work on our goals or to get the rest we need. I know a creator who swears constantly. They refuse to tone it down for any reason—it doesn't matter if they're at a fancy speaking engagement or if there are young kids around. "It's just who I am," they say, confident and uncaring. Now, I'll swear in conversation as well, but I keep it out of my videos. Is that inauthentic—adjusting my behavior, censoring myself? Not at all. In those moments, I'm being faithful to a deeper authentic intent—to spread all this musical knowledge and joy. Swearing isn't important to me, and it's easy to find other words to use. That occasional adjustment to how I express myself is something I absolutely want to do so that my videos can be enjoyed in classrooms and shared between parents and their kids. For a much broader example: I wrote in Part One about my platonic ideal for sharing music, how I'd like the work I create to speak for itself. I still hold on to that—and I've compromised on it with every step I've taken. Because I *also* love sharing about the process. I've *also* seen how powerful it is to attach a personality or a face to something that is otherwise invisible and ephemeral, and building my brand has given me the resources and ability to create a hundred times as much. And something I never would have anticipated but that I cherish so much: I've made some of my closest friends through my online content, and it wasn't just by sharing my work but by sharing myself that we were able to connect.

We're always balancing between countless possibilities, and many more than one of them can be authentic, even if they seem at odds or *are* at odds. It may be extra tricky when it comes to art, business, and branding, where, as discussed earlier, simplicity has a tremendous advantage. Simplicity of concept, messaging, and expectations leaves so much less room for someone in the audience to feel the friction of a nuance they don't yet understand. More than simply tapping into what's authentic for us, we're trying to find an *authentic balance* between many parts of us that sometimes seem like they can't coexist.

Appearing to be real sometimes works better than realness itself. Being a little outside-the-box, what's genuine for me has often clashed with what people expect. For example, exploring a huge range of genres—one of my core passions—is sometimes seen not as a love of all music but as an attempt to capitalize on trends. Those who enjoy my experimental tendencies think my "pop" output must be disingenuous, a cheap grab at a broader audience. On the other end of the spectrum, for some folks who are deeply involved in experimental music scenes, my more traditional music or even just the size of my YouTube channel rule me out as an authentic participant. They conceive of me as either traditional or popular, and so my interest in more niche subjects like tape loops or obscure synthesizers must only be novelty seeking, a way to create sensational content. But I always return to that deep openness; despite any appearances, it would be much less authentic for me to confine my output to a narrower band. Ironically, expressing all your individuality works best when your authenticity looks similar to that of the average person.

It gets thornier as you dig deeper. The strength of a brand relies on what it truly values and represents, as well as on omitting anything that would dilute its message or image. And for many artists there's a bit of make-believe in their brand: otherworldly imagery, a dramatized backstory, or simply—harbinger of the fake-jet-cabin selfie—renting luxury vehicles to pose with in music videos. Artifice, mythmaking, fantasy . . . but I think they *authentically* want to project these things!

I wrestled directly with these themes in my project *Spacetime*, a multimedia experiment that took over all my platforms for six months in 2020, blending reality and fantasy in the online space where it's all too easy to fabricate and falsify. Over the course of those months, my YouTube videos and social media posts descended further and further into an alternate reality, until they were completely and obviously a work of fiction. While *Spacetime* was still about all the things my usual content is about—having fun, creating and sharing music, inspiring and educating viewers—it had numerous additional aims. I wanted to experiment with form and push the boundaries of YouTube content, bringing a story arc and cinematic production values to my usual videos. I also set out to parody the ways we behave on social media, and raise questions about its performative nature. I would be taking a performed reality to the absolute extremes: costumes, set design, green screens, visual effects, computer-generated characters, "casual" posts planned years in advance, and a journey to another galaxy.

Much of the project stemmed from my growing need to explore authenticity itself in my art as I was figuring out my values and my place in this industry. When I first came up with the concept, I was in my most intense period of YouTube creation, and all those questions about authenticity were snaking to the surface. I had met hundreds of other creators in a few short years, and seen how common it was to misrepresent reality or to become an entirely different person on camera. I could feel the pull to create things that were less authentic, even to become less authentic in how I presented myself, in ways that I knew would lead to higher views, more engagement, and increased revenue. In my own weird way of addressing these issues and working through my feelings, I came up with an eighteen-episode space opera and spent four years bringing it to life with my team.

*Spacetime* began with me announcing in a YouTube video, with complete earnestness, that I had an opportunity to go to space. At the end of that video, you see me being driven to a launch facility, going through various tests conducted by people in lab coats, getting suited up, and then, sitting in the driver's seat of a very sci-fi-looking cockpit, blasting off into the sky. My intention was to have people fooled for a moment and then hopefully delighted as they realized I was embarking on some new kind of fun on my channel. For some viewers, that was the experience. But for others, the series was a turnoff—too cryptic for too long, and too far of a departure from my usual output. To my astonishment, in the earliest videos of the series—before the interdimensional alien and time-travel-endowed crystals came into the picture—our storytelling and visual effects were a little *too* good. For many of the viewers who didn't know anything about the realities of spaceflight, the announcement video was absolutely convincing. They took it at face value—that I as an untrained civilian could hop into a skintight suit and be the lone passenger on a ship that looks like it's from *Star Wars*—and they really thought I was in space. Even a few of my friends told me they thought it was real at first! And with each subsequent upload, I would be surprised that some people still weren't catching on that it was all theater. Many must have been playing along with the gag, I'm sure, but for the first couple of weeks, when I tweeted about being in space, when I posted photos "from space," there was a lot of debate in the comments about whether it was real. *Newsweek* even published an article to debunk it.

Much further down the line, these responses would aid in my overall goals with the project, demonstrating the potency of the ways we choose to portray ourselves online. If there are people who believe me when I tell them I'm *going to outer space*, what are the effects of a much more believable dab of exaggeration here, touch of Photoshop there, misquoted words or snippets of video out of context, compounded again and again in a torrent of posts beamed into our brains daily?

Throughout *Spacetime* I used a lot of the online tropes we've become accustomed to, but executed them within an increasingly fictional world. I posted selfies in my new outfit: a spacesuit. I did a home tour—of my intergalactic vehicle. I did the "goodbye" video and the "apology" video. (Creators will often rack up views with videos about supposedly retiring, or controversial events in their lives; my "goodbye" video was about leaving Earth for space, and my "apology" video was about realizing that I'd been depleting my new alien friend's most precious resource for the sake of time travel.) I even parodied myself, making music out of the "everyday" sounds around me, like cockpit controls and pneumatic sliding doors—all sound effects that I'd artificially created for my show, of course.

I was dismayed by the audience response as the project progressed. Many people were enjoying it, but it seemed just as many actively disliked it. Views declined as less invested viewers checked out; comments were more negative than I'd ever experienced. For many people, much of what I'd set out to do wasn't landing as intended. The inclusion of an overarching story was confusing rather than coherent; the social media commentary was barely picked up on; the cinematography and visual effects we'd worked so hard on were written off as merely an attention-seeking gimmick. Most artists who work long enough hear some version of "I wish they went back to what they were doing before"—never in my career had I heard it so frequently. It was the first time I felt I might have made a major strategic error. Up until that point, every move I'd made (whether through astuteness or sheer luck) had led to forward leaps in my career that often surprised me. I had been used to downturns in views before, but they had been minor, or deliberate, as when I severely reduced my publishing frequency. Here I was sharing not only a passion project but by far my most ambitious undertaking ever, and it was being met with the worst reception I'd ever experienced.

But I was committed to seeing it through for the full six months as planned. I had gone into it knowing it would challenge many viewers—I just didn't anticipate how much. And the heart of the project *was* its extremeness. A few videos with a story line or special effects is not uncommon for many creators. Half a year of elaborately scripted content being presented as your "real life" on every platform, with multiple sets, locations, and computer-generated backdrops; with costumes, props, voice actors, foley, and a soundtrack—that was a massive operation. I was searching for and playing with the line where authenticity ends—or shatters. Some part of me always has to learn through this type of extreme process, as when I spent a year exploring noise. I need to go until I find the limit or until something breaks. I need to go so far past the line of where I think I should be, or even in the opposite direction of where I think I should be, in order to *know* where I should be.

In the end, by numbers, *Spacetime* performed no better or worse than any other season of my content. There were lows, yet there were also highs. But the response was polarized, and it had demanded immeasurably more of my team and myself than any other project. It was entirely self-funded; I turned down all sponsors while it ran. The crew was *tiny*, involving my usual team—Essa overseeing logistics, Kyah helping me develop the story, Phil doing a mountain of Hollywood-level visual effects, and he and his partner, Kit, creating a spacesuit costume from scratch. We were augmented further by a few friends I hired: Joy and Rose Broadbent, a sister artist duo who fabricated set pieces, and Berkeley Pickell and Stephanie Malek in voice-acting roles.

*Spacetime* was "fake," but it was also what I truly wanted to make. Nothing about its reception was going to discourage me from taking it to the finish line. Though the social media commentary didn't make it through to most people, and many viewers were confused or turned off, it was some of the most fun I'd ever had in my career, and I was thrilled with how all of the creative aspects turned out. Interestingly, it was only after the final episode was published that the bulk of the appreciation came in, and viewers shared how inspired they were at our attempts to expand and elevate the online video form—especially after the credits rolled and they saw what a small team worked on it. While the series was unfolding I sometimes thought that I was confusing and alienating viewers; it turns out that I was also strengthening my connection to others, many of whom ended up saying it was my best work.

Long after the project was over, it surprised me with a lesson about authenticity. My team and I put together a behind-the-scenes documentary—which, due to the huge amount of footage to sort through and the fact that we were also working on lots of other regular videos again, came out more than two years after *Spacetime*'s finale. It was nice to be able to document my aims with the project and the hard work and resourcefulness behind it, and give its fans a deeper understanding of how and why it came to be. It was gratifying to hear from so many of them that they *loved* it, in many cases more than anything else I'd done, and the behind-the-scenes content only increased their appreciation of it. But now, having seen what I went through to make it, and how high I had aimed, there was also a new sentiment being expressed: many loved that I had clearly done exactly what I wanted to do, a passion project that threw the rule book out the window, something so uniquely *me*. And due to the nature of this project—and also the way we share and experience art in general—I'd simply never had a glimpse of this side of my work's impact. The most inspiring thing for the audience was not the resourcefulness of the team, the beauty of the visuals, or the richness of the music. It was the fact that, despite doubts and detractors, I had a singular vision that I saw through to the end.

# Conclusion

Anyone can tell you, as I've tried to do, what they believe to be the circumstances, events, principles, and choices that led to their success. I wanted to be transparent so that you can glean anything that might be useful. But no one can tell you what success means for you, and you can't follow another's steps like a map. There *is* no map. It's always going to be a jumble of luck and work and weirdness. Our days, dreams, and contexts are different, as are the things that feed our souls. We all have to forge our own path—or risk simply being nudged along whichever one the people around us have already worn into the dirt. So while I can't give you the answers that are right for you, I can encourage you to nurture your sense of openness, so you can find perspectives and approaches that work best for you—and act on them. I wrote this book to suggest you consider letting go of what you think it means to be an artist, creator, or success.

The openness with which I approach life is something I learned, along with so many other things, from music. In music we can touch the infinite. I'm open because I found myself in music, and music was open in a world that seemed closed. Music is transformative. It's an experience through time; it demands change in order to be expressed. Even a single note being held embodies movement: it is air oscillating between compression

305

and rarefaction; its rise and fall mirrors the arc of our lives. Music is multitudinous, embodying the vastness of human culture. It can express emotions we can't even name. Every voice in the choir adds its own timbre, and each person is a microcosm for that harmony—countless disparate parts that fit together in a way that is equally beautiful and impossible to comprehend. Music is like each of us, ever changing and ever growing, a complex, joyous, tragic, miraculous story unfolding with every moment.

Being artists makes us particularly prepared to embrace our identities wholeheartedly. Our work deals in malleability and manifestation. To create anything meaningful we have to tap into what's deep inside. It's so life-giving to recognize our multifaceted natures and to accept that all aspects of ourselves are valid, as different as they may be from the molds we're presented with. We're not all supposed to be just one way. There's not even just one way *you're* supposed to be *you*. So if there's only one lesson you take away from this book, it's one of openness. I hope you'll be open to defining your own path.

Make your own rules!

# Acknowledgments

Natasha Yglesias, this book would not exist without you. Your invitation to me to write this has been the fulfillment of a lifelong dream, and your perspective and guidance throughout the process have been a support far beyond what I would have ever believed possible. Pretty sure you were genetically engineered to do this. Thank you for the long chats, the answers to complicated questions, and for holding my hand through all the unexpected twists we encountered on the road.

Ronnie Alvarado, you've been a grounding force in shaping everything I wanted to communicate. Thank you for keeping the bigger picture in mind, and bearing with all my first-time-author quirks (and many other quirks).

To my team, you're all incredible and I don't take it for granted that I get to work exclusively with people I love. Philip Bowser, you are the unsung hero of the videos that go out under my name, and have brought a polish and a flair to them—and to the online video space—that no one else could. Thanks for a decade (!!!) of weirdness and fun. Sophie Flattum, thank you for always going above and beyond to make sure we're sharing things of joy and meaning. Marty Bernie, your ears are on permanent loan to me—thank you for your talent, dedication, and attention to detail. Kyah Green, you have such a unique perspective and sense of humor—thanks for bringing it to my world. Galen Drinnan, you're the glue that binds us and the foundation that holds us up. I'm constantly astonished at how effortlessly you seem to roll with everything that gets thrown your way. You're also very handsome and have an amazing personality. I'll write anything you want me to here as long as you never leave us.

Thank you to the teachers, mentors, and friends who helped my creativity flourish: Jen Grantham, Lionel Tanod, Nancy Jowett, Eric Hardie, John Merritt, Angus Armstrong, Brenda Eisner, Shane Simpson, Iain Farrell, Adil Johan, Colin McGuire, Burke Carroll, and Rick Lazar.

Thank you to my partners in creating tools and resources that propel the creativity of others: Oliver Greschke, Christian Blombert, Aaron DeRoche, Matt Davey, Pascal Kaap, Andreas Zhukovsky, Julia Bondar, Caspar Bock, Luke Brennan, and Max Deutsch.

Since I started publishing work online two decades ago, I've connected with hundreds of other creators with whom I've felt a special kinship—all the radiant souls who share my wonder for life and play by their own rules. Thanks especially to Rob Scallon for your bulldozer of friendship; Rachel K. Collier for celebrating and commiserating with me; Scott Harper for all the late-night noisemaking; Malinda Kathleen Reese for your empathy and joy; Nahre Sol for your sincerity and brilliance; Hank and Katherine Green for your kindness; Paul and Joe DeGeorge and Mike Harpring for all the goop; Dan Wilson for your wisdom, and Jad Abumrad for your encouragement. Thanks also to Jamie Lidell, Greg White, Dotan Negrin, Andreas Paleologos, the Hadfield family, TWRP, Keeley Bumford, Bill Day, Dylan Lane, Lee Bates, Val Brunn, Joshua Steele, Grant Stinnett, Jesse Hanson, Chuck Sutton, Kay Oko, Mary Spender, Danae Greenfield, Ben Levin, Adam Neely, Rick Beato, Andrew Gunadie, Hannah Hart, Joel Berghult, Ariel Bissett, Vi Hart, Jeremy Leaird-Koch, Alex Theakson, Ben Wilson, Bo Nurmi, Stephen Fitzgerald, Bryan Noll, James Cigler, Stefan Paul Goetsch, Andreas Plab, Mark Hadley, Laura Escudé, Sofia degli Alessandri-Hultquist, Luke Pretty, Alfred Darlington, and many more. You inspire me endlessly.

Thank you to my family for being behind me, even though you don't understand what I'm doing half the time. To my parents, I love you and I owe you everything. Mom, you instilled in me both the grit to march headlong toward my vision and the generosity to bring others with me. Dad, in anything big or small, I have never felt without your support. Thank you both for showing me what a life of integrity and contentment looks like. Lucas, you will never know just how much I look up to you for your heart. Evelyn and Dorian, when you eventually learn how to read, this is one more place where I'll tell you I love you.

Essa: In a life full of luck you've been the luckiest thing to happen to me. Everything I've done has been made better by being with you. I love being your partner, I love every day with you, I love you.

# About the Author

**Andrew Huang** is a creator of music, videos about music, and tools with which music can be made. An early adopter of the internet as a means of growing both an audience and a client base, he sustained an online music career before the existence of social media, where he now has over two million followers. He's known for taking a broad and eccentric range of approaches to music, particularly on his YouTube channel, where his videos explore concepts in an entertaining and accessible way and have been viewed over 300 million times. He lives in Toronto with his family. This is his first book.